Understanding Adoption

Understanding Adoption

Clinical Work with Adults, Children, and Parents

Edited by Kathleen Hushion,
Susan B. Sherman, and Diana Siskind

JASON ARONSON
Lanham • Boulder • New York • Toronto • Oxford

Published in the United States of America
by Jason Aronson
An imprint of Rowman & Littlefield Publishers, Inc.

A wholly owned subsidiary of
The Rowman & Littlefield Publishing Group, Inc.
4501 Forbes Boulevard, Suite 200, Lanham, Maryland 20706
www.rowmanlittlefield.com

PO Box 317
Oxford
OX2 9RU, UK

British Library Cataloguing in Publication Information Available

Library of Congress Cataloging-in-Publication Data

Understanding adoption : clinical work with adults, children, and parents / edited by
Kathleen Hushion, Susan Sherman, and Diana Siskind.
   p. cm.
 ISBN-13: 978-0-7657-0425-2 (cloth : alk. paper)
 ISBN-10: 0-7657-0425-0 (cloth : alk. paper)
 ISBN-13: 978-0-7657-0426-9 (pbk. : alk. paper)
 ISBN-10: 0-7657-0426-9 (pbk. : alk. paper)
 1. Adoption. 2. Adoption—Psychological aspects. I. Hushion, Kathleen, 1950– II.
Sherman, Susan, 1946– III. Siskind, Diana.

HV875.U48 2006
362.734—dc22   2006014195

Printed in the United States of America

⊗™ The paper used in this publication meets the minimum requirements of American
National Standard for Information Sciences—Permanence of Paper for Printed Library
Materials, ANSI/NISO Z39.48-1992.

For our children:

Summer

Rachel and Bill

. . . and in memory of Paul

Contents

Part I

CLINICAL ISSUES

Chapter One

The World of Adoption

An Introduction

Diana Siskind

There are certain words that immediately evoke powerful effects and associations, and I believe that the word *adoption* belongs in that group. Consider how we react when we learn that a child was adopted, or that someone we know is about to adopt a child, or that a woman has decided to surrender her child for adoption. Often a mixture of feelings are aroused, some strong and unexpected, some contradictory, and some very subtle. Awe, curiosity, fear, interest, pity, disapproval, discomfort, and compassion are among the many reactions we experience. Members of our profession are not exempt from reacting to this potent word and to the story that will follow. Adoption is a shadow that never completely goes away. Its presence remains an eternal factor in the life of the adoptee and in the lives of the adoptive parents; but the impact of that shadow varies enormously, and that is what this book is going to address and explore.

The chapters of this book will describe and discuss the effect of adoption on children and on their parents through the perspective of the clinicians who work with them. We feel this to be an important area of investigation and one that very much fits the climate of our times. The beginning of the twenty-first century is a time of great flux and upheaval. Family life has undergone substantial changes over the past several decades, and one of these changes is that the traditional family, consisting of a man and a woman married and the parents of their biological children, has lost exclusivity. Adoption has become widely practiced, accepted, *and* accessible. Consequently, we as clinicians find ourselves being consulted by a growing number of patients for whom adoption is part of the presented problem. Also, we are being consulted by an increasing number of people in related professions: teachers, guidance workers, case workers, lawyers, pediatricians, and other people whose work puts them in contact with families where adoption is an important factor.

In some of the cases that find their way to our consulting rooms, the circumstances leading to adoption are no different from those of the past. In these more traditional situations, a man and a woman, married and wishing to have a child but unable to conceive due to infertility or some other reason, adopt a newborn child through an adoption agency or through a lawyer who specializes in arranging adoptions within the United States. But many of the adoption-related cases we see differ from this traditional model both in the nature of the adoptive parent's or parents' life circumstances, and in the method by which the adoption takes place.

For some nontraditional adoptive parents, adopting a newborn or young child born in the United States is not an option open to them. Consequently, many have turned to international adoption as a more accessible path to adopting a child, but one involving a lengthy and complex process and the knowledge that their child will not be a newborn infant and that they might know very little about the child's history prior to the adoption. International adoption also often results in a child racially different from the adoptive parents, and the complicated feelings this evokes in both the child and parents are brought to our attention over and over again as we find ourselves being consulted by these racially mixed adoptive families.

Among the growing group of adoptive parents who do not fit the *traditional* picture and who seek our help are single men and women, who may be heterosexual, gay, or lesbian, all wishing to form a family and parent a child. We are also consulted by adoptive couples who are gay or lesbian, and by older, married, heterosexual couples who are past childbearing age and adopt their child late in life. Once the adoption has taken place, many of these nontraditional adoptive families find themselves faced with difficult and confusing situations and seek our help; and we, in turn, often find ourselves challenged by the atypical picture they present and by their description of circumstances that are bound to profoundly affect their children's development but in ways we have to struggle to grasp and understand.

Another current change pertains to the fate of the adopted child's contact with the birth mother. Whereas in the past it was rare for an adopted child to meet the biological parents, this too is no longer necessarily so. Increasingly, new regulations make it possible for the adopted child to locate the biological parents, and in our practices we encounter more and more situations of searches by adoptees for their biological parents and searches by parents who have surrendered their child and now long to meet the child they never knew. A growing trend toward *open adoption* exists as well, and in this arrangement the biological parents are allowed to be in contact with the adoptive parents and their "shared" child from the beginning.

The adoption of older foster children is often underrepresented in psychodynamic[1] books and journals, and we are fortunate that this will not be the case in this volume. These children, who do not often appear in the offices of private practitioners, have suffered trauma and abuse and their needs must be recognized and met by developing better ways of working with them.

The changing face of adoption as described so far has focused on the external circumstances and arrangements, the reality-based aspects of adoption, and these are easy to describe. However, understanding how both the more traditional as well as the more unusual circumstances of adoption might affect the psychic development of the adopted child and the development of the capacity *to parent* in the adoptive parent is no simple matter at all. Our goal is to keep in mind both the external and internal worlds of these children and to explore the interplay of all the forces that shape their development. Of equal importance is the harnessing of our knowledge and skills to reflect and organize our thinking in ways that will help us give these parents the insight and grounding they need to parent their child with a measure of confidence.

I now will take a short detour and make a few relevant comments about the history and evolution of our profession. We the authors and editors of this book are psychodynamically trained psychotherapists. Our training is based on a theory and technique that in the first half of the twentieth century, in its original form, was created to address unconscious conflict and identity issues, and required that the adult or child patient attend frequent appointments, usually over a long period of time. Although this continues to be the treatment modality for many patients, our field has branched out, and we use our training and skills in other situations as well. Indeed, in the second half of the twentieth century, much was written about the need to adapt theory and technique to meet the needs of the large population of people, adults and children, who could not be fitted into the earlier psychotherapeutic model. Psychodynamic psychotherapy has been gradually and carefully formulated to meet the needs of the wide variety of conditions and situations that are presented to us in our consulting rooms. Some of our colleagues have moved away from psychodynamic theory and technique and prefer cognitive, behavioral, and psychopharmacological approaches to treatment. We, however, find that contemporary psychodynamic therapy— a therapy that has evolved to include salient features of ego psychology including object relations theory, self psychology, relational and attachment

---

1. *Psychodynamic* is used as shorthand for *contemporary psychoanalytic theory and technique*, which broadly defined may include aspects of ego psychology, attachment theory, intersubjectivity, and relational theory.

theory, and intersubjectivity—offers us a theoretical foundation and a professional attitude capable of addressing whatever diagnostic issues or life circumstances are presented to us.

The widening scope of our profession has naturally brought about some changes in the way we work, and one of these changes is in the attitude of many child therapists toward the parents of their young patients. We have come to appreciate that parents can play an important role in their child's treatment. No longer, as in the past, are parents viewed primarily as providers of information about their children and of transportation to and from appointments. We now find that our work with parents (J. Novick and K. Novick 2005; Siskind 1997; and Slade 2006) can play a key role in their ability to parent, which of course has an enormous impact on the child's treatment and on the child's life. We also find ourselves increasingly consulted by parents for a variety of developmental snags that in the past might have been handled by a wise grandmother. Intergenerational wisdom is not as available as it once was, with wise grandmothers now flocking to retirement communities in warm climates, and perhaps would not be as sought after by a generation of parents many of whom reject the traditional childrearing attitudes of their elders. With this and other changes in family life, parental confidence is at a low point in many of the parents we see, and I have found this observation to be echoed by teachers and school administrators. Consequently, parents increasingly rely on us for help in dealing with their anxiety in raising children.

As clinicians we know that the roots of anxiety are deep and complicated and that parenthood both reawakens conflictual issues and affords new avenues for growth and the resolution of these issues. However, we do need to also understand that being an adoptive parent can be even more challenging and daunting than being the biological parent of a healthy child. That adoptive parents consult us even when their child appears to be doing well is a wise move on their part. After all, becoming a parent took a very different path for them than the one available to biological parents. Not only do most adoptive parents need to deal with the disappointment of not being able to have a biological child, they also miss out on the ordinary progression of conception, pregnancy, birth, nursing, and early symbiosis, which under optimal circumstances allows the mother (and to a degree the father) to regress, to *fit together* (Hartmann 1958) with her infant and to experience a state of motherliness. Adoptive mothers and fathers do not experience this gradual preparation for parenthood. Their preparation is more along the lines of dealing with agencies, lawyers, documents, money, and such—a cold climate at best. And while all parents take a leap of faith in having a child, clearly adoptive parents take a more precipitous one. Their induction into parenthood is punctuated by unfamiliar experiences all the way.

And what about the babies and children who were not adopted at birth and whose early months and sometimes years are not known? Their moms or dads cannot say to them "When you were a very tiny baby how you loved your bath," or "There was one lullaby I had to sing over and over again." What happens when one's history is unknown? What happens to those early, inter-rupted experiences of sound and smell and touch? How, with the lack of con-tinuity, do early object experiences translate into self and object representa-tions? And later, when these children construct fantasies about their biological mothers and fathers, how does that affect their identifications and identity formation? And being of a different race than his adoptive parents surely is a complex hurdle for both child and parents.

The chapters to follow will illustrate how in the treatment of these varying situations the clinician-authors of this book have adapted their training to fit the psychic and life circumstances before them. That is what we do, and that is a given. However, when the situation before us strays very far from what is customary, when life circumstances impose extraordinary obstacles to the ordinary progression of development of children, we as clinicians can some-times feel overwhelmed.

Our work also requires that we pay attention to the fact that some of the sit-uations we encounter are tragic and impose formidable demands and wrench-ing responsibilities on us. For instance, we may at times feel that the child be-fore us, usually a child who has already suffered a great deal, is all alone in the world except for our concern for him. When that happens, we need to ask ourselves whether the job before us is too big to be done alone. It takes a lot of discipline, self-scrutiny, and creativity for us to *not* become seriously dis-tracted by extraordinary circumstances and, to despite them, maintain our psychodynamic approach and our professionalism. But sometimes when that seems perilously beyond our grasp, for countertransferential and other rea-sons, we professionals need to seek help from our colleagues, from our own therapists, and from reading books and papers that afford us the chance to share the experiences and insights of our fellow therapists.

Here is an example of a dramatic situation I encountered many years ago in my practice that taught me a great deal. It had to do with the search by a mother for the daughter she had surrendered right after delivery when she was nineteen years old. The daughter, now also nineteen, lived on another continent, the one her mother had fled right after having surrendered her child. The mother con-sulted me just as she had located her daughter and was making arrangements to go meet her. She needed my help because, as much as she longed for the reunion, it terrified her. Over the past nineteen years there had not been a day that she had not thought about the child she had "abandoned," and her longing for her daugh-ter had a primal quality that also deeply affected me. Her only comforting thought was the belief that her daughter's adoptive parents had given her a much better home than she could have provided.

Their reunion finally took place in that faraway land, and I learned by phone contact that while her daughter's response to her was positive, my patient did learn that the adoptive home had been far from ideal. This was a grave disappointment. Over the next two years we worked on what all this meant to my patient. During that time, mother and daughter stayed in constant communication, and my patient visited her several times. Then one day the daughter came to the United States to visit her mother, and my patient brought her to my office. Although the daughter was shorter than her mother, these two women looked so alike and had such similar speech patterns and mannerisms that it was hard to believe that they had been apart for all those years. After my patient moved out West, she wrote and told me that her daughter had moved to the United States and that they now lived close to each other.

This case, unusual insofar as such reunions do not usually bring about the degree of closeness and permanence that developed between my patient and her child, taught me a great deal on many levels. It taught me not to make general assumptions about the plight of adopted children or about the mothers who surrendered them. My patient's daughter, a young woman who had been adopted at birth by a dysfunctional family, nonetheless appeared to be a pretty intact person. She even had the emotional resources to forgive her birth mother for having surrendered her, to make peace with her, and to allow their physical reunion to develop into an emotional connection. In turn her mother, my patient, despite severe abuse and neglect suffered in her early years, seemed to have within her, against all odds, those deep qualities of motherliness whose source eludes us. These two women and what happened to them and between them taught me that the effect of adoption is never fully known, that what we might attribute to adoption may be the result of other factors, and how humble we must be lest we think we know and understand more than we possibly can. But not the least of what this case taught me is to never make assumptions about a bond that we don't know much about, and that is barely mentioned in the literature: the bond that sometimes exists between the mother who surrenders and the baby who lives forever in her mind.

In the chapters that follow, you will become acquainted with a variety of treatment situations[2] that have adoption as their central factor. You will read about the adoption of babies and toddlers, of latency-age children, and of adolescents, and about the parents, in various family configurations, who adopt them. You will read about adults in treatment who were adopted as children.

---

2. All cases and case vignettes in this book have either been disguised beyond recognition or are presented with the permission of the patient (or patient's parent if the patient is a minor).

You will read about adoption issues in forensic work and about consultation to adoption programs. You will delve into an exploration of what parenthood is about. And you will discover that certain recurring themes emerge no matter how different the circumstances. There is trauma, dislocation, loss, grief, and mourning; there is the feeling of being different and not belonging; there is living with secrets and living out fantasies rather than finding a way to live life; and there is unmanageable anger, distrust, self-hatred, shame, feelings of doom, pervasive self-doubt, and the identity confusion that so often festers. It is these affective states and conflicts, this emotional landscape that is the root of the shadow of adoption that never completely goes away. But you will also read about how, with hard work and the necessary help, the possibility of change and growth also exists, and with it, that of *finding one's place, the hope of a good future and the ambition to find it*. And when the fact of adoption becomes one of the many factors in the life of a person and not the overriding fact, then the shadow of adoption recedes, and life moves on.

REFERENCES

Hartmann, Heinz. 1958. *Ego Psychology and the Problem of Adaptation*. New York: International University Press.

Novick, Jack, and Kerry Kelly Novick. 2005. *Working with Parents Makes Therapy Work*. Lanham, MD: Jason Aronson.

Siskind, Diana. 1997. *Working with Parents: Establishing the Essential Alliance in Child Psychotherapy and Consultation*. Northvale, NJ: Jason Aronson.

Slade, Arietta. 2006. "Working with Parents in Child Psychotherapy: Engaging the Reflective Function." *Psychoanalytic Inquiry*.

Chapter Two

Unconscious Communication and the Transmission of Loss

Christopher Bonovitz

In my clinical experience, it appears that there are two extremes when it comes to adoption: it is either overemphasized in explaining a child's symptoms or overlooked and minimized. Wagner (2001) makes the point that adoption is often used as the "Coat-Rack Defense," meaning adoption is the coat rack, or hook, that one can hang anything or everything on. She points out how adoption becomes equated with psychopathology and personality disorders. On the other hand, there is the danger of dismissing adoption as an integral part of a person's identity and developmental struggles.

Much of the psychoanalytic literature on adoption focuses almost exclusively on the emotional world and fantasy life of the adoptee, often disregarding the adoptive parents' unconscious fantasies concerning adoption. There has been very little consideration given to how the parents' unconscious lives shape the child's adoption fantasies. In this chapter, I will examine a specific adoption scenario in which a couple decides to adopt a child at infancy following their prolonged attempts to conceive a child. I am interested in how the sense of loss of the adoptive parents who are unable to conceive a child due to infertility influences the attachment with the adopted child and shapes the adoptee's self-representation and adoption fantasies, including representations of the birth parents. Hodges et al. (1984) begs the question as to how a child can construct a mental representation of a parent without memory or real experience of that parent. She goes on to explore this question with the assumption that "the mental representation of the biological parents is, very largely, a locus of feelings and fantasies, not modified by everyday reality experience" (50). I would add that these feelings and fantasies are at least partially influenced by the adoptive parents' own representations (Glenn 1985).

Similarly, I am interested in exploring how the child's understanding of his origins interacts with the parents' own sense of inadequacy and loss related to infertility, most notably the loss of the wished-for child. In some cases, the parents' inability to mourn their imagined infant, along with the frequently traumatic process of trying unsuccessfully for many years to conceive, is transmitted to the adopted child. The multiple losses associated with infertility interact with the young child's understanding of his origins, his self-representation, his fantasies of where babies come from, and the conscious and unconscious meanings of adoption within the family constellation.

In instances where the adopted child begins to experience behavioral problems, these dormant issues may surface in some families. In these situations, it becomes necessary to work with both the child and the parents to set in motion the process of mourning. This includes the acknowledgment and mourning of the losses associated both with the absence of the biological parent and with the infertility. Mourning in these instances does not necessarily mean a "giving up," but rather that the acknowledgment and eventual acceptance of the loss allows for the continuation of the absent object to exist and remain alive alongside the physically present child or parent.

For example, in the case of the adoptive parent, mourning the loss of the wished-for child permits a greater acceptance of the adoptee and a psychic integration that allows both to coexist in the same person. This process on the part of the parents reduces parental projective identification, allowing the parents to better tolerate the child's own sense of loss rather than deny the child's birth history, and aids the young child in establishing a sense of continuity that connects his birth mother to his parents. In general, parents of adopted children may be resistant to treatment as it threatens to confirm their own sense of inadequacy stemming from infertility and, in some cases, the adoption screening process, during which the parents are placed under a microscope. Later in this chapter, I will offer clinical material involving parents who, initially resistant to treatment, gradually became more engaged and were eventually able to reflect on their sense of loss.

Up to this point, much of the psychoanalytic literature has focused on disclosure of adoption (see Wieder 1977a), antisocial behavior found among adoptees (see Kirschner 1988; Kirschner 1992), Oedipal configurations related to having two sets of parents (see Feder 1974), the splitting of good and bad parental images (see Brinich 1980; Priel, Kantor, and Besser 2000), genealogical bewilderment (see Sants 1964), family romance fantasies (see Wieder 1977b), the loss of the birth mother (see Deeg 1989, 1990), attachment disorders (Schechter 2000; Silverman 2000), and, outside the psychoanalytic discourse, the search for the birth parent (see Lifton 1998). In contrast, less exploration has been made concerning the interaction of psychic worlds between the adopted child and the adoptive parents (see Schneider and Rimmer 1984). This is with respect to, more specifically, their shared unconscious, the transmission of trauma and loss (transmission of trauma and loss occurs in both directions: parent to child, and child to parent), interaction between the child's representations, and the unconscious meanings of the adoption for the parents.

I am interested in how the reality of adoption becomes organized in the internal worlds of each of the family members and in the relational patterning that emerges out of subsequent interaction. What were the motivations that went into the decision to adopt a child (Clothier 1939)? How does the adoption situation reactivate old parent-child and intergenerational conflicts (Blum 1983)? And, how does adoption interact with preexisting conflicts, anxieties, and fears in the parents that can eventually come to haunt the child?

In this chapter, I will seek to do the following: (1) discuss infertility in the context of object loss; (2) outline an interpersonal/relational theoretical perspective, including the current concept of projective identification as this stands in the background of my thinking on adoption; (3) speculate about the loss associated with infertility for the parents who adopt and how this intersects with the child's ambiguous loss of the birth mother; and (4) present case material to illustrate how the parents' unmourned loss of the wished-for child shapes the adoptee's internal world and the construction of his adoption narrative.

INFERTILITY AND OBJECT LOSS

Carol Munschauer (1997) describes infertility as the "dark shadow," referring to the deep-seated shame and sense of failure associated with chronic infertility. For both men and women who are unable to conceive children, feelings of potency and sexuality come under attack as failed fertilizations and failed implantations accrue over time. Munschauer notes that there is a "gradual erosion in confidence in one's body-self and one's sexual-self that can be likened to a slow and painful psychic demise" (315). For some couples, the experience of infertility can include the painful struggle of trying to conceive a child for many years, being forced to undergo invasive medical procedures, and investing much of their savings in reproductive technologies to combat infertility problems (Schechter 1970). Couples who go through this kind of process and then decide to adopt are left with penetrating narcissistic injury, wounded bodies and sexuality, and a dampened sexual life, as well as feelings of rage, despair, grief, and contempt for the other who is "at fault" (D. Brodzinsky, Smith, and A. Brodzinsky 1998; Deutsch 1945; Schechter 1970).

For females in particular, there is the devastating blow to the dream of giving birth to a baby, and the psychic assault on the conception of herself as a woman. Everyday living—in which the possibility of pregnancy from the time of being a little girl is taken for granted and unquestioned—drastically changes upon a woman's not being able to bear a child. Infertile women may feel as though they are "broken" as their reproductive organs fail them or are deemed "defective." For a man, not being able to impregnate his wife may leave him with feelings of castration, doubts about his own masculinity, and a sense of loss in not being able to perpetuate the family line. Deutsch (1945) asserts that the adoptive mother's inability to conceive interferes with her developing a sense of motherliness in relation to her child. Eventually disclosing the adoption to her child revives the conflicts associated with this "failure" (Toussieng 1962).

In not being able to conceive, couples are faced with mourning the child they could not have and the loss of the fantasized child. In some cases, however, an absence of mourning may result in the disowning of the parents' conscious and unconscious wishes for a biological child. With the arrival of their adopted child, the parents' inability to mourn their loss interferes with their being able to accept the gift of the adoptee, that gift being his arrival followed by later offerings from the child such as his love or caring (Shabad 1993). One adoptive mother expressed that she was unable to tolerate her daughter's love for her and feared her daughter's dependence on her as "her mother." This mother came to understand her frequent, rage-filled outbursts toward her daughter as a rejection of her daughter's love.

For both the couple and the child, their respective losses are characterized by their having little to no real experience with the lost object. Thus in each case, their representations are largely based on their own feelings and fantasies. The inability of the couple to mourn the losses associated with infertility may be transmitted to the child, intermingling then with the adoptee's own ambiguous loss of the birth mother. The adoptee may come to stand for the wished-for child who was never mourned, and may exist as a reminder of the couple's infertility. In defending against their own loss, the parents may initially be, as Diane Ehrensaft (1997) states, "awash in the desire for perfection" (31), only then to become gradually disillusioned with their "majestic baby," as he or she falls short of their wishes. For instance, the mother of a ten-year-old boy adopted at birth who had been recently diagnosed with multiple learning disabilities shamefully admitted to me that she had threatened to cast her son off to an orphanage. This mother later went on to explore her wish that she could return her son for a "Gerber baby," meaning one not riddled with so many problems.

Beyond the painful struggle of trying to conceive their own child, couples who then decide to adopt, depending on their chosen route, are often dragged through the process of being investigated and screened by the adoption agency in the agency's homestudy to determine if they are suitable parents (D. Brodzinsky, Smith, and A. Brodzinsky 1998). This kind of process gives rise to anxiety, confusion, and helplessness, and further erodes the parents' confidence, planting seeds of doubt about their right to be parents at all. Parents are forced to market themselves to the agency or birth parent, presenting themselves in as favorable a light as possible. In comparison to pregnancy, where the time line is roughly known and where the attachment process begins with the baby in utero, adoption often entails a dreaded and prolonged wait for the actual arrival of a child. During the sometimes long waiting period, parents may experience significant life changes as well as changes in their attitude toward the adoption itself (Winnicott 1954a). With the absence of pregnancy, when the adoptee and parent first meet, they are complete strangers to each other. With couples who adopt through private agencies, there is a heavy financial investment, and the adoption culture within these agencies that the parent is inducted into. While such a community can provide support for the parents and a social network among the families and children, there is also the economic reality and financial interest of the company, implemented through marketing strategies, that can turn the child into a commodity.

AN INTERPERSONAL/RELATIONAL PERSPECTIVE: PROJECTIVE IDENTIFICATION AND THE INTERGENERATIONAL TRANSMISSION OF TRAUMA

Although a comprehensive review of an interpersonal/relational perspective and projective identification is beyond the scope of this chapter, I would like to touch briefly on how such a perspective, along with contemporary thought on the processes of projective identification, informs clinical work with adopted children. Interpersonal and relational child analysts have been in the forefront of offering an alternative theoretical model to the once predominant ego-psychological perspective (see Warshaw 1992; Gaines 1995; Kantor 1995; Pantone 1995; Spiegel 1996; Frankel 1998; Krimendahl 1998; Aronson 2001; Altman 2002; Altman et al. 2002; Bonovitz 2003). Interpersonal and relational theorists seek to integrate the internal and external, interpersonal and intrapersonal relations. The premise for these theorists is that relationships, or contact with others, are a central motivating force, while drives, or instincts, enter into psychological life through the relational matrix in which they arise (Greenberg and Mitchell 1983; Mitchell 2000). Child and parent, like patient and analyst, are understood as a dyadic system where there is mutual influence within an asymmetrical relationship—both are embedded in a dynamic relational field co-constructed by each participant (Beebe and Lachmann 1988; Aron 1996). Mind is fundamentally dyadic, with an unconscious comprised of relational configurations, or matrices, which begin developing during early life, and are reshaped and contoured by ongoing "real" interactions with others (Mitchell 1988; Aron 1996; D. B. Stern 1997; Hoffman 1998; Hirsch 2003).

An interpersonal/relational perspective also takes into account the larger systems outside the dyad, namely, the social and institutional contexts (Altman [1995] refers to these contexts as the "third") that are acting influences on the psyche, and imbue human experience with meaning (Sullivan 1940, 1953). Experience is always context dependent. This is especially important when considering adoption, as adoption itself is a social construction that bears a stigma in our society that must be taken into account in understanding a person's relationship to their adoptive identity. Even before the child is adopted, parents often undergo a sometimes humiliating pre-adoption process that reactivates and reaffirms their self-doubt and feelings of inadequacy. I consider this, and the adoption culture in general, as acting influences and important contexts with which to understand the meanings of adoption for the child and the parents.

The Kleinian concept of projective identification has undergone a transformation, moving from an omnipotent fantasy that is body-based and instinctually driven within a one-person psychology to a more current formulation. Now, projective identification is understood as an interpersonal event between two participants that is observable, with affective and behavioral concomitants (Seligman 1999). The integration of contemporary infant research with psychoanalytic theory has transformed this concept. Through the microanalyses of mother-infant interactions, infant researchers demonstrate how relational scripts develop out of preverbal, kinesthetic, affective-based interactions located in the nonverbal mode of experience that govern one's internal object world (Beebe, Lachmann, and Jaffe 1997). The infant research shows how projective identification has its behavioral concomitants in actual observable behavior.

Seligman's seminal contribution (1999), along with the work of others, illustrates how projective identification, in contrast to the Kleinian concept, moves from parent to child. From this point of view, the child is pressured or coerced via asymmetrical influence into the position of complying with the preverbal relational script projected by the parent. The child comes to experience himself or herself as the parent's inner selves or objects along the lines of the relational rules that characterize the parent's internal object world. Similarly, the child's own representational world, cognition, physiology, constitution, temperament, and so on are all acting influences on the interaction with the parent and the projective/introjective processes that flow between parent and child. The parent-infant model (Fraiberg, Adelson, and Shapiro 1975; Lieberman 1992; D. N. Stern 1995), along with the neo-Kleinians, has contributed to a theoretical framework where the representational worlds of all family members are interacting within the same sphere and interpenetrating each other through projective and introjective identifications (D. N. Stern 1995; Pantone 2000; Bonovitz 2001; Altman 2002). With these more recent contributions, the Kleinian concept of projective identification has become one where projection and projective identification flow from parent to child, and child to parent, within a dynamic field of reciprocal influence. Klauber (1991), a neo-Kleinian, in a paper that describes her work with an adopted girl and her family, makes the compelling case that her work with the child and family enabled her to make sense of the projections and see the unconscious matching between the family's psychopathology and the child's.

Similarly, family systems theorists who integrate psychoanalytic theory speak of how family members collusively carry psychic functions for each other, or how a child may identify with projected parental images of him (Zinner and Shapiro 1972; Framo 1992). Fraiberg, Adelson, and Shapiro's (1975) "Ghosts in the Nursery" poignantly captures how parents are susceptible to the intergenerational transmission of trauma in that their unresolved difficulties from their own families of origin come to haunt the next generation. For example, a mother who was abandoned by her own father recently told me that she used a suitcase as a crib for her adopted daughter for the first several weeks upon the baby's arrival in her home. Thus, this mother's own abandonment history generated ambivalence toward her newly adopted child, and eventually had a profound influence on the attachment process and the symbolic meanings of the adoption for both child and mother.

The extent to which parents have mentalized, or reflected on their own traumas, will determine the extent to which their projections, or their rigid negative attributions, interfere in the ability to see their child as his own person (Fonagy and Target 1998; Silverman and Lieberman 1999; Altman 2002). If too much of the mother's psychic terrain is occupied by her own trauma, there is then little space available to see the baby in his own right. Main and Hesse (1990) link the adult's unresolved trauma and continuing state of fear to the infant's display of disorganized/disoriented attachment behavior. In this situation, the baby becomes confused and disoriented in response to parental expressions of fear or anxiety as the mother is responding to her own internal cues as sources of her frightened behavior. With children of disorganized/disoriented attachment behavior, one way in which they may attempt to master their own helplessness is by becoming punitive and controlling of their parents (Hopkins 2000). In the case of adoptees and their parents, treatment along with individual development may allow for a greater capacity to tolerate ambivalence and the integration of love and hate, thus reducing projections and creating a space that provides the opportunity to mourn painful loss (Waterman 2001).

In light of this theoretical perspective, child psychoanalytic psychotherapy involves working closely with parents to better understand how their own history, childhood, and so forth influence their relationship with the child. It also utilizes the child's play to understand the unconscious communication between parent and child. Often the child's play and its unconscious derivatives may elucidate psychic terrain that has been blocked out, dissociated, or repressed by a parent. Similarly, the child's play may be a conduit into understanding the impact of cumulative trauma on the family. Additionally, unforeseen family enactments that take place during the course of treatment may shed light on the projections circulating in the atmosphere and provide a lens into the conflicts, fears, anxieties, and traumas that have not been mentalized or reflected upon.

INTERMINGLING OF LOSS BETWEEN PARENT AND CHILD

The age group of children I will be focusing on here is latency, roughly between the ages of six years to ten years. In addition to the more traditional psychoanalytic conceptions of latency as a developmental period that involves the Oedipus complex, family romance fantasies, and the development of a stable and positive ego identity (see Freud 1950; Brinich 1980; Blum 1983; Kernberg 1985; Priel, Kantor, and Besser 2000), there are also significant cognitive changes that take place during this time that contribute to the child's increased knowledge about his adoption. Studies demonstrate that the full impact of adoption is felt when the child reaches latency (Brodzinsky, Lang, and Smith 1995; Priel, Kantor, and Besser 2000).

The development of newly emerging cognitive skills related to problem solving, logical reasoning, and differentiation enable the child to begin making distinctions between adoption and birth. Children during this period may exhibit anxiety and confusion as they struggle to grasp the idea of being relinquished, or given away, by the birth mother, realizing that they are not biologically tied to their adoptive parents (Nickman 1985; D. Brodzinsky, Smith, and A. Brodzinsky 1998). Frequently, relinquishment by one's birth parents is internalized as having been abandoned or rejected, leaving the child feeling unloved and unwanted. Nancy Verrier (1993) refers to this postnatal separation from the birth mother as the "primal wound," a wound that leaves holes in one's sense of self and confusion about one's own origins.

Depending on where a child is in his or her emotional and cognitive development, the act of having been given up and then chosen has many different meanings. In the case of the adoptee who has emotional and behavioral difficulties, the parents may experience guilt in response to feelings of hate or fantasies of getting rid of the child, driving parents to disown such thoughts or feelings and project them into the child. Adoptees, in turn, test out their own abandonment fears by repeatedly provoking rejection from their parents, what Laura Bass Wagner refers to as the "preemptive strike" (2001). These parents may allow themselves to be subjected to the child's punitive behavior so as not to realize the child's fears and to avoid their own aggression and powerful sadistic fantasies. The parents' disowning of their hate then interferes with their ability to truly love the child, as hate becomes split from love. Or, as Winnicott (1949) poignantly remarks, in not being able to reach the mother's hate, the child does not come to feel loved.

In the adoption scenario, there are multiple losses circulating for everyone involved. For the child who is adopted at infancy as part of a closed adoption where there is no contact with the birth mother, losing the mother or father is an ambiguous loss, as the child will have no organized experience or memory of them, yet may have knowledge that they exist. Kernberg (1985) holds that the state of being adopted makes the child feel deceived by his birth parents and lied to by his adoptive parents for having kept the adoption a secret.

Along with the loss of the birth mother, the child has also lost his extended birth family and genealogy. In play therapy with latency-age children who are adopted, themes of loss, separation, death, and reunion often emerge. For example, we may meet with themes that deal with missing or stolen mothers, fantasized reunions with the birth mother or family (Kernberg 1985), the fantasy of being rescued or stolen back by the birth mother, the taking of responsibility for the loss of the birth parent, the harboring of aggressive wishes toward the birth parent, or the fear that the parent is dead. The child, for instance, may feel as though he "killed" or destroyed his parents (Hodges et al. 1984, Hodges 1989).

For the birth mother who relinquishes her parental rights and gives up her child for adoption, there is the profound loss of her child whom she may never see again. Depending on the circumstances of the adoption, she will be faced with guilt, shame, and other sets of feelings connected with her decision, regardless of whether she thinks it was in the best interest of her child and her own well-being. For the adoptive parents, in situations where they decide to adopt because they cannot have their own children, there is the loss for each of them in being unable to bear their own child, the loss of not being able to experience pregnancy, and the loss of the wished-for, or imagined, child.

The *common ground of loss* that both the parents and the adoptee share represents their respective losses (wished-for-child, and birth mother) as well as a point of identification. In her discussion of an earlier version of this paper, Diane Ehrensaft (2002) highlights the dialectic that exists for adopted children and parents, the dialectic of sameness and difference, with therapy then becoming a place to create a potential space where these tensions can be linked and transformed. For instance, the child's mourning of his birth mother not only concerns the relationship to his "other mother," but may also be seen as an attempt to identify with his adoptive mother's sense of loss, namely the loss in being unable to get pregnant and conceive. It is this kind of identification that allows the child to develop a sense of belonging, or sameness, with his adoptive parent. The respective individual traumas are not only about difference; they are attempts toward identifications and feelings of sameness. Loss for the adoptee and parent is not only about separation, loss, or otherness, but is also about making room for birth, life, and sameness. For the adoptee, there is the "death," or loss, of the birth parent, but at the same time the birth of the relationship with the adoptive mother. Similarly, for the adoptive mother there is the loss, or "death," of the wished-for child as well as the birth of the adoptee.

BUILDING BRIDGES

In the treatment of Billy I am about to describe, I will home in on the interaction between Billy's play, specifically the themes that emerged in relation to his understanding of adoption, and his parents' unmourned loss of not being able to conceive. There were at least two levels to Billy's treatment: Billy's play in the context of our relationship, and the enactments that I became caught up in with his parents and the family as a whole. I see both the play and the family enactments as projections of the internal worlds of everyone involved and inroads to the unconscious meanings of the adoption.

In my first encounter with Billy's parents, his mother and father appeared beleaguered and battle fatigued. When describing the explosive and tyrannical behavior of their seven-year-old son, his mother and father rolled up their sleeves to display their battle wounds. Bite marks, bruises, and scratches marred their arms. They went on to tell me how Billy had been brutalizing them for the past year. He had violent explosions during which he physically lashed out at them, pulled their hair, hit them, bit into their flesh, and randomly threw objects that stood in his path. Billy was experiencing frightening nightmares of monsters, and was refusing to attend school or leave home. As they described their son's behavior, Mr. and Mrs. C created a chaotic atmosphere, talking over each other and anxiously jumping from one thought to the next so that the chronology and history they gave was jumbled together with details that appeared vague and confusing. They portrayed themselves as victims of a child who was violent and uncontrollable, yet who also was afraid to be left alone and desperately fearful of being abandoned. Mr. C was a passive, somewhat jittery man in his late thirties with a large frame and a quiet presence. He was a former professional athlete who had been forced into early retirement because of a career-ending knee injury. He clearly loved his son very much, but struggled with owning his parental authority, often surrendering it as if it did not legitimately belong to him. He was concerned with repeating the physical abuse that had been inflicted on him by his own father, but in his efforts to restrain himself, was reexperiencing the abuse once again as his child "walked all over" him, as well as unconsciously experiencing his own aggression vicariously through his son's explosions.

Mrs. C was a highly anxious, self-absorbed woman with somatic preoccupations who had a long history of physical ailments and frequent doctor visits. Mrs. C was an only child whose mother was chronically depressed throughout Mrs. C's childhood, and whose father expected nothing less than perfection of his daughter. From the time she was very young, she assumed parental responsibilities for her mother and actively sought out her father's praise and affection, grasping for some kind of recognition. Mrs. C organized her life around caring for Billy, yet also managed to have a moderately successful career as a veterinarian. Billy's difficulties engendered in her a feeling of having been "gypped," of being envious of others who had easier lives. Mr. and Mrs. C explained that they had decided to adopt a child after six years of trying to get pregnant. Despite fertility treatments in which they invested much of their savings, they were unsuccessful in their attempts to conceive, apparently because of Mrs. C's ovaries, although the exact reasons were never identified. After this painful and exhausting six years of trying to conceive that extracted a considerable toll on their marriage, they embarked on what came to be a four-year process of trying to adopt a child. They vaguely recalled the humiliating experience of being screened by the adoption agency, an experience that left them questioning whether they were suitable to be parents, reinforcing their sense of inadequacy and damage from their failed attempt to bear a child. These feelings were never adequately dealt with during this phase of their lives.

Although Billy's early developmental history was unremarkable, Mrs. C had worried about his physical health from his early childhood onward. He was taken to many doctors for cold-like symptoms and "allergic" reactions, with Mrs. C convinced that there was something wrong with him that was going undetected. There was a lack of stability in Billy's contact with the outside world as his parents perpetuated a pattern of moving him from one location to the next. For instance, through his early school years he was forced to change schools several times, as his parents were dissatisfied with the teaching. They moved from one apartment to the next and in moving repeatedly made it difficult for Billy to establish stable relationships with others. They had also abruptly terminated Billy's prior treatment, apparently because they felt the therapist to be incompetent. While Billy quickly adapted to new situations, his attachments to objects were fragile and always on the verge of ending.

I suggested to Mr. and Mrs. C that we meet several times before my meeting Billy in order to familiarize myself with their family history and the course of Billy's development. They were reluctant to do so and felt that I needed to see Billy immediately or else they might not make it to the next day. They were determined to foist him onto me with no further questions asked. Feeling the sense of urgency, I acquiesced.

In my first meeting with Billy, he wheeled a suitcase into my office. Billy immediately unpacked his suitcase and introduced me to his stuffed animals, explaining their origins, where they came from, and characterizing them as either "legendary, extinct, or rare." I learned that one of the animals I met was born at a manufacturing plant, and lived on a conveyor belt as part of an assembly line until it was sold by its owner. After meeting several of Billy's companions, I heard a loud click. I glanced up to see a smirk cross Billy's face. He chuckled as he proudly displayed a tape recorder that up until then had been tucked away in his bag. I suddenly realized that I had been duped. Billy had managed to record our session together unbeknownst to me. Billy smiled from across the room and, heightening my anxiety even more, rewound the tape and played our voices. As Billy laughed and took stock of the ease with which he had fooled me, I had the fleeting fantasy that he planned to play this tape for his parents. Or maybe his parents were coconspirators? I dreaded the thought that they would now hear what we child therapists really do with kids. When I asked Billy what he intended to do with the tape, a question partially arising out of my own anxiety, he explained that he planned to play it to himself in between sessions.

Glancing at this moment through an adoption lens, I believe that Billy was actively trying to make sense of his own history and to figure out whether he was "legendary, extinct, or rare" as explored through his animals. Was he the product of an assembly line, a meaningless object akin to his animal on a conveyor belt that was then sold off? In packing his suitcase for our first meeting, was he preparing to be shipped off somewhere, or unsure where he might end up or what he might need? Did objects have any sort of permanence or security for Billy, I wondered? Or, could we see the suitcase as a womb, symbolic of a reconstruction of his birth and a new beginning (Elizabeth Kandall, personal communication)? He came with all his belongings and left with my recorded voice in his pocket. And what about the element of secrecy and deception? Did Billy feel he had been tricked somewhere along the way? In documenting our time together with the use of a tape recorder, was he trying to establish a clear and accurate historical record of events as a corrective to his own history that was bewildering and too confusing to reconstruct? There was the feeling in me that he was trying to hold on to a new relationship and have a memento of it in the event that it was abruptly snatched away from him.

In my subsequent meeting with Billy's parents, they informed me that at the urging of the adoption agency, they had told Billy of his adoption when he was four years of age. Mrs. C had told Billy that she was unable to bear children because of there being something wrong with her stomach, an explanation that she repeated quite frequently to Billy. Billy had been informed that his birth mother was an older woman who was unmarried and financially unable to take care of him. Mrs. C remembered that once when Billy was five he was standing alone in his preschool classroom and he suddenly started "hysterically crying." Referring to his birth mother, he asked, "Why did she give me away?"

Mr. and Mrs. C stated that following the disclosure of his adoption, Billy had become quite fearful and desperately clung to them and objects around him, afraid that if they were to leave his sight they could vanish forever. He angrily protested anytime his parents wanted to get rid of old toys or stuffed animals, and in passing other people's piles of trash on the street curb, he begged his parents to "rescue" the objects no longer considered of value by others, dangling the question, "Would you give me away if I was broken?" Mr. and Mrs. C reported that there were apparently no complications during the birth mother's pregnancy and labor. Billy spent the first two months of his life in an orphanage with other babies and was then adopted at eight weeks by Mr. and Mrs. C. (An attachment theory perspective might use this piece of data to suggest that Billy's symptoms were indicative of an attachment disorder.)

As Billy settled into therapy, he became increasingly more destructive at home. Mrs. C called several times a day reporting the mayhem and reprimanding me for not doing enough. We were all caught up in a chronic state of crisis. The split between Mr. and Mrs. C and myself became more pronounced—Billy was good with me and a terror with them. Although Billy initially protected me from his own destructiveness, he gradually re-created the chaos that permeated his own mind and the relationship with his parents. In his play, he spoke of cyclones and tornadoes that devastated houses, villages, and entire communities. Flicking the lights on and off, he made sounds and noises that evoked a feeling in me of being overcome by powerful forces. In one session, Billy reported a frightening dream:

> There is a cyclone, water is spilling over onto the beaches and houses, and I had to do something or I would die. It was life or death. So I went and bought 20 lbs. of food. Then I saw this boy drowning in the ocean, and I went to save him on a rescue boat. The whole beach was covered with rescue trucks and cars. We needed a helicopter too. I saved the boy.

The dream may suggest, among an array of possible interpretations, that Billy lived inside a cyclone, with the overwhelming responsibility of having to rescue others, yet also harboring the wish to be saved himself. He lived in constant preparation for a disaster, the kind of cyclone that threatened to kill off those whom he depended on for survival. And, in some way, he understood himself both to be the drowning boy who was rescued by his parents from his birth mother and who, at the same time, gave his parents the experience of drowning in a wave of helplessness.

To more fully understand Billy's play and the meanings of his adoption, we need to consider how Mr. and Mrs. C's representations of the adoption and their own loss were interwoven with Billy's attempt to symbolize it. As I tried to work with Mr. and Mrs. C, they became increasingly disappointed with my inability to help them, nudging me into a position of complete and utter ineffectualness. They had left Billy's prior therapist after a short period of time, and appeared determined to repeat this with me. Because they felt that I was not witnessing what Billy was truly like with them (which I sometimes felt was the case as well), Mr. and Mrs. C were concerned that I did not believe their reports. They informed me of books I should read if I really wanted to understand their child, books about attention deficit disorder (ADD) or aggressive children, and made references to their need for a "real expert." They insinuated that I was, in fact, making Billy worse, as he usually fell apart upon leaving his session with me, leaving them to pick up the pieces. In short, they questioned the value of the therapy, and in turn, I felt my own hope begin to crumble and was beginning to buy into the feeling of hopelessness that pervaded the treatment.

If we look at this through the adoption lens and with the idea of there being two sets of parents, perhaps I represented the birth mother, the rival, and in this vein was a threat to Mr. and Mrs. C's parental authority and legitimacy.

It appeared that, just as Billy felt himself to be worthless and unlovable like trash thrown out on the curb, Mr. and Mrs. C felt damaged themselves and sought to inflict these wounds on me. In addition, at the time I myself was a parent for the first time and felt vulnerable to the projections swirling about.

Through all of this, Mr. and Mrs. C made it impossible for me to see beyond the crisis, refusing to elaborate on their marital history or family background in my meetings with them. However, what did come to light was Billy's dominant status in the family and his lack of safety from his overwhelming amount of power. Mr. C, afraid of becoming violent like his own father, disowned his paternal authority and allowed Billy to manipulate him. Mr. C deeply cared for Billy, but his inability to set any sort of limit left him at Billy's mercy; Mr. C was strangled by his own rage for fear of its destructiveness. In contrast, Mrs. C felt more competent with Billy, but turned to him rather than her husband for reassurance and validation. She portrayed herself as a martyr who had sacrificed so much for others (her son, her husband, sick animals), yet who received little in return. She saw Billy as a sick boy who had a "special illness" that required a unique form of treatment.

In one session, Billy created a story about owners and parents. His play involved a five-year-old child who was sold off by its owners to parents in exchange for money, as though the child were a cash crop. In elaborating on this story and speaking as the five-year-old child, Billy remarked, "I lived on a farm with my owners, who then sold me when I was five years old. My parents bought me. They gave me food, milk and are nice to me." It is interesting to note that he chose the age of five. As mentioned earlier on, Mrs. C remembered Billy first mentioning his adoption at the age of five, following their disclosure of it when he was four. In this same session, Billy moved from the idea of being sold to his fear of being abandoned. Remarking that he knew kids who had been sold, he said, "I saw this girl once standing in the train station, alone, left by her parents." The understanding that he had been bought and sold left him with the overriding fear that this kind of transaction would repeat itself again someday.

Associated with the theme of sales and transactions was Billy's ongoing experience of annual reunions at the adoption agency with other children adopted through the agency. These reunions were organized by the adoption agency in order to create a support network among the children adopted through this agency, as well as to invite prospective parents who were in the process of deciding on an agency to use in their attempt to adopt. In the context of his play, Billy shamefully remarked on being brought up on stage in front of a large group of people where he was then introduced along with other kids to prospective parents. In his story, he is reluctantly paraded on stage while those in the audience look him over. The commoditization of the adoption world cast meaning on Billy's relationship to his adopted self, as suggested in the experience of this part of himself as a marketing tool for the agency.

Parallel to this, Mr. and Mrs. C's financial woes were exacerbated during the treatment due to Mr. C's sporadic employment and his financial losses incurred in the stock market. They became delinquent on their payments, and were unsure about the possibility of being able to continue the treatment. As their balance increased, I was approaching the dreaded, yet unavoidable, reality of possibly having to suspend the treatment, leaving me feeling as though I was on the verge of having to abandon them. It appeared that Billy was aware of his parents' dire financial position, and that this for him was actively influencing his own adoption narrative. There was guilt attached to the sense of gratitude he felt toward his parents, and Billy felt himself to be a financial burden.

Although Billy was now attending school on a regular basis and his violent tantrums had subsided, they had been replaced by more manipulative behavior that served to intensify Mr. and Mrs. C's hostility and unconscious wish to get rid of Billy, thus realizing Billy's greatest fear. Billy repeatedly tested his parents and his expectation that they would inevitably reject him. To protect himself against further dependence on them, he sought to control his parents as a means of managing his sense of helplessness. Mr. and Mrs. C were still elusive, and at the same time working both for and against the treatment.

However, a shift occurred as Billy's play shed light on his parents' own object loss. Billy arrived for his session one day with one of his favorite animals and explained to me that this particular animal lived in a place called Roach Alley. In response to my inquiry about the intriguing name, Billy, sounding like a professor of biology pontificating about the origins of the species, looked out from the podium and explained that Roach Alley is famous for the birthplace of roach eggs. When the roach eggs are hatching, he went on to explain, their mothers leave *before* the babies are born. A few moments later, Billy mentioned that penises are for peeing and making babies, and inquired about the conception of babies. In my asking him about the roach eggs, Billy blurted out, "My mommy can't have babies, something is wrong with her stomach and that's why I'm adopted." This was immediately followed by a game of earthquake in which his character becomes preoccupied with contracting Lyme disease. His play here and its associative links suggests that Billy struggled to make sense of where babies come from given his own historical circumstances. Billy's understanding of there being something wrong with his mother's stomach stood in relation to his own birth from a roach, the roach-like connotations possibly both an allusion to his birth from a spoiled, dirty egg left by his birth mother to hatch alone, as well as an unconscious reference to his adoptive mother's defective ovaries or to his adoptive father's penis that could pee, but not make babies.

Billy saw his mother's body as damaged, a representation constructed from his mother's repeated explanation to him that the deficiencies of her body had prevented her from conceiving. His mother also had frequent medical visits and illness in her extended family that she halfheartedly tried to hide from Billy (for instance, whispering about these events to others in his presence). The effect of this knowing and not knowing, as well as the mystifying explanations of the obvious, left Billy feeling paranoid and with a deep-seated fear of his mother dying. He worried about her health, and identified with her as sickly, as hinted at by his contraction of Lyme disease in the play and his frequent somatic excuses as reasons why he sometimes did not want to leave home. Billy's "sickness" may not only be seen as an identification with his mother's "broken" body, it can also be taken as a desire to find elements of sameness and points of similarity with his mother (Ehrensaft 2002).

Billy's reference to Roach Alley led me to more actively pursue contact with Mr. and Mrs. C, and to directly confront their avoidance of the past and their absorption in the present state of affairs. In my commenting on this with each of them, each began to speak with me more openly about the traumatic impact of trying to conceive a child over the course of six years. In their own way, each acknowledged the magnitude of the loss of the wished-for child. When I spoke with Mrs. C, she reflected on her chronic medical problems that first started when she was a child and that when she was an adult involved several cancer scares that turned out to be false alarms. Over the years of trying to get pregnant, her marriage and sexual life with Mr. C deteriorated. Mrs. C came to feel that her female organs were "damaged," and not being able to bear a child made her question her own womanhood. Each time she menstruated, she was reminded of being unable to conceive a child and would fall into a depressive state for days. She carried all sorts of beliefs about her risk for cancer that were not medically founded, and she lived with the constant fear that she might die at an early age. She was extremely envious of other women around her who had been able to bear their own children, including Billy's birth mother. Over the last few years she felt that she had "stopped living," and that she was waiting for terminal illness to appear. She considered how her preoccupation with her fears of somatic illness may have impacted Billy's relationship to the world around him.

Mr. C, somewhat less available in our work together, reflected on his own feeling of impotence in connection with male expectations within his own conservative, traditional upbringing. He recalled how the many years of trying to impregnate his wife had chipped away at his self-image, already weakened by his sporadic employment and difficulty in supporting their family.

Mr. and Mrs. C went into more detail about the humiliating process of being screened and interviewed during the pre-adoption process, and the frustrating wait to learn if they would ever indeed receive a child. This arduous process left them feeling empty, and took its toll on their marriage, with each questioning their own as well as the other's sense of adequacy. Both Mr. and Mrs. C were forthcoming for the first time about their hostility toward Billy, hostility that had been festering and manifesting in the form of guilt and atonement. Mr. and Mrs. C each revealed their own fantasized child, speaking of how Billy fell short of this. For Mr. C, he was gravely disappointed that Billy was not more coordinated, and he cringed each time Billy exhibited any sort of clumsiness. Mrs. C spoke of her wish that Billy would be more like her: "socially outgoing" and "driven." In allowing themselves to experience their disillusionment with Billy and by acknowledging their hostility, Mr. and Mrs. C reconnected with their unconscious wishes associated with conceiving a child, therefore beginning the process of mourning these wishes and creating a space for their love of their living son. Our exploration of these sets of concerns and the path that led to Billy's adoption allowed for a shift in their perspective toward one in which they could begin to see Billy as his own person while at the same time allowing them to embrace their own parental efforts.

Through my parent work with Mr. and Mrs. C, important shifts took place. It seemed as though the crisis that had pervaded the treatment abated, and a sense of continuity reigned for the first time, as though time, with its past, present, and future, had been restored. Mrs. C sought out her own therapy for the first time, and was becoming more aware of the extent to which she used Billy to meet her own needs, rather than turning to others such as her husband. Mr. C became active in a self-help group, and spoke openly about Billy's adoption in contrast to hiding it in the past out of shame and embarrassment. He was also becoming more comfortable with asserting his authority. In Billy's play, roach eggs and cyclones evolved into bridges that connected people from one destination to the next. Although these bridges were not immune to catastrophic surprises that threatened both the people crossing and the stability of the bridges themselves, the surprises became less devastating over time. Billy's bridges seemed to symbolize a link between his adoptive history (his birth mother) and his adoptive parents. At home, Billy's violent tantrums dramatically subsided, and he became significantly less fearful.

CONCLUSION

Adoption is an inherently confusing process for children, no matter what the circumstances. Although one cannot and should not reduce an entire family's constellation of symptoms to an adoption, and should hold in mind that adoption is one context among many, including "normal" developmental struggles (Winnicott 1954b), adoption nonetheless has particular meanings for each individual. Its unconscious representations in the parents interact with the young child's own representation of it. I think we have a tendency in the psychoanalytic literature to forget what we know when it comes to making sense of events such as adoption. We tend in these situations to isolate the child in relation to the large fact, and to forget things like unconscious communication and the "ghosts in the nursery" (Fraiberg, Adelson, and Shapiro 1975).

In situations where a couple has tried to conceive a child and has in some cases turned to fertility treatment, this painful endeavor then sets the stage for trying to adopt a child. Infertility and the loss of not being able to bear one's own child may then exert their influence on the couple's attachment to their adoptive child and the child's understanding of where he comes from. The extent to which these parents have mourned their loss will greatly shape the young child's conscious and unconscious knowledge and understanding of his own adoptive history. The adoptive parents' mourning of their wishes and the experience of disillusionment on the part of the adoptive parents allow for the child's own mourning, a process that allows the parents to accept the gift of their child and, in turn, allows the child to adopt his adoptive parents (Kernberg 1985).

REFERENCES

Altman, N. 1995. *The Analyst in the Inner City*. Hillsdale, NJ: Analytic Press.
———. 2002. "Relational Horizons in Child Psychoanalysis." *Journal of Infant, Child, and Adolescent Psychotherapy* 2, no. 1: 29–39.
Altman, N., R. Briggs, J. Frankel, D. Gensler, and P. Pantone. 2002. *Relational Child Psychotherapy*. New York: Other Press.
Aron, L. 1996. *A Meeting of Minds*. Hillsdale, NJ: Analytic Press.
Aronson, S. 2001. "Only Connect: The Mutuality of an Attachment in the Treatment of a Resilient Adolescent." *Contemporary Psychoanalysis* 37, no. 3: 427–41.
Beebe, B., and F. M. Lachmann. 1988. "The Contribution of Mother-Infant Mutual Influence to the Origins of Self- and Object Representations." *Psychoanalytic Psychology* 5, no. 4: 305–37.
Beebe, B., F. M. Lachmann, and J. Jaffe. 1997. "Mother-Infant Interaction Structures and Presymbolic Self- and Object Representations." *Psychoanalytic Dialogues* 7, no. 2: 133–82.
Blum, H. P. 1983. "Adoptive Parents: Generative Conflict and Generational Continuity." *Psychoanalytic Study of the Child* 38:141–63.
Bonovitz, C. 2001. "Treating the Child, Treating the System: Weathering the Storm." Paper presented at the annual meeting of the American Psychological Association, San Francisco, California.

———. 2003. "Treating Children Who Do Not Play or Talk: Finding a Pathway to Intersubjective Relatedness." *Psychoanalytic Psychology* 20, no. 2: 315–28.

———. 2005. "The Cocreation of Fantasy and the Transformation of Psychic Structure." *Psychoanalytic Dialogues* 14, no. 5: 553–80.

Brinich, P. M. 1980. "Some Potential Effects of Adoption on Self and Object Representations." *Psychoanalytic Study of the Child* 35:107–33.

Brodzinsky, D. M., R. Lang, and D. W. Smith. 1995. "Parenting Adopted Children." In *Status and Social Conditions of Parenting*. Vol. 3 of *Handbook of Parenting*. Ed. M. Bornstein. Mahwah, NJ: Lawrence Erlbaum, 209–32.

Brodzinsky, D. M., D. W. Smith, and A. B. Brodzinsky. 1998. *Children's Adjustment to Adoption: Developmental and Clinical Issues*. London: Sage.

Clothier, F. 1939. "Some Aspects of the Problem of Adoption." *American Journal of Orthopsychiatry* 9:558–615.

Deeg, C. 1989. "On the Adoptee's Cathexis of the Lost Object." *Psychoanalysis and Psychotherapy* 7, no. 2: 152–61.

———. 1990. "Defensive Functions of the Adoptee's Cathexes of the Lost Object." *Psychoanalysis and Psychotherapy* 8, no. 2: 145–56.

Deutsch, H. 1945. *Psychology of Women*. Vol. 2. New York: Grune and Stratton.

Ehrensaft, D. 1997. *How Well-Meaning Parents Are Giving Children Too Much—But Not What They Need*. New York: Guilford.

———. 2002. "Where Do Babies Come From: Some Thoughts on the Unconscious Meanings of Infertility, Fertility, and Adoption." Paper presented at the spring meeting of the Division of Psychoanalysis, American Psychological Association, New York.

Feder, L. 1974. "Adoption Trauma: Oedipus Myth/Clinical Reality." *International Journal of Psychoanalysis* 55:491–93.

Fonagy, P., and M. Target. 1998. "Mentalization and the Changing Aims of Child Psychoanalysis." *Psychoanalytic Dialogues* 8, no. 1: 87–114.

Fraiberg, S., E. Adelson, and V. Shapiro. 1975. "Ghosts in the Nursery: A Psychoanalytic Approach to the Problem of Impaired Infant-Mother Relationships." *Journal of the American Academy of Child Psychiatry* 14:387–422.

Framo, J. L. 1992. *Family-of-Origin Therapy: An Intergenerational Approach*. New York: Brunner/Mazel.

Frankel, J. 1998. "The Play's the Thing: How the Essential Processes of Therapy Are Seen Most Clearly in Child Therapy." *Psychoanalytic Dialogues* 8, no. 1: 149–82.

Freud, S. 1950. "Family Romances." Orig. pub. 1908. In *Collected Papers*. Vol. 5. Ed. J. Strachey. London: Hogarth, 74–78.

Gaines, R. 1995. "The Treatment of Children." In *The Handbook of Interpersonal Psychoanalysis*. Ed. M. Lionells, J. Fiscalini, C. Mann, and D. B. Stern. Hillsdale, NJ: Analytic Press, 761–69.

Glenn, J. 1985. "The Adopted Child's Self and Object Representations: Discussion of Dr. Kernberg's Paper." *International Journal of Psychoanalytic Psychotherapy* 11:309–13.

Greenberg, J. R., and S. A. Mitchell. 1983. *Object Relations in Psychoanalytic Theory*. Cambridge, MA: Harvard University Press.

Hirsch, I. 2003. "Analysts' Observing-Participation with Theory." *Psychoanalytic Quarterly* 72:217–40.

Hodges, J. 1989. "Aspects of the Relationship to Self and Objects in Early Maternal Deprivation and Adoption." *Bulletin of the Anna Freud Center* 12, no. 1: 5–27.

Hodges, J., M. Berger, S. Melzak, R. Oldeschulte, S. Rabb, and F. Salo. 1984. "Two Crucial Questions: Adopted Children in Psychoanalytic Treatment." *Journal of Child Psychotherapy* 10:47–56.

Hoffman, I. Z. 1998. *Ritual and Spontaneity in the Psychoanalytic Process: A Dialectical Constructivist View*. Hillsdale, NJ: Analytic Press.

Hopkins, J. 2000. "Overcoming a Child's Resistance to Late Adoption: How One New Attachment Can Facilitate Another." *Journal of Child Psychotherapy* 26, no. 3: 335–49.

Joseph, B. 1987. "Projective Identification—Some Clinical Aspects." In *Melanie Klein Today*. Vol. 1. Ed. E. B. Spillius. London: Routledge, 138–53.

Kantor, S. 1995. "Interpersonal Treatment of Adolescents." In *The Handbook of Interpersonal Psychoanalysis*. Ed. M. Lionells, J. Fiscalini, C. Mann, and D. B. Stern. Hillsdale, NJ: Analytic Press, 771–92.

Kernberg, P. F. 1985. "Child Analysis with a Severely Disturbed Adopted Child." *International Journal of Psychoanalytic Psychotherapy* 11:277–99.

Kirschner, D. 1992. "Understanding Adoptees Who Kill: Dissociation, Patricide, and the Psychodynamics of Adoption." *International Journal of Offender Therapy and Comparative Criminology* 36, no. 4: 323–33.

———. 1988. "Antisocial Behavior in Adoptees: Patterns and Dynamics." *Child and Adolescent Social Work* 5, no. 4: 300–312.

Klauber, T. 1991. "Ill Treatment in the Countertransference: Some Thoughts on Concurrent Work with an Adopted Girl and with Her Family by the Same Psychotherapist." *Journal of Child Psychotherapy* 17:45–61.

Krimendahl, E. K. 1998. "Metaphor in Child Psychoanalysis: Not Simply a Means to an End." *Contemporary Psychoanalysis* 34:49–66.

Lieberman, A. F. 1992. "Infant-Parent Psychotherapy with Toddlers." *Development and Psychopathology* 4:559–74.

Lifton, B. J. 1998. *Journey of the Adopted Self: A Quest for Wholeness*. New York: Basic Books.

Main, M., and E. Hesse. 1990. "Parents' Unresolved Traumatic Experiences Are Related to Infants' Disorganized Attachment Status: Is Frightened and/or Frightening Parental Behavior the Linking Mechanism?" In *Attachment in the Preschool Years: Theory, Research, and Intervention*. Ed. M. T. Greenberg, D. Cicchetti, and E. M. Cummings. Chicago: University of Chicago Press, 161–82.

Mitchell, S. A. 1988. *Relational Concepts in Psychoanalysis: An Integration*. Cambridge, MA: Harvard University Press.

———. 2000. *Relationality: From Attachment to Intersubjectivity*. Hillsdale, NJ: Analytic Press.

Munschauer, C. A. 1997. "Shame: The Dark Shadow of Infertility." In *The Widening Scope of Shame*. Ed. M. R. Lansky and A. P. Morrison. Hillsdale, NJ: Analytic Press, 313–23.

Nickman, S. 1985. "Losses in Adoption." *Psychoanalytic Study of the Child* 40:365–98.

Pantone, P. 1995. "Preadolescence and Adolescence." In *The Handbook of Interpersonal Psychoanalysis*. Ed. M. Lionells, J. Fiscalini, C. Mann, and D. B. Stern. Hillsdale, NJ: Analytic Press, 277–92.

———. 2000. "Treating the Parental Relationship as the Identified Patient in Child Psychotherapy." *Journal of Infant, Child, and Adolescent Psychotherapy* 1, no. 1: 19–38.

Priel, B., B. Kantor, and A. Besser. 2000. "Two Maternal Representations: A Study of Israeli Adopted Children." *Psychoanalytic Psychology* 17, no. 1: 128–45.

Sants, H. J. 1964. "Genealogical Bewilderment in Children with Substitute Parents." *British Journal of Medical Psychology* 37:133–41.

Schechter, M. D. 1970. "About Adoptive Parents." In *Parenthood: Its Psychology and Psychopathology*. Ed. E. J. Anthony and T. Benedek. Boston: Little, Brown, 353–73.

———. 2000. "Attachment Theory in the Light of Adoption Research." In *Thicker Than Blood*. Ed. S. Akhtar and S. Kramer. Northvale, NJ: Jason Aronson, 139–53.

Schneider, S., and Rimmer, E. 1984. "Adoptive Parents' Hostility Toward Their Adopted Children." *Children and Youth Services Review* 6: 345–52.

Seligman, S. 1999. "Integrating Kleinian Theory and Intersubjective Infant Research Observing Projective Identification." *Psychoanalytic Dialogues* 9, no. 2: 129–59.

Shabad, P. 1993. "Repetition and Incomplete Mourning: The Intergenerational Transmission of Traumatic Themes." *Psychoanalytic Psychology* 10, no. 1: 61–75.

Silverman, M. A. 2000. "Adoption, Insecurity, and Fear of Attachment: An Illustrative Psychoanalytic Case Study." In *Thicker Than Blood*. Ed. S. Akhtar and S. Kramer. Northvale, NJ: Jason Aronson, 171–99.

Silverman, R. C., and A. F. Lieberman. 1999. "Negative Maternal Attributions, Projective Identification, and the Intergenerational Transmission of Violent Relational Patterns." *Psychoanalytic Dialogues* 9, no. 2: 161–86.

Spiegel, S. 1996. *An Interpersonal Approach to Child and Adolescent Psychotherapy*. New York: Columbia University Press.

Stern, D. B. 1997. *Unformulated Experience: From Dissociation to Imagination in Psychoanalysis*. Hillsdale, NJ: Analytic Press.

Stern, D. N. 1995. *The Motherhood Constellation*. New York: Basic Books.

Sullivan, H. S. 1940. *Conceptions of Modern Psychiatry*. New York: Norton.

———. 1953. *Interpersonal Theory of Psychiatry*. New York: Norton.

Toussieng, P. W. 1962. "Thoughts Regarding the Etiology of Psychological Difficulties in Adopted Children." *Child Welfare* 41: 59–71.

Verrier, N. N. 1993. *The Primal Wound*. Baltimore, MD: Gateway Press.

Wagner, L. B. 2001. "Contemporary Perspectives on Adoption." Paper presented at the spring meeting of the Division of Psychoanalysis, American Psychological Association, Santa Fe, New Mexico.

Warshaw, S. 1992. "Mutative Factors in Child Psychoanalysis: A Comparison of Diverse Relational Perspectives." In *Relational Perspectives in Psychoanalysis*. Ed. N. Skolnick and S. Warshaw. Hillsdale, NJ: Analytic Press, 147–74.

Waterman, B. 2001. "Mourning the Loss Builds the Bond: Primal Communication between Foster, Adoptive, or Stepmother and Child." *Journal of Loss and Trauma* 6:277–300.

Wieder, H. 1977a. "On Being Told of Adoption." *Psychoanalytic Quarterly* 46:1–22.

———. 1977b. "The Family Romance Fantasies of Adoptees." *Psychoanalytic Quarterly* 46: 185–200.

———. 1978. "On When and Whether to Disclose about Adoption." *Journal of the American Psychoanalytic Association* 26, no. 4: 793–811.

Winnicott, D. W. 1949. "Hate in the Countertransference." *International Journal of Psychoanalysis* 30:69–75.

———. 1954a. "Pitfalls in Adoption." In *Child and the Outside World*. London: Tavistock, 45–52.

———. 1954b. "Two Adopted Children." In *Child and the Outside World*. London: Tavistock, 52–69.

Zinner, J., and R. Shapiro. 1972. "Projective Identification as a Mode of Perception and Behavior in Families of Adolescents." *International Journal of Psychoanalysis* 53:523–30.

Chapter Three

International Adoption

Projection and Externalization in the Treatment of a Four-Year-Old Girl and Her Parents

Kathleen Hushion

Parents who create or expand their families through international adoption often find themselves particularly vulnerable to the insecurities that plague parenthood. I recently saw four-year-old Natasha who presented with temper tantrums that included hitting her mother and throwing a block at a boy in preschool. The parents, who had adopted her from Kazakhstan at seven months of age, could not understand why I needed to take their family history or discuss Natasha's post-adoption development. They felt that this aggressive behavior was a product of the "Russian in her" and had no connection to their relationship with their child.

As a child therapist, it is certainly not the first time I have heard a parent attribute their child's problems to external influence. So often, it is the other kids, an inexperienced teacher, or too much sugar in the diet, all of which serve as a reminder of how difficult it is to acknowledge when a child needs help and how narcissistic vulnerabilities can distort reality. In this chapter, I will discuss how the experience of adopting and raising their child may provide adoptive parents with unique opportunities to displace, deny, and disguise their own insecurities and conflicts. And, through case vignettes and one extensive case example, I will show how this impacts on the parent-child relationship and the child's development.

Children adopted from foreign countries arrive in their parents' arms with innate temperaments and a short developmental history, and they come from a cultural milieu usually very different from that of their new family. Adoption professionals encourage parents to help their child maintain a connection to the customs and mores of the country of origin. Ethnic identity and differences in appearance can emerge as issues in the course of a child's life, to some degree, in the same way that they occur in biological families. For example, a blond-haired, fair-skinned mother can have a daughter who has the olive skin and dark complexion of her South American father. In my experience, cultural and physical differences are either overemphasized or denied, both of which can indicate an underlying struggle for the parents. For example, ten-year-old Jessica was adopted from Guatemala at six months of age by a couple who were both Irish-American attorneys. Jessica was referred for therapy due to symptoms of depression and experiences of being scapegoated by her peers. When I asked the parents to tell me about their daughter's experience of looking so different from them, the mother laughed defensively and said that they don't like to harp on the differences, and in fact, Jessica believed that her skin was the same color as her parents. This blatant disavowal by the parents revealed their own difficulties with this issue and, unfortunately, left their child with no psychic space to explore the differences and what they meant to her.

The opposite can also be true. When parents overemphasize cultural connections for their child, it is often a red flag that they are experiencing some conflict and denying it through a defensive overemphasis that serves to highlight the difference between parents and child. Adoptees from Asian countries have a wealth of opportunity to be involved in their culture through agencies like Families with Children from China (FCC) and the Chinese-American community. But a parent can unconsciously utilize these opportunities to mask a problem. For example, Ms. J brought her five-year-old daughter for evaluation when her daughter refused to separate at the start of kindergarten. In my discussions with this single mom, Ms. J proudly emphasized the degree of her involvement in the adoption community and cultural activities. She created a playgroup for adopted children, sent her daughter to a Chinese school for art, dance, and language, and never missed any cultural event. When first arriving home with her daughter she tried to find a Chinese nanny but was unsuccessful. When I asked her about soccer or gymnastics for her feisty and athletic little girl, she said it had never occurred to her. This mom's impediment to making a connection to her daughter was complex but manifested in her overinvolvement in things that emphasized their differences and separateness and in an inability to tune in to her daughter's unique temperament and personality. Upon exploration, it emerged that this mother was extremely self-conscious and guilt-ridden regarding her status as a single, older mom. Her immersion in the adoption community and cultural events helped her to avoid more mainstream families in the community at large where she felt odd and uncomfortable. But when her daughter regressed at the start of kindergarten, this mother was thrown into the spotlight that illuminates all mothers who struggle with separation.

Every parent struggles with the task of helping their infant or toddler separate and become comfortably independent. Adoptive parents have a more complex task because they are beginning to develop an attachment to their new son or daughter who is already involved in the separation/individuation process. The child's attachment to external objects may have already changed multiple times while their internalized object representation has been in process. As will be discussed in chapter 4, parents must be acutely attuned to their child's behaviors, which can provide important clues to the child's unique needs for attachment, separation, and affect regulation. It is hard to hear your fifteen-month-old whimper at bedtime and during the night without jumping up to soothe them. Adoptive parents who know their child spent the first year of life in an orphanage with little individual attention can find it particularly difficult to say, "No" and help their child achieve the sense of internal regulation necessary for healthy growth and independent functioning. Parents who struggle with their own aggression or dependency needs often utilize their child's early deprivation as an excuse to overindulge and thereby avoid their own struggle.

Quite often, internationally adopted children have developmental delays and medical conditions when they first arrive in this country. Pediatricians who specialize in international adoption can identify and treat problems, and early intervention is often necessary to bring muscle tone, speech, and sensory-motor delays up to snuff. Many parents experience severe narcissistic injury when their child is less than perfect, resulting in parental depression and feelings of alienation. The fact that their child was adopted can be used as a way to distance bruised psyches from any connection to this child that they perceive as less than perfect. By contrast, defensive hypervigilance to a potential problem can be a manifestation of a mother or father who needs to project her or his insecurities, or of a reaction formation disguising conflicts. As I will show in the case example, the child can become the repository for a parent's negative projections.

Adoptive parents often feel they are in a fishbowl and subject to constant scrutiny by the agency, family, other professionals, or even any passerby who might notice that their son or daughter has a different appearance from the parents. This factor only exacerbates any anxiety that is natural to parents with a new baby or toddler and lends itself to an excessive or hyper concern about problems that may be visible to others. Whether the child has a temper tantrum in the grocery store or a facial rash, it is somehow highlighted when he or she is an internationally adopted child. And however striking or adorable the child may appear, their differentness serves as a red flag to the public that this is not the parents' biological child. For some mothers whose self-worth has been chipped away by years of fertility treatments or who delayed motherhood for conflictual reasons, their adopted child can be a constant reminder of their inadequacy.

The issue of birth parents is complex and emotionally charged for both adopted children and their parents, and in international adoption it is even more complicated. For example, in China it is virtually impossible to locate the biological parents because the children have been abandoned with no identifying data. This factor can lend itself to excessive fantasy for both the child and the adoptive parents. In my experience, I have observed both defensive idealization and blatant denigration of the birth parents. While I will not take up this important issue in this chapter, suffice it to say that the existence of another mother can be psychologically maneuvered in a variety of ways by an adoptive parent who needs to disguise or project his or her own related feelings and fantasies, particularly unconscious conflicts with one's own parents.

The following clinical example highlights many of these issues and shows how parents' conflicts can interact with their adopted child and exert a powerful influence upon the developmental tasks of childhood.

CLINICAL EXAMPLE

Katie was adopted from China at thirteen months of age. She was abandoned at birth and placed in an institution in a rural area where she spent the next thirteen months with the exception of a two-week stay in a hospital for reasons that were unclear. When Katie's adoptive parents arrived in China, they were not permitted to visit the orphanage. Katie was delivered to them in their hotel, so they had no information about the conditions or staff of the institution. But by all accounts Katie was relatively healthy, and her development was grossly within normal range for her age.

When I first met Katie she was three years and seven months old, an adorable, wide-eyed little girl who appeared vibrant and healthy. Her parents, Mr. and Mrs. T, were an Irish-Catholic couple in their midthirties: Mrs. T was an accountant, and Mr. T was a school administrator. They brought Katie for evaluation due to problems with separation and unresolved toilet training. They were also concerned about her angry outbursts at home contrasted with excessive shyness in public. Mrs. T felt that Katie's speech and fine motor development were delayed despite the fact that she had been evaluated by early intervention services and found to be functioning within normal limits. At twenty-one months, Katie did not have a large repertoire of words, and Mrs. T felt she was lagging behind her peers. She arranged for private speech therapy as well as occupational therapy for a slight fine motor deficit.

My first impression of Katie's mother was of an intelligent, concerned parent who was unsure of her parenting skills and overly vigilant regarding potential problems in her daughter. Both parents were very sensitive to adoption issues and attended seminars and read many books to make sure they were doing the right thing. Mrs. T took a leave from her job for the first six months that Katie was home and made arrangements for the many services that she felt Katie needed, but described feeling almost relieved to return to work and share the caretaking with a nanny. Mr. T was a very pleasant, gentle man who seemed more comfortable in the nurturing role and was protective of his wife's self-critical tendencies. Neither of the parents was very comfortable with anger and both sought concrete solutions for the presenting problems.

Katie had been sleeping in her parents' bed regularly since she was about sixteen months old. Initially she would cry at bedtime, and her parents had great difficulty allowing her to learn to soothe herself and could not tolerate her crying for more than a few minutes. They described being indulgent for the first year as a way to compensate for Katie's early deprivation and lack of individual attention. By the time Katie was three, Mr. and Mrs. T realized that this could not continue but were unable to find a solution. Every night she would be allowed to fall asleep in her parents' bed, and they would carry her back to her room. When she awoke during the night, she would angrily jump back into their bed. Bleary-eyed from sleep deprivation, the T's *wanted* Katie to sleep in her own bed, but it became apparent that both parents had a hard time setting limits and establishing boundaries.

Toilet training was problematic for similar reasons. According to both parents, Katie was essentially trained but insisted on wearing her diaper to bed at night even though she woke up dry every morning. In addition she was adamant about wearing her diaper to preschool. Mrs. T had read that children who spend their first year of life in an institution often achieve developmental milestones on a different timetable so they should not be pushed. Therefore she felt that Katie would give up the diaper when she was ready and did not address the issue any further. Mrs. T was surprised when the preschool teacher suggested that she just send Katie to school in underpants.

In my sessions with Katie, she took total control of the play as well as the contact between us. She was intense and would often act angry to the point where I wondered if she was teasing me. But her play themes were appropriate for her age and reflected much of her real-life experience. She engaged me in enactments of mother-baby relationships with bedtime scenarios and diapering scenes. Since Katie was becoming very verbal, she was able to use this play to talk about her bedtime worries and diaper problems, with me and with her mom. Her aggression was most evident in her domineering style, and at this point I attributed it to a defensive structure that may have had its origins in the first year of life (Cohen 1996; Fraiberg 1982).

Over the next six months, I worked with Mr. and Mrs. T on the toilet-training and sleeping issues. Since both parents were so unsure of their parenting skills, I felt that I needed to advise them in a fairly concrete way. I told Mrs. T to simply tell Katie that she was not going to buy any more diapers since she did not need them anymore, and we worked out a behavioral plan to help Katie sleep in her own bed and to separate at preschool. Since these parents were highly motivated, they followed my advice to the letter and the presenting problems began to resolve. In my next meeting with the parents, I felt confident that the case was moving along well, but to my surprise they were frustrated and critical. They expressed concern about Katie's "mood swings," or outbursts, at home and what they still believed to be a speech delay. At this point, I began to question my competence and wondered if I was underestimating Katie's pathology. As I examined this countertransference, I also wondered if I had underestimated the parents' pathology and the degree of stress that they were experiencing. It seems that all their corrective action had raised their anxiety and taken its toll on their internal worlds. The parents, particularly the mother, could not accept that the problems were improving, and they focused solely on the areas that were not. I realized that while able to follow directions, these parents needed to be able to reflect on the meaning of Katie's behavior, as well as their own responses to her (Slade, forthcoming).

In one session with Mrs. T, I asked if she was aware that she did not seem to derive any gratification from Katie's improvements and only focused on the difficulties. She responded with a sense of resignation that she felt it was her fate to have a child with problems. She described it as an old feeling that had resurfaced during her fertility struggle and again when she adopted Katie. She discussed powerful feelings of inadequacy that I suspect had been projected onto me. I wondered how these feelings were affecting her relationship with Katie. Was she looking for defects in her daughter as a way to rid herself of a painful, defective sense of self? And did Katie's adopted status, which can allow for a degree of distance as well as the potential for certain problems, provide a unique opportunity for these projections?

I suggested that Mrs. T meet with me more frequently, and she agreed. It was in these sessions that I learned more about her background and the source of these difficulties. She was raised in a moderately religious family described as quite chaotic and unstructured. Her father was a college professor, an alcoholic given to severe mood swings. Mrs. T began to realize that her difficulty tolerating aggression, or any instinctual expression, was related to her fear of losing control and becoming like her father: erratic and explosive. Her mother was tense and distant, raising six children and returning to work as a nurse when Mrs. T was six years old. It would seem that Mrs. T's experiences of neglect by her own parents left her with an emotional void and narcissistic vulnerabilities that had an effect on her functioning from early on. She said that growing up she kept to herself most of the time, was a good student, and had no boyfriends until college where she met her future husband. They married when they were both twenty-five, and hoped to start a family by the time they were thirty. When this did not happen, they began the long and painful process of fertility intervention. Mrs. T described being withdrawn and feeling depressed during this time, but "resigned to my fate." Mr. T was extremely supportive of his wife's feelings and always thought of adoption as a good option. Mrs. T did not accept it until five years and many disappointments later.

Mrs. T's long-standing narcissistic vulnerabilities were exacerbated by her inability to conceive a child. Her feelings of inadequacy were acutely focused on her experience of mothering and resulted in her need to separate good and bad and, apparently, project her negative self-representation onto her daughter. Mrs. T would vacillate between internalizing Katie's problems as a reflection of her own bad mothering and reinforcement of her negative self-image, and externalizing it as an *adoption issue*. Katie remained highly ambivalent toward her mom and had great difficulty reconciling the ambivalent feelings that are a normal part of this stage of development. Several authors (Brinich 1985; Glenn 1985; Kernberg 1985) discuss splitting in adoptive families; Brinich emphasizes that ambivalence exists in all parent-child relationships but that "adoption offers some special opportunities for developmental anomalies in the management of ambivalence" (196).

Mr. and Mrs. T would often bring up examples of behaviors that they interpreted as Katie's search for her birth mother. For example, they reported that Katie would often talk about her preschool teacher, a pretty young woman with long, straight, dark hair. In my mind, it is not unusual for a little girl to idealize a teacher, but both parents believed that this reflected a fantasy about her biological mother. A few weeks later in the midst of a struggle over bedtime, Katie angrily exclaimed, "I wish I had two mommies." Mrs. T said, "I asked her who else besides me, fully expecting she was going to talk about her mother in China." To her surprise, Katie responded, "A good mommy." Mrs. T's difficulty in accepting her daughter's aggressive feelings or potential idealization of her made it difficult for Katie to internalize a stable identification of her adoptive mother. Mrs. T displaced the entire issue onto the birth mother and kept it at a safe distance. Katie's splitting reflected her difficulty resolving ambivalent feelings toward her adoptive mom and her ongoing wish for an omnipotent mommy.

At this point, Mrs. T accepted a referral for individual psychotherapy, but continued to meet with me monthly to work on parenting issues. Katie, who was now four and one-half years old, had become increasingly angry and controlling with me. She would start the sessions in an almost paranoid stance and turn into different variations of monsters and bad guys that she had to push away, tie up, or imprison, sometimes even physically pushing or hitting me. When I announced the end of our time she would say, "Good," but then would start to ask for objects to take home. Any verbal intervention from me was met with a negative barrier. She would not allow anything to penetrate this primitive defense and risk exposure of the affective turmoil underneath.

As Mrs. T addressed these issues in her own treatment, she was able to be increasingly reflective, and she began to discuss with me the guilt and frustration she experienced in her relationship with Katie. She acknowledged her inability to feel close to her daughter and discussed feeling responsible for all of Katie's difficulties. She worried that Katie would never measure up to her peers and would be at a disadvantage all her life. At other times, she would complain about Katie's behaviors at home and express intolerance for minor problems. My countertransference would often resurface at these times and serve as a red flag that Mrs. T's insecurities were aroused. Mr. T was more tolerant of Katie's erratic behavior but could become passive in his approach to his daughter and his wife.

Up to this time, Mrs. T had allowed the nanny to bring Katie to school, thereby avoiding the struggle of separation. Like many adoptive parents, she did not fully realize that her daughter's current separation anxiety was not just related to early attachment deficits but was also a product of the adoptive parent-child relationship. Her growing ability to understand this issue resulted in some positive changes that improved her relationship with her daughter. She arranged her work schedule so that she could take Katie to school every morning. And as her self-esteem improved, she was able to confront her own and Katie's ambivalence more directly. Arietta Slade defines parental reflective functioning as the mother's "capacity to reflect on the current mental state of the child and upon her own mental states as these pertain to her relationship with her child, as opposed, for instance, to her capacity to reflect upon her childhood relationship with her own parents" (Slade, forthcoming). As Mrs. T was able to contain and regulate her own internal experience more effectively, she could begin to move beyond the concrete, observable aspects of her daughter's behavior and understand what lay beneath.

By the time Katie started kindergarten, she had made outward improvement in all areas, but her personality still bore the burden of her difficulty integrating the loving and hating aspects of her self. She continued to have difficulty managing frustration, and bedtime fears would occasionally resurface. Her early life had left her with vulnerabilities in affect regulation that were further complicated by parents who had severe difficulties expressing their emotions. The competitive feelings that now emerged with the entrance of the

Oedipal phase were intense and powerful. At school, Katie created triangles with classmates and developed rivalries with several friends over which one of them was the favorite of the new music teacher. In our sessions, my role was most often the evil competitor who took her away from an idealized teacher, friend, or parent. She would giggle with sadistic pleasure as she devalued and defeated me.

As we entered the third year of treatment, Katie, who was now six years old, was chronologically entering the latency stage of development. The transference continued to reflect her inner struggle with extremes of loving and hating feelings as well as the residue of an omnipotent three-year-old who could not accept my authority. She needed to feel powerful and superior. Her need to control and devalue me clearly defended against her fear of feeling weak and damaged. Even my words were experienced as magical and powerful, so she would not let me speak without her permission. She played out fantasies where she could see through me and impose magic spells, and did so with such confidence that I wondered about her reality testing. At times, I felt impotent in my effort to have some effect on our relationship and wondered if I truly had underestimated the degree of pathology.

I questioned whether this seemingly borderline pathology was an inevitable outcome of early damage that would leave intractable traces on Katie's developing character. Or was it the product of early vulnerabilities in collision with her mother's difficulties, which could lead to a more benign outcome? Thinking in Kleinian terms, I would say Katie seemed to be entrenched in the paranoid-schizoid position, a normative developmental phase, but in a six-year-old this raised serious questions. I wondered if the treatment could provide the opportunity for Katie to move beyond this position. At this point I accepted my role as "damaged goods," and over the next year, while acting as a container for Katie's negative projections, I made consistent interventions that were designed to chip away at her primitive defenses. Slowly and sporadically, Katie allowed me to speak, which resulted in more reciprocity in our interactions. She began to share information about her friends, events at school, and weekend activities, but often would pepper it with remarks like "And you missed it" or "Nobody invited you because you are so stupid." As her need to devalue me lessened, the comments became "Woops, I can't believe I told you that." She became increasingly curious about my life and my family. She invited me into her fantasy play, which often involved magic carpet rides. And then during one session she acted out a fantasy voyage that took us to China, to the castle of a king and queen, who she said were her "biological parents." Her primitive defenses were beginning to give way to more appropriate latency structures, and she felt safer to use me as a partner on her journey and less as an object of projection. This ushered in another level of treatment where the door was opened to unravel the elaborate construction Katie had made of her life.

Unfortunately, my work with the T family had to end prematurely. For financial reasons, they decided to move to another state where much of Mr. T's family lived. While sad and disappointed that I could not continue the work with Katie, the T's accepted my recommendation and continued treatment with a new therapist at their new location. By all reports, Katie continues to improve and is increasingly prepared for the upsurge of conflict that adolescence will inevitably bring.

CONCLUSION

The reciprocal patterns that are established between a mother and child begin in the first day of life, or even before, and lay the groundwork for all future development. Infants raised in orphanages, hospitals, and foster homes with multiple caretakers do not have this advantage, and their degree of emotional and physical deprivation varies widely. Many authors have written about their observations of infants who, for a variety of reasons, have been deprived of adequate parenting in the first year of life (Ainsworth et al. 1978; Fraiberg 1982; Spitz 1965). Fraiberg describes those who were abandoned at birth and spent their early life in orphanages, hospitals, or other institutions with no consistent caregiver available to deal with "external threats or physiological distress" (184). These children must learn to cope with ongoing feelings of helplessness through defensive reactions like freezing, avoidance, fighting, reversal, and transformation of affect. Many of these primitive mechanisms are the forerunners of serious pathology, and as clinicians, we do see internationally adopted children who suffer from pervasive developmental disorders and reactive attachment disorders. But in my experience, many children adopted internationally develop a means of coping with less than optimal circumstances, and in ways that are quite healthy and adaptive.

Adoptive parents need to be well prepared with the psychological strength and openness needed to tune in and respond appropriately to their child's unique needs and vulnerabilities. The more adaptive child will have developed some method of coping with his or her pre-adoptive environment, but these defenses can be overly rigid or too fragile and can curtail the development of self-regulatory mechanisms and impair basic trust in the object world. Offering a true holding environment (Winnicott 1965) is crucial in these circumstances, so that the child can reorganize and continue development within the fluid, reciprocal relationship of the new dyad.

Parents who are limited in the capacity to reflect and who remain unaware of their own conflicts can add a further complication to their child's development, whether the child is biological or adopted. Parental narcissism is particularly problematic in adoption when so many factors related to the adoption process can erode self-esteem and exacerbate any existing difficulties. And as outlined in this chapter and illustrated in the case material, the adoption process itself can provide unique opportunities for parents to perpetuate the avoidance and denial of their own conflicts, thereby protecting themselves against excessive anxiety or the profound wounds of narcissistic injury.

For those internationally adopted children and their parents who do present in our offices, the clinician's task involves a complex assessment, acknowledging what we do not and perhaps can never know about the child's first year of life, and therefore, suspending our conclusions about the effects of early deprivation, while integrating the multiplicity of factors both pre- and post-adoption. In addition, parental history, which is always part of assessment in child treatment, is equally important when trying to understand the subtle intermingling of experience between an adopted child and his or her new parents. But as mental health professionals expand their knowledge of the unique joys and struggles of international adoption, parents and children will derive the benefit of effective therapeutic treatment, and together they will grow and flourish.

REFERENCES

Ainsworth, M. D. S., Blehar, M. C., Waters, E., and Wall, S. 1978. *Patterns of Attachment: A Psychological Study of the Strange Situation*. Hillsdale, NJ: Erlbaum.

Brinich, Paul. 1985. "Psychoanalytic Perspectives on Adoption and Ambivalence." *Psychoanalytic Psychology* 12, no. 2:181–99.

Cohen, Shlomith. 1996. "Trauma and the Developmental Process: Excerpts from an Analysis of an Adopted Child." *Psychoanalytic Study of the Child* 51:287–302.

Fraiberg, Selma. 1982. "Pathological Defenses in Infancy." *Psychoanalytic Quarterly* 51:612–35.

Glenn, Jules. 1985. "The Adopted Child's Self and Object Representations: Discussion of Dr. Kernberg's Paper." *International Journal of Psychoanalytic Psychotherapy* 11:309–13.

Kernberg, Paulina. 1985. "Psychoanalysis with an Extremely Disturbed Adopted Child." *International Journal of Psychoanalytic Psychotherapy* 11:277–99.

Slade, Arietta. Forthcoming. "Working with Parents in Child Psychotherapy: Engaging the Reflective Function." *Psychoanalytic Inquiry*.

Spitz, Rene. 1965. *The First Year of Life: A Psychoanalytic Study of Normal and Deviant Development of Object Relations.* New York: International Universities Press.

Winnicott, D. W. 1965. *Maturational Processes and the Facilitating Environment.* New York: International Universities Press.

Chapter Four

Working with Parents of Internationally Adopted Infants and Toddlers

Carole Lapidus

In this chapter I will explore the challenges of becoming a parent through adoption, with attention to international adoptions of infants over six months of age, and of toddlers. I will consider reasons for the adoption, parental states of mind before and after the adoption, and the impact of the implicit and explicit memory of the baby or toddler on the attachment and parenting process. One theme of the chapter will be the critical need for emotional support of the parent prior to the adoption, during infancy, and in the early childhood years.

Before the birth of a baby, all parents have a fantasy of what the new family member will be like, from physical attributes to temperament makeup. Adoptive parents share with biological parents thoughts about their fantasy child and parenting preferences. Given that there are no inherited biological similarities in an adopted child, adoptive parents will need opportunity and encouragement to come to know the potential for disappointment, to give voice to their fears, and if necessary, to grieve for their fantasy child. The unique challenges of bonding and forming a solid attachment with an older infant or toddler will therefore be addressed in this chapter. Finally, the role of the baby or toddler's early memory and that memory's relevance to the attachment and parenting process will be explored.

The current generation of child therapists has had increasing contact with families who have adopted children from other countries. During the years 1992–2002, 100,000 international adoptions were processed in the United States (*Pediatrics* 2004). During that ten-year period, the babies and children came primarily from Eastern Europe and the former Soviet Union, Central

With greatest appreciation to the parents and children who shared their stories with me. And many thanks to Drs. Cheryl Lehman and Sarah Zarem who with thoughtfulness and generosity shared their expertise.

America, and Asia. Most had been living in orphanages with care ranging
from extremely neglectful to minimally adequate. It has been known for more
than half a century that physical care alone is not sufficient for a newborn to
thrive. The work of John Bowlby (1969), Sally Provence and Rose Lipton
(1962), and Rene Spitz (1945) has chronicled how modern, antiseptically
clean, and well-equipped orphanages do not in themselves assure progressive
development of constitutionally intact newborns and babies. The unalterable
link found to be critical to development in all domains (social, emotional, motor, language, sensory/affective) was that each baby or toddler be cared for by
someone who was *emotionally* invested in the baby or toddler's well-being.

In some countries, foster-care placement was provided as a transition to
family life during the months before the adoption was legally finalized. Presumably, this placement would expose the baby to a more intimate relationship providing more attentive care and more frequent communication. Pediatricians and other child-development specialists have noted that those babies
and toddlers who have been adopted directly from an orphanage or from other
care that was not developmentally appropriate have greater delays in language acquisition, cognitive and motor development, and sensory integration.
These children also have difficulties in regulating mood, particularly when
under the stress of fatigue, frustration, or transitions.

Many referrals have come to me during the child's third year, although the
adoption may have occurred when the baby was anywhere from six to thirteen months of age. At three years, the emotional storms and perhaps what
parents experience as intentionally provocative behaviors have been occurring for some time, and have reached a level arousing strong feelings in the
parents. A child therapist is often sought out when parents feel helpless and
outraged, though the latter may be thinly veiled. As with so many of those
who seek child therapy consultations, the parents may have resisted calling a
mental health professional, hoping that they would be able to solve the issues
on their own. For some, contacting a child therapist is regarded as failure on
their part as parents. For others, the pain and feeling of failure is so great that
they are fearful of beginning to open up what seems like a Pandora's box. In
both short-term consultations and long-term work with parents and child, I
see my role as one of developing a partnership: joining parents in coming to
know who their child is by examining what they *do* know and what behavioral patterns seem mystifying. Some parents also find themselves stymied by
their own behaviors and are eager for an opportunity to share their thoughts
and feelings about how they have been reacting to their children.

My goal is to draw parents into thinking about what life was like for the
baby or toddler before the adoption and how this child coped with what was
likely to have been unattuned and inconsistent care. Together we will hy-

pothesize about the huge, empty space representing the child's past, an emptiness that is made up of all that is not known and never will be known. This huge space leaves room for the adults in the child's life to reflect on their hopes, dreams, and yes, fears. However, the reality is that a child's adaptive capacities and physical and psychological resilience override negative influences and the majority of babies who have spent up to one year in an institutional or otherwise neglectful setting are able to reach age-appropriate milestones in a catch-up pattern once adequate nutrition and emotional nurturing have been put in place (*Pediatrics* 2004). We often learn that not all that seems difficult about a baby or toddler is explained by the factor of adoption and unknown biological contributions.

PHASE ONE: BECOMING A PARENT THROUGH ADOPTION—WHO IS MY BABY?

It is not unusual for the advice given to soon-to-be adoptive parents to be something on the order of "Just take the baby home and love it." Indeed, embedded in that belief is the notion that love is everything. By embracing the notion that all the baby needs is love, there is, in one fell swoop, an eradication of the lived reality preceding the adoption. Parents adopting a baby or toddler frequently struggle with contradictory feelings, feelings not fully available to the conscious mind but more likely to make themselves known in fleeting moments of thought that all too readily can be pushed aside as too complex, too worrisome, or too frightening to hold in the mind. The inchoate feeling described by parents retrospectively is often *I didn't want to think about why I didn't want to think about my baby's earlier life*. Typically, parents meet their child well aware that the child has had experiences they, the parents, have not been privy to, but about which they want to be respectful. At the very same time they are eager to begin their life as adoptive parents. It is not easy for them to keep in mind the fact that the child had a previous life, the memory of which lingers as the child is beginning a new life with them.

Exactly how memories are expressed by a baby or toddler with little or no language is a question that many have asked even as attentive parents and students of early development have been amassing a wealth of anecdotal evidence supporting the existence of a working memory in babies and toddlers. The burgeoning field of research on brain development in the early years has brought to the foreground new questions and the potential for new understandings. Daniel Siegel, a neuropsychiatrist, has been thinking and writing about memory and brain development in both the parenting process and child development. His hypotheses, regarding mental functioning beginning from birth, have created interest in those whose attention is on the newborn-to-three-year-old population. Fundamental to his hypotheses and to our interest in the place of memory in the adoption of older infants and of toddlers is the notion of the two types of memory: *implicit* and *explicit*. Siegel believes that implicit memory begins forming during the first days of life when the infant begins to perceive the environment. All aspects of the sensory system are active and all experiences become encoded in the brain. The brain, being experience dependent, responds to new events by changing the connections between neurons, the basic building blocks of the brain. These connections become the structure of the brain and are believed to be the means through which experiences are recalled (Siegel 1999, 22). When implicit memories are retrieved, there is *no awareness* that something is being recalled. An example is one family's discovery that singing the same Chinese lullaby repeatedly was helpful in calming their three-year-old. The soothing sounds of the familiar words and the melody, from almost two years before, halted the crying, relaxed her body, and allowed sleep to take over. Siegel hypothesizes that explicit memory becomes possible by one and one-half years and feels like a *recollection*. An explicit memory may be triggered by an experience that associates to a recollection. The toddler may not be able to fully explain the recollection, but is nevertheless aware of it as a memory. The toddler, having few if any words, will not be able to explain the memory, but his or her activity will make clear to the attuned caregiver that a previous experience has come to mind, as in the following vignettes.

A grandparent, having bathed a fourteen-month-old in the afternoon, found that at bedtime the toddler was unwilling to stay in his crib. Upon noting that the little boy repeatedly walked into the bathroom and looked into the tub, the grandparent suspected that the communication indicated that the child expected a bath before bedtime. Sure enough, after a bath, going to sleep was easy.

A small boy, adopted at two and one-half years, cried frantically when placed in his crib at night. Eventually he cried himself to sleep and was found curled into a ball in a corner of the crib. After two months, his mom, feeling sad and frustrated, wondered aloud about how she could help him fall sleep without his being so upset. After the third story that night, the small boy threw himself onto his mom's lap with his little arms clasped around her neck. She interpreted this to mean that he wanted to be held until he fell asleep. Perhaps this was the way he was accustomed to falling asleep.

In thinking about memory, consider the impact of a change of environment or caregiver at twelve to eighteen months. The toddler has already established mental models of daily life and activity. The toddler is in the cognitive process of creating order, of making sense of the world. These mental models or schemata represent generalizations that result from events occurring throughout the period of infancy (Piaget 1969).

One ten-month-old expects to see her dad when she awakens in the morning. One morning, her mom enters the room and the baby, looking at her says, "Dada." She might be thinking something on the order of "What are you doing here? My Dada usually comes at this time."

With an adoption taking place in the second half of the first year and through toddlerhood, there are many behaviors that the child brings that can be incomprehensible and challenging. Using Siegel's paradigm, these behaviors represent either implicit or explicit memory based on the mental models that have already developed and are encoded (stored) in the infant or toddler brain. New experiences will create new mental models even as some older schemata remain in the memory reserves.

The following vignette is most likely an implicit memory recollection appearing as a dream or possibly a night terror.

Liza, now four and one-half years old, was adopted at eleven months from an orphanage in China. At four and one-half she still awakened some nights, though less frequently than in the first year, screaming with her arms outstretched above her head. She was not readily calmed even when picked up, often flailing her arms and legs. In the morning she had no memory of a dream or what had occurred during the night.

Parents whose stories reveal their assumption that their toddler's behavior pattern was established as a coping mechanism are curious to ferret out a meaning for the circumstances creating the need for that adaptive behavior pattern. They are likely to be more empathic and more open to avoiding a power struggle when their toddler is clearly upset by an implicit or explicit memory.

Diego's adoptive mom, Jeanine, was told that he was toilet trained. But beginning with the trip back to the United States, he refused to enter a public bathroom. Was it the noise of the toilets flushing? The hand-drying machines? The people?

One day, Jeanine was angry at Diego (then three years and two months, and about six months after he was adopted), and scolded him. She picked him up to take him to his room. He still had very little language, but he shrieked with fear in his voice, "No, cuna [crib]!" Jeanine had the realization in that moment that he was letting her know that he knew what it was like to be put into his crib. She wondered if he also feared being left alone in a room.

The following is an example of a mental model that a little girl clung to for a year after adoption. It illustrates the range and power of an experience that structures a mental model.

Adopted at thirteen months from an orphanage in China, Aisha for one year refused to be placed in a prone position to have her diaper changed or to go to sleep. Her parents accommodated the baby's need, understanding that being prone had a meaning to Aisha. They knew that in the orphanage Aisha had shared a crib with three other babies, and they assumed that while human contact was important for sensory and social development, Aisha might have used an upright position to distinguish herself and capture the limited attention of an adult. Perhaps for Aisha, to lie down was to be unnoticed. Clearly the prone position made her very anxious. This same little girl was outgoing and engaging from the start of her new life. The vendors and shopkeepers she befriended from her stroller were the same people she ran to, as if they were old friends, as soon as she was ambling about. Her expressive eyes and broad smile drew people to her before she knew English and before she was walking. Her parents wondered if these same capacities were able to draw people to her in the orphanage.

Grief and Loss

Each parent brings to the decision to adopt a many-faceted personal story deeply embedded with hope and fantasy. Memories from the distant and not so distant past along with the present state of mind interact to create complex feelings and thoughts about adopting an infant or toddler. Parents also bring the history of how they came to adopt a child. Whether the path was through the frustration and disappointment of infertility or the lack of a suitable partner, or whether it was to complete an already existing family, each parent brings acknowledged or buried emotions to the adoption process. The details of infertility, the visits with medical professionals, the tests and treatments may be recalled in painful detail along with palpable emotion. The disappointments in relationship building, in the effort to bond with a suitable parenting partner, are similarly recounted. Ultimately, these parents are faced with grieving a tremendous loss. The women need to come to terms with the realization that they will experience neither pregnancy nor nursing; the men, with the realization that they will neither sire a child nor pass on their genes. There will not be a newborn with which to bond. Older couples know that this child is likely to be their only long-awaited child. Older single women may decide to adopt a toddler because they are aware of the reality of age discrimination.

In all cases of adoption, it is unlikely that the child will have the curly locks, kinky hair, fine features, or glowing smile captured in the parent's own baby photos. Choosing to adopt from outside the United States sometimes brings with it the reality of adopting a child who will be racially different. For some, the complexity of that decision is known only in the form of uneasy feelings, some spoken, others inchoate. The parent may be troubled that *Everyone will know that she is adopted, that she's not really my child*. Racial differences stand as a constant reminder to the family, and as a flag to all others, that the child is adopted.

While parenthood is known to be a marker experience, for some, having a biological child is so central to this marker event that if adoption is ultimately decided upon, it occurs only after much soul searching and possibly emotional coercion by a partner. The many concrete issues that adopting parents must face are easier to deal with than the actual experience that includes their awareness and containment of loss. For adoptive parents, to live through a grieving period that ultimately prepares them for bringing a baby into their hearts and home is a formidable challenge. The grieving may not be complete or even acknowledged at the time of the adoption.

PHASE TWO: HOW WILL I KNOW HOW TO BE A GOOD PARENT? MY PARENTS WERE SO AWFUL

Adoptive parents, as well as those parenting a biological child, attribute significance to their own experience of being parented. Nonetheless, many are not open to bringing this subject to discussion and are uncomfortable when it is raised. Does a familiarity with one's experience of childhood have anything to do with effective parenting? This question has been explored by psychologist Mary Main through an interview protocol used in exploration of parents' memories of their own parents as parents. The Adult Attachment Interview (AAI; Main, George, and Kaplan 1985) has become noted for having a predictive correlation with a parent's own attachment style. Main and others have attributed the greatest value to the emotional clarity of the narrative constructed from the interview questions. Their research has established that *how* one was parented is not as relevant as developing a coherent narrative of one's childhood experience. Keeping this notion in mind while working with parents, we are looking for opportunities to assist in their recalling childhood events. Some of the questions we might ask are "What do you think happened in your early relationship with your mother? With your father?" "What did you do when you were emotionally upset as a child, and to whom did you turn when you were hurt or upset?" or "Were there situations of loss, separation, abuse?" The ultimate and pivotal questions are "What do you make of these recollections?" and "How has your childhood influenced who you are today?" Such questions can facilitate recollections along with affect and thoughts about current parenting style. These moments can become opportunities to imagine other ways of reacting.

It is the clarity of the narrative that opens the potential of being a different parent with one's own child. If the narrative flows without confusion or conflict, it can be looked at and reflected upon. The power of reflection and of wondering opens the path to imagining other ways and trying new possibilities.

Daniel Siegel writes of parents attaining clarity about their own childhood narratives, particularly of their own parents' emotional interactions with them. This awareness may open parents to the path toward a more individuated way of parenting their own children.

Siegel's understanding of the way the brain records experience and the way in which the neural pathways set familiar behavior into motion suggests one way of understanding how behavior patterns repeat. As with infants and toddlers, new neural pathways in the adult are constructed through new experiences. Siegel offers therapeutic techniques practiced along with psychotherapy that have been useful in assisting adults who can become explosive or passive in reaction to some toddler behaviors, helping them to maintain greater calm and find less dramatic avenues of reaction (Siegel and Hartzell 2003).

Mothers who do not feel that they have been adequately parented seem to need more support. They are subject to more frequent bouts of disappointment, despair, and feelings of hostility toward the child. Indeed, while there have been few parents who have said to me that they wished they could give their child back, those who did were women who experienced their own mothers as unempathic and unwilling or unable to meet their emotional needs. They sensed their own mothers' emotional depletion. Sadly, they had not taken advantage of psychotherapy to help them with these feelings.

PHASE THREE: THE TRANSITION

Children who are adopted after the second half of their first year may begin their new relationship with an initial caution and wariness. In addition, adoption from another country exposes them to unfamiliar sensory experiences: the sounds of different music and language, the odors of new foods, the sensations of an unfamiliar climate, and so forth. In addition, and most dramatic, is the experience of being cared for by the unfamiliar people who are now their parents, who hold them and feed them and perhaps give them a degree of attention hitherto never experienced in their early lives. These new experiences are as foreign as the sights, the smells, and the language. We know that the development of object relations is built out of contingent responses and consistent patterns of care. This cornerstone of care, of a nurturing and attuned environment, is an experience precious few infants and toddlers experience in orphanages. The paucity of care in the early lives of these babies is in some cases apparent in their constricted affect. Take for example, Lily.

Lily was adopted at six months from a Chinese orphanage. She was aloof and solemn, and she had an unchanging expression. She didn't smile spontaneously or responsively until she was nine months old.

What did this mean? Thinking about object relations, the therapist and Lily's parents reminded one another that the expression of a smile evolves in the context of a relationship. Lily's parents confessed their disappointment that their beautiful baby girl was not the typically social six-month-old they had been expecting.

While some parents are worried about early relational deprivation and its implications, others have reported tender moments after meeting their baby as they observed her reach for a caregiver, the caregiver then brushing a tear aside as she placed the baby into the adoptive mother's arms. There *had* been an attachment; the child *had* been cared about. Or take the case of a toddler, who will be introduced below, who was seen to visually check for the where-abouts of his foster mother and to turn to her for permission (social referencing) when he wanted to touch something new, both of which were signs of a developing relationship.

Most parents acknowledge during the transitional phase that they are starting an uncharted journey and are expecting a winding path with unexpected curves. Many appear optimistic, even though some admit retrospectively that along with the optimism were apprehensions they tried to minimize or wish away. They hope that they can be accepting and empathic. At the start they are clear that their child had a previous life, and they want very much to be able to hold that in mind as they are getting to know the child. While they expect patterns of behavior stemming from previous experiences, they are not always prepared for the unexpected moments they encounter. Most who adopt an infant or toddler from another country know little about the child's previous life experience or the biological mother's prenatal care. Even when there is information, it rarely speaks to the subjective, the emotional, the qualitative. The following describes a small boy about whom more information than usual was known.

Diego

Diego was adopted at two years eight months by a single older mother, a widow. He had been born into a family living in severe poverty in a Central American country. The poverty of the family changed from severe to desperate with the death of the father soon after the birth of a younger brother, prompting the immediate placement of Diego. Diego was the sixth of seven children.

Three older sisters, ages four, six, and eight, would be placed for adoption within the year of Diego's placement. Diego was released for adoption when he was two years old, and at the instructions of the lawyer handling the adoption case, was brought to the home of a *nunera* (foster mother).

Carried by his eight-year-old sister, Diego arrived barefoot and unwashed, and dressed in ragged but clean clothing. He had the bloated abdomen of so many poor children with parasites. Diego clung to his sister when she placed him on the floor, and his cries became uncontrollable sobs when she said good-bye. The foster mother reported that Diego was lethargic and sad for the first week, brightening only when in the company of her five-year-old grandson.

Medical evaluation established Diego's general health as typical given the level of poverty from which he had emerged. His parasites and anemia were treated and the recommendation for a diet rich in protein, calcium, fruits, and vegetables was given to the foster mother. An informal cognitive and social/emotional assessment at two years four months (he had been in foster care for four months) suggested that Diego was a physically well-endowed boy with at least average intelligence. His expressive language was markedly delayed although his receptive language skills appeared age-appropriate. He pointed to objects while saying, "What?" in Spanish and repeated all words, followed one-step directions, kicked a ball, stacked more blocks than expected for his age, engaged in symbolic play, and pointed to pictures of familiar people and animals when named. He was able to listen attentively to a story. In play with an agemate, he took turns and shared a ball.

There were no observable behavioral problems. He was reported to be toilet trained during the day and night. During the time that his prospective adoptive mother, Jeanine, spent with Diego and the foster mother, Jeanine's one concern was that he seemed to be too good, too obedient. Her thoughts were filled with the same questions over and over again. What does he do when he is frustrated? Does he ever cry? Under what circumstances? Does he ever get angry? Emotionally, he did not seem like two-year-olds she knew from either life or books.

It is difficult even for an experienced parent to fathom what more than one adoptive parent has described: dramatic mood swings in a child that starkly contrast with sunny and responsive moments. While cheerfulness predominates, the child's mood can switch in a split second from content and serene to intensely angry, with rapid escalation transforming the mood into a full-blown emotional storm. The accompanying intense crying seems to have a life of its own with no acceptance of efforts to console. Many a young child, adopted as an older toddler, has been described as preferring to cry alone, often moving to a private space until the emotional upheaval has run its course, or the child falls asleep. It seems as though the established mental model of reaction to frustration, anger, or being left alone is to cry long and hard with no expectation of comfort. These periods are excruciatingly painful for new adoptive parents, but with support, they are able to maintain a presence for the child either quietly, or by talking softly or sometimes humming, and always as physically present as is possible. Each parent is encouraged to find a way that works for the duo.

THE ROAD TO ATTACHMENT

It takes time to trust, time to make a new friend, and it takes time to learn what it means to have a mom. It also takes time to believe that there won't be another loss. The goal in developing and deepening an attachment is to sense the attachment stages that represent lacunae in the infant's or toddler's attachment history and to work to fill in the missed stages. Ideally, there is a long period of time before a parent leaves the infant or toddler and returns to work, if that is necessary. The new parent is needed to supply experiences of attunement, mutual enjoyment, consistency, and empathy for as long as possible. These contribute to the development of trust and form the bedrock of the attachment.

Building Diego's Trust

Diego needed daily playtimes on the floor. Diego was a good player, he already had the ability to play symbolically, and it was fun to play with him while sharing the attention of the idea or the task and the reciprocal communication as ideas were exchanged (Greenspan and Weider 1998). He also needed the sensory input of deep pressure supplied by robust hugging and playing a "sandwich" game with pillows. Diego and Jeanine lived in a semi-rural area of a northeastern state. While there was an Early Intervention Program for both assessment and service provision as required by federal law, it was possible to get neither a speech evaluation in Spanish nor the services of an occupational therapist trained in sensory integration. Part of every day included the pre-verbal gestures and communications of gazing, smiling with fixed eye contact, nose wriggling, and touching parts of the face: re-creations of play and nonverbal communication with an infant.

It was necessary for Jeanine to return to work within a month after the adoption. Diego was appropriately phased in to a warm and welcoming family daycare setting. Each day he allowed himself to be carried from the car and placed into the arms of the daycare provider. Separation issues were revealed again at the day's end when Jeanine arrived to fetch him. He ran, he hid, he wriggled and giggled while she creatively worked to put on his jacket. When they finally were outdoors, she needed to hold his hand firmly to keep him from running away. Getting Diego into the car and his car seat and buckling him up was a struggle. Separation was a daily challenge played out with regression in the morning, when leaving day care at the end of the day, and again before bedtime.

Once work and day care were woven into each day, mornings were scheduled to include time together apart from washing and dressing. A schedule was made for evening time. While there was daily time for floortime (Greenspan and Salmon 1995, 66) and physical play, it was on weekends that there was the luxury of seemingly endless play and snuggling. For a long time, much of Saturday was stay-at-home time, which included the luxury of no schedule.

WHEN PARENTS BECOME INCREASINGLY REFLECTIVE

I have mentioned that many children adopted between the middle of their first year and through toddlerhood have challenges in regulating their moods, and this is particularly noticeable when the child is under the stress of fatigue, transitions, or frustration. For many children, simply being told "No" can set off an emotional storm. It is often when thinking about one of these moments that a parent will say, "Why does she get so angry at me, when she's so cooperative in school?" or "We've given her so much, we love her so much. Why is this *so* hard?" These poignant moments reveal both how hard parents work at the relationship and how readily they can feel despair and grief, perhaps even wondering if they can be a parent to the child in these difficult moments. My work with these parents identifies the signs of attachment that may not always be encountered in the most comfortable and comforting moments. For the toddler, beginning to feel trust in a relationship includes the freedom to express *many* feelings and moods.

Relationships are solidified through sharing many such moments, communication mismatches, and repairs. These adopted infants and toddlers have missed out on the most critical part of learning self-regulation: the connection and the relationship. Let's think together about how babies learn to become emotionally regulated, the precursor to being able to self-regulate as a preschooler. I think that you, the reader, will recognize how much of this work is done in the development of attachment with the newly adopted child. The new parent must first learn to read and understand the child's needs; that is, the way the child signals different states of comfort or distress. The parent must have the creativity and energy to respond in helpful ways to the daily routines of sleeping, waking, and soothing. The second function of the parent is to provide titrated experiences so that the baby can begin to take over some of these daily tasks (Shonkoff and Phillips 2000). One challenge exists because the child already has established mental models that the new parent will take some time to make sense of. And since the relationship is beginning later than it would have had the adoption occurred at birth or had the baby been a biological child, there is a delay in the capacity for self-soothing. An additional challenge occurs when the child is less adept at forming connections as a result of previously unpredictable and unreliable caregiving. Such children may initially be fussy during social interactions, may make less eye contact, and may smile and vocalize less.

Over time and through daily grappling with the emotional states of fatigue, hunger, wetness, and frustration, the differing states will be managed through a repertoire of interventions created by the new parents. Gradually, as security and confidence in the predictability and reliability of the relationship develops in both child and parents, new mental models will form, and emotional regulation and self-soothing will become possible. Long before self-soothing occurs, however, emotional states have been managed within the relationship. A preschooler with differentiated feelings of anger, shame, and embarrassment is a child whose environment has been attuned to his affective states and whose parents have helped him identify these states.

CONCLUSION

In this chapter I have focused on several overlapping themes: (1) the international adoption of infants and toddlers, (2) aspects of early development, and (3) critical issues for adoptive parents. My experience in working with adoptive families has taught me that it is a daunting task for adoptive parents to become fully prepared for the behavior of an infant or toddler whose world has changed overnight. Adoptive parents struggle to make sense of their child's behavior and hope that what they are doing meets the needs of their child. I, along with other experienced therapists, recommend that parents consult with a therapist who specializes in early development and in parent work, and who is familiar with the behaviors of infants and toddlers whose emotional needs have been neglected. By forming a therapeutic alliance with a competent professional, these parents can be helped to understand and respond to emotional cues whose origins may be orphanage-related or more currently induced. Together, therapist and parents will begin to learn to understand the child's responses to changes in routine, language, and other customs. With a solid working alliance in place, the therapist will be able to provide a holding environment (Winnicott 1965, 43) for the parents, aid them in dealing with their worries and fears, and enable them to develop a repertoire of responses that allows attachment and growth to unfold and deepen.

REFERENCES

Bowlby, John. 1969. *Attachment and Loss*. Vol. 1. London: Hogarth Press.

Gray, Deborah D. 2002. *Attaching in Adoption*. Indianapolis, IN: Perspectives Press.

Greenspan, Stanley, and T. Nancy Greenspan. 1985. *First Feelings*. New York: Viking.

Greenspan, Stanley, and Jacqueline Salmon. 1995. *The Challenging Child*. New York: Addison-Wesley.

Greenspan, Stanley, and Serena Weider. 1998. *The Child with Special Needs*. Reading, MA: Addison-Wesley.

Main, M., C. George, and N. Kaplan. 1985. "Adult Attachment Interview." Paper.

Pediatrics. 2004. "International Adoption: A Four-Year-Old Child with Unusual Behaviors Adopted at 5 Months of Age." Vol. 114, no. 5 (November).

Piaget, Jean. 1969. *The Psychology of the Child*. New York: Basic Books.

Provence, Sally, and Rose Lipton. 1962. *Infants in Institutions*. New York: International Universities Press.

Shahmoon Shanok, Rebecca. 1999. "Adopting Parenthood: An Enduring Transformation Marking Identity and Intimacy Capacities." *Zero to Three* 19 (4).

Shonkoff, Jack P., and Deborah A. Phillips. 2000. "Acquiring Self-Regulation." In *From Neurons to Neighborhoods: The Science of Early Childhood Development*. Washington, D.C.: National Academy Press, 93–123.

Siegel, Daniel. 1999. *The Developing Mind*. New York: Guilford.

Siegel, Daniel, and Mary Hartzell. 2003. *Parenting from the Inside Out*. New York: J. P. Tarcher/Penguin.

Spitz, Rene. 1945. "Hospitalism: An Inquiry into the Genesis of Psychiatric Conditions in Early Childhood." *Psychoanalytic Study of the Child* 1:53–74.

Winnicott, D. W. 1965. *The Maturational Processes and the Facilitating Environment*. New York: International Universities Press.

Chapter Five

Gay and Lesbian Parents in the World of Adoption

Sandra Silverman

Historically, being gay and becoming a parent were considered mutually exclusive. Many lesbians and gay men had children, but the vast majority of those children were born of a heterosexual marriage prior to the parent's coming out. But times have changed. Currently there are an estimated 6 million to 10 million lesbian or gay parents in the United States (Buell 2001). Only a decade or two ago it was considered a radical act for a lesbian to decide to have a child. More recently, as I have observed in my practice, the question "Do you want to have kids?" has become as much a part of the early stages of a lesbian relationship as it is a part of a new heterosexual relationship. And it is becoming more and more common that gay men as well are creating their own families. Although becoming a parent no longer feels quite as radical for lesbians or for gay men as it once did, it still carries an element of amazement. For most gay or lesbian parents, as opposed to their heterosexual counterparts, parenthood has been more of a fantasy than an expectation.

When a gay or a lesbian couple considers having children, they begin that process from a place akin to that of an infertile couple: they cannot make a baby together. For the gay or lesbian couple, the first step in becoming parents is figuring out where the baby will come from. Will one member of the couple be the biological parent to the child? If so, which one? If they are a lesbian couple, will they use a known or unknown donor? If they choose a known donor, will that man function as a father to the child, or simply as a friend who helped them to conceive the child? If they are a gay male couple, will they use a surrogate to carry their child, or will they find a friend, perhaps a gay woman, who would like to coparent?

Or more to the point of this chapter, will the couple adopt? If they want to adopt as an openly gay or lesbian couple, then their options become much more limited, and their chances of getting a baby decrease significantly. In all likelihood they will have to choose one member of the couple who will become the legally adoptive parent. How will they decide which one of them it will be? How will this decision impact their relationship and the way in which they attach to the baby? In this chapter I look at the experience of gay men and lesbians who have made the decision to become adoptive parents, and who are living daily life as same-sex parents to their children. It appears that the adoption experience of gay and lesbian parents can have a direct and significant impact on the formation of the family if unresolved feelings are left lingering in the minds of the parents. I am interested in how the experience of adopting a child is lived in the internal and external worlds of gay men and lesbians who decide to go against the grain of much of our culture and create their own families.

Adoption presents unique issues that will affect any family, regardless of the sexual orientation of the parents. The same-sex parented family has its own set of unique issues, whether the child is biological or adopted. Before I look at how these issues overlap, that is, how gay and lesbian parented families are affected by the adoption experience, I'd like to focus on some of the issues and challenges that may be found in gay and lesbian parented families in general.

Parenting and privacy about one's sexual orientation do not generally go hand-in-hand. Parenting requires much more intense involvement in mainstream society than many gay men and lesbians may have had in years. There are soccer games, PTA meetings, and informal conversations with other—usually heterosexual—mothers and fathers at preschool and on the playground. When a gay or lesbian couple seriously considers having a child and they picture themselves in these settings, it is not unusual for issues that seemed resolved, such as fears of being judged or anxiety about exposure of one's sexual orientation, to reemerge. Suddenly, old and seemingly resolved feelings may feel surprisingly alive. It's as if they had been living in exile, and have suddenly and unexpectedly made an unwelcome return. This can be quite jarring for the gay or lesbian individual who felt certain that his or her feelings of internalized homophobia had been worked through.

Adding to the challenges the prospective parents may face is the response many receive when they announce their decision to have a child. When a gay or lesbian couple makes the decision to become parents, that announcement is often met with curiosity and questions from others as to why the couple wants to have a child. A heterosexual couple, on the other hand, is expected to have children, and the announcement of impending parenthood is considered a time for celebration. It is only when a heterosexual couple decides not to become parents that they are questioned about how they made that decision. This difference is reflective of the norms and expectations that we take for granted in the culture in which we live. Having to defend or explain a decision that goes unquestioned for heterosexual couples can leave the gay or lesbian couple with the feeling that they are not fully entitled to become parents. In the case of adoption, the domestic and international adoption laws that make it difficult, if not impossible, for gay people to adopt can profoundly intensify these feelings.

Once the baby arrives, the adjustment to parenting is, for the same-sex parented family, similar in many ways to that of any other new family. There is joy, excitement, and surprise at what is involved in taking care of a new baby. In roles and responsibilities with regard to the new baby, the gay or lesbian parented family faces unique and complex challenges that, if they are not addressed, may lead to intense conflict.

If one looks closely at most families where a mother and a father are present, it is generally true that the mother, even if she works full time, feels a sense of primary responsibility for the children and the father feels a primary responsibility for the income. The father in the heterosexually parented family, even if he is less connected to the child during infancy due to time spent at work, has a clear and socially recognized role in relation to the child. In the lesbian couple, on the other hand, the mother who is not the primary caretaker to the child and whose partner is another woman may feel that she receives no social recognition as a parent to the child. This can lead to resentment within the couple. The question "Can a child really have two mothers, or two fathers?" hovers around gay or lesbian parented families on both a personal and a societal level.

It's not unusual for envy and competition to develop between same-sex parents (Glazer 1998; Crespi 1995; Schwartz 1998). This is particularly true for women because they have been raised to be caretakers and may both have a wish, be it conscious or unconscious, to be the primary mother to the child. The social benefits of being a mother are also quite significant. While being a mother is not of terribly high social status, it is certainly of much higher status than being a lesbian or being a childless woman. The social benefits of being a father, on the other hand, are not quite as weighty. The gay man who chooses to become parent and nurturer to a child is often viewed as less of a man because men in our culture continue to be defined by how much they earn and how well they are able to financially provide for their families rather than by how nurturing they are to their children. These issues are important to keep in mind when working with individuals or couples in two-mom or two-dad families. The following vignette illustrates some of the issues that may arise in the two-mom family.

CATHERINE AND SUZANNE

Catherine and Suzanne began couples treatment when Gus, the child they were raising together, was nine months old. Gus was adopted from Latin America two weeks after he was born. Catherine was the legal parent to Gus. Catherine's previous relationship had ended because she wanted a child and her partner did not. Shortly after the breakup, Catherine began the process of adopting as a single parent, and it was during that time that she met Suzanne. Catherine put her plans to adopt on hold for a brief period of time, but then decided she did not want to wait until she and Suzanne had solidified their relationship before pursuing her adopting as a single parent. She had the hope that things would work out between her and Suzanne, and they would ultimately be able to parent the child together. Catherine waited more than a year for a baby to become available, and during that time she and Suzanne moved in together and both of them eagerly awaited the opportunity to become new mothers. The couple began treatment because tension and conflict had rapidly intensified between them in the months since the baby had arrived in their home.

It did not take long for the struggles between Catherine and Suzanne to take shape in the treatment room. Catherine described feeling pressured by Suzanne to "do things her way." She felt that Suzanne was insensitive to her wishes when it came to issues such as how to get Gus to sleep, whether to bring him into their bed when he woke during the night, and who should comfort him when he was crying. She said she felt as if Suzanne was always correcting or questioning how she was caring for Gus. Suzanne, on the other hand, described a feeling of being "pushed out." She felt that any suggestion she offered about how to care for Gus was rejected without even being considered. She felt that whenever she was holding, feeding, or soothing Gus, Catherine was always waiting to get him back into her arms, as if this was where he truly belonged. She described feelings of alienation from Catherine and Gus: "He is with Catherine more and she is the one who legally adopted him but even so, I feel like an outsider, like I don't matter."

As we looked more deeply at the issues between Catherine and Suzanne, it became clear that each of them felt threatened in the role of mother to Gus. Catherine described feeling overwhelmed by the process of adopting Gus, and she said she had feared she would be deemed unsuitable to adopt him because she was not married to a man. Catherine's family history included a critical mother who persistently told her that she could have done things in a better or different way, and it became clear in our work that she was reliving that experience whenever Suzanne made a suggestion to her.

Suzanne expressed her own anxiety about how much she could possibly matter to Gus. She did not feel Catherine allowed her to have any say in Gus's caretaking. She acknowledged that her response to feeling on the outside was to become quite forceful, which caused further conflict between her and Catherine. What made things even harder for Suzanne was that when friends or family members spoke about how cute Gus was or had questions about him, they directed those questions to Catherine rather than to Suzanne. She feared they would never feel like a family.

Shortly into treatment Catherine sheepishly revealed what she described as an "irrational fantasy" that she often had. "I just feel if I were with a man it would be so much easier. I would do my thing and he would do his. I feel like Suzanne is encroaching on my motherhood." It became clear that Catherine had an idea about motherhood that was unrealistic even in a heterosexually parented family. Suzanne felt hurt and angry, but things became even more complicated when, upon exploration, it became clear that she had her own feelings about being in a two-mom family. Suzanne felt fearful that Gus would need a father and that they were depriving him of one. There was so much feeling of inadequacy floating around in their relationship that it was, at times, difficult to establish where any given feeling had originated. It seemed that many of these feelings had been disavowed by one woman in the couple and projected into the other.

An enduring strength in Catherine and Suzanne's relationship was their commitment to working at improving their relationship and creating the best possible environment in which to raise their son. They were able to take pleasure in watching Gus grow and develop. They responded well to treatment and worked to understand and empathize with the experience of the "other mother." Over time Suzanne was able to tolerate being the less central parent to Gus. She hoped that when he was a little older her relationship with him would develop, and that turned out to be true. Catherine worked through many of her feelings of anger, sadness, and alienation related to the adoption experience. As she became more confident in her role as mother, she stopped seeing Suzanne as someone who would intrude on her mother-baby relationship and began to see her instead as another mother in her own right whose relationship with Gus was separate and meaningful. As Catherine made this psychological shift, Gus began to connect more to Suzanne. It was as if she had been unconsciously communicating to Gus that she would be threatened if he bonded too closely with Suzanne. In other words, the two women came to realize that a child can in fact have two mothers.

We traced to Suzanne's family history some of her fear that she was doing something damaging to Gus by not providing him with a father. In addition, she and Catherine worked to accept that they could not provide everything for

Gus. They realized that not having a father would probably be an area of difficulty at some points in his life, and they would do whatever they could to help him through that time.

THE DECISION TO ADOPT

In the overwhelming majority of heterosexual couples, the decision to adopt follows an experience of infertility that carries with it shock, despair, and painful disappointment because of their inability to make a baby together. Same-sex couples know from the beginning that they cannot, together, have a biological child. For some couples this is a source of considerable pain and sadness, and in order to move forward in becoming parents they must mourn their inability to have a child who shares both their genetic heritages (Crespi 1995). But for many who have been gay for years before deciding to have children, the idea of creating a biological child with their partner was given up and mourned when they came out. Those who choose the route of adoption sometimes do so after the disappointing discovery that there is a fertility problem in one or both of them. For the gay male couple, the complications involved in locating a surrogate or friend to carry their child sometimes makes adoption a more desirable option. Other same-sex couples choose adoption because they want to provide a home for a child who is in need of one rather than bring another child into the world.

Those lesbian couples that make the shift to adoption after having first planned to have a biological child and to raise that child with the involvement of the biological father are now faced, not only with the adoption process, but with a new parenting arrangement. If they adopt a child, then they will be raising that child in a family with two moms and without a father in the child's life. In my practice I have had more than one lesbian patient who has faced fertility problems after having planned to have a biological child with a man who would be present as the father to the child. These women experienced an array of unanticipated feelings as they made the shift to adoption. While they may have been certain that they were comfortable with their plan to be lesbian mothers by raising their children in a two-mom family with peripheral involvement from the biological father, suddenly they become very anxious at the thought of not having a father involved in parenting their children. The women I have worked with who moved to adoption after having planned to have a child using an unknown donor had already worked through their feelings about raising a child without any involvement from the father. If the wish to have a father for the child is not mourned and if feelings of inadequacy about being a lesbian parent are not well explored, then there will inevitably be an unconscious transmission of those feelings to the child and to the partner.

Similarly, the gay man (single or in a couple) who is planning to be the biological father to a child birthed by a friend is giving up the possibility of a mother for the child. Many gay and lesbian couples do not plan to have the egg or sperm donor involved in the raising of their child. For those who do, and for whom biological parenthood is important, there is an added loss when deciding to adopt. Two recent books written by gay fathers describe the experience of making the decision to adopt rather than to participate in a coparenting arrangement with a lesbian couple. In *The Kid* (1999) by Dan Savage, the author writes that he realized he was "functionally infertile" when he came out, which was years before he considered being a parent. He spends a period of time considering coparenting arrangements with a lesbian couple but is relieved to let go of the idea because, among other things, it makes him feel powerless. Jesse Green, author of *The Velveteen Father* (1999), writes about his partner's journey to adopt a child just prior to meeting Green. His partner had been intent on having a biological child so that the mother could be involved in the raising of the child. Green describes his partner's attempts to conceive a child with a lesbian couple. Green's partner realizes that it is a doomed process. The women seem to have all of the control because "the one thing a man lacked in order to give birth to a child was so vast and mysterious that religions were built around it; a woman lacked only a teaspoon full of something men wasted by the gallon" (20).

THE ADOPTION PROCESS

The process of adoption includes being interviewed, screened, and evaluated by an agency for which one has to provide extensive documentation, fingerprints, and personal references, in addition to allowing a social worker into one's home to conduct a homestudy. The effort to prove that the potential adoptive parents are not in any way criminal can carry with it an offensive quality of its own. This whole process can be a source of humiliation, stress, and anger for any potential adoptive parent. For those who have experienced years of infertility, they can be made to feel as if they are not deserving of a child in the same way as those who have been able to conceive a child. For the gay or lesbian couple who wants to adopt, the thought of allowing someone else to determine whether they are fit to become parents and raise a child with two moms or two dads can be daunting. Many agencies refuse to work with gay or lesbian couples. The two-mom or two-dad family is viewed by many in our society, and many with the power to make legal decisions, as a family that is not fit to raise children. As a result, the gay man or lesbian who chooses to become a parent must be able to live with difficult social realities and still feel entitled to pursue his or her wish to have children.

Gay or lesbian couples and individuals who have made the decision to become parents have usually moved from a place of hiding and shame to a place of pride and openness with regard to their sexual orientation. Generally, or perhaps I should say hopefully, they are aware that to become parents as a same-sex couple will involve being out in a bigger and more uncontrollable way than they have ever known. The subsequent discovery that they may not be able to adopt internationally or, in some cases, domestically because of their sexual orientation may leave them feeling demoralized and depleted of hope.

The experience of the gay or lesbian person who has decided to adopt a child may be one of disbelief accompanied by a sense of profound injustice. Adoption laws within the United States vary widely. In most states, single gay or lesbian people are not explicitly barred from adopting; in other states it is unclear whether single gay or lesbian persons are permitted to adopt, and in Florida single gay or lesbian people are explicitly prohibited from adopting. In nine states, same-sex couples are permitted to jointly adopt, but in other states it is either clearly prohibited for same-sex couples to adopt or it is unpredictable and decided on a case-by-case basis. In some states, *second-parent adoption* is legal, meaning that a person can adopt the child that his or her same-sex partner has already adopted. Domestic adoption laws sometimes even vary from district to district within a state. International adoption continues to be particularly challenging for the gay or lesbian person. No countries allow a same-sex couple to adopt. In some countries, such as China, a single person who wants to adopt is required to sign a form stating that he or she is not homosexual.

Picture yourself as a gay man or woman who has made the decision to become an adoptive parent. You then learn that it may be quite difficult for you to adopt a child, and that your options are severely limited because of your sexual orientation. You may in fact be unable to become a parent because somewhere it has been decided that the fit parent is not the gay or lesbian parent. At this moment you may wonder if there is something seriously wrong with the world. Depending on your own psychology and background, and, if you are in a couple, depending on how things are worked out between you and your partner, you may feel defeated. At this point you may feel you are truly flawed, and feelings of hope may be replaced with self-hatred. All of this may occur unconsciously and may lead to a decision not to pursue parenthood, a decision you are never able to fully explain to yourself or to others, but a decision nonetheless. On the other hand, the experience of being treated as a second-class citizen because of your sexual orientation may increase your determination to pursue an adoption. For it is true that unless those who are gay or lesbian adopt children and prove to the world they are perfectly capable of creating healthy families, it will be even more difficult to make adoption by gay or lesbian adults widely accessible.

What does it mean for a gay or lesbian couple to go through the adoption process? How does it impact their feelings of pride in the family they have formed? If the adoptive parent does not work through the feelings associated with the adoption, such as anger, shame, and helplessness, then where do those feelings go? Do they live on in the child? Does one parent disavow those feelings and project them into the other, causing conflict in the couple? How do the parents learn to talk about these painful feelings with each other rather than burying them or enacting them?

Christopher Bonovitz (2004) notes that adoptive parents "may harbor guilt and shame associated with the fantasy of having 'stolen' or 'kidnapped' their child (6)." He is referring to heterosexual families, but it is important to consider how these feelings might be compounded for the gay or lesbian parent. A gay or lesbian couple may feel guilt or shame related to their knowledge that, in all likelihood, if they had not adopted their baby, then he or she would have been adopted by heterosexual parents. If the gay or lesbian parent has shameful feelings related to the process of adoption or if they have feelings of inadequacy as same-sex parents to their child, then it is imperative that these emotions be explored and worked through in order to provide the child with an environment that is not contaminated by the parent's shame. Being able to feel proud, strong, and secure about the family one is forming is imperative for any parent; for the parent who is both gay and adopting, feeling fully real, legitimate, and respected as a capable parent may be an especially tender issue. This is particularly true in the early stages of parenthood. The following vignette describes my work with a patient who was in the process of adopting a baby with his partner.

ADAM AND NATHAN

Adam entered treatment stating that at the age of thirty-five he was unsure whether he would ever find a meaningful and fulfilling relationship in life. He said that his relationships would start out well, but he inevitably became disillusioned with the men he chose. He would begin to feel alone and misunderstood, and then leave the relationship. He said that he was beginning to give up hope that one day he would have a fulfilling relationship and possibly even raise a child with a partner.

In our first session Adam told me that he had heard that I was a lesbian and that I had children. He asked me to confirm that this was true. It is not unusual for gay or lesbian patients to inquire about their therapist's sexual orientation. Most heterosexual patients enter treatment assuming that they share the same sexual orientation as their analyst, and so they do not even consider asking about it but instead assume that this is an area in which they and their analyst have similar experiences. Gay and lesbian patients have likely lived a life in which they have felt like an alien other: different and misunderstood. They are wondering whether their analyst might be better able to understand them. While sharing the same sexual orientation with one's analyst may provide a deeper understanding by the analyst of what it means to live as a gay or lesbian person, part of the analytic work may also be realizing that a shared sexual orientation does not guarantee perfect attunement or understanding between patient and analyst.

My decision to disclose my sexual orientation to Adam was based in part on my work as a relational analyst. Following the tenets of relational theory (Aron 1996; Mitchell 1988), it is my belief that the analytic relationship is one in which both members are continuously affecting each other, often in the subtlest of ways. It is impossible for the analyst to remove him- or herself and to observe what is occurring in the treatment because the analyst's role is inevitable and continuous. In light of this, I believe it is important that the analyst allow space for the patient to talk about his or her experience of the subjectivity of the analyst, that is, who the analyst is as a person. Talking about what was occurring between Adam and me was a crucial part of our work. This included his thoughts and feelings about having an analyst who was gay and who was a parent, as well as revealing, when appropriate, my countertransferential reactions to him.

At the point in the treatment where I will begin, Adam and I had been working together for five years. Adam arrived for this particular session looking different than usual. He seemed unsettled, a word I would not generally use to describe him. Regardless of what he felt inside, Adam's exterior was almost always one of confidence, control, and calm. We had spent much of our time combing through the tangles beneath his "I can handle anything" appearance. Many changes had taken place in Adam's life. He could now speak of his areas of insecurity or fear without feeling he was confessing something shameful, but rather that he was revealing parts of himself he no longer feared knowing. After many disappointing and brief involvements with various men, Adam had met a man for whom he felt a rich and growing love, and most recently, the two of them had made the decision to become parents.

So why did he seem so unsettled today? I wondered, in fact, worried, that his expression indicated that something had gone awry with the adoption. It was early May. The baby was due in June. Three months ago the birth mother had responded to an ad in an upstate New York newspaper. She had called the 1-800 number in the ad and the call went directly to Elise, the woman Adam and his partner Nathan had hired to help them adopt a child. In most cases Elise would suggest that the prospective adoptive parents set up a 1-800 number in their own home. She would advise that the woman in the couple answer the calls. But because Adam and Nathan were a gay male couple, she felt it best that she take the calls, screen them, and send the most promising callers on to Adam and Nathan. There had been a few possibilities, mostly teenage girls, one of whom suggested that Adam might like one of her dog's new puppies as well as the child she was carrying. Then Sarah called. She was twenty-six. She had a five-year-old son whom she was raising on her own, and this was her third pregnancy. She had given up one child for adoption less than two years ago. According to Elise that was good news. It indicated that Sarah was capable of going through with an adoption.

Initially, Adam and Nathan had planned to adopt a child who was in the foster-care system. It did not matter to them what race the child was as long as he or she was young and relatively healthy. They wanted to provide a home to a child in need. They had gone through all of the required steps to become foster parents and were working with an agency that reassured them that it would be happy to place a very young child in a home with two gay men as parents. Adam and Nathan waited a long time for a call, but they never received one. The only child ever offered to them was one with a terminal illness, a situation that both men had clearly informed the agency would be untenable for them. Where were all of the babies in need of homes? It became clear that the foster-care agency was not going to place a child with them, and so Adam and Nathan decided to pursue a private adoption, which they knew would involve considerable financial cost.

In the three months since the agreement had been made for Adam and Nathan to adopt Sarah's baby, there had been many late-night phone calls and emergency payments. Sarah was suddenly out of food, or she was facing imminent eviction from her studio apartment. Although Sarah had contact with both Adam and Nathan, it was Adam, because of his calm and in-control demeanor, who handled the majority of their interactions. He'd had groceries delivered to her house, arranged for a taxi to take her to and from doctor's appointments—including a recent one for a sonogram where they'd found out the baby would be a girl—and he'd been patient with her in moments when it seemed like the adoption might fall through. And so it was a bit of a surprise to me when he arrived in a less than calm and confident state. He seemed to be experiencing uncertainty and confusion rather than anxiety. He was quiet for a moment and then he told me about Jennifer and her offer.

Jennifer was Adam's closest friend. She had been supportive of the adoption from the first moment that Adam and Nathan told her about their plans. She and her husband had two small children of their own. She was more than willing to share her babysitter with Adam and Nathan, had given them many of the baby items they might need, and most importantly, she had provided them with consistent support and encouragement.

"Jennifer called last night," Adam said. "She told me that she realized she could continue nursing her eighteen-month-old son until our baby is born and then she could nurse our baby. You know, so the baby will get breast milk." He was quiet for a moment. He looked distressed. "I don't want it," he said firmly. "Even if she pumps it into a bottle. I just don't want it."

The room was quiet, and more than a little tense. Adam looked at me and I remember feeling like he was sizing me up, studying my face for a reaction. We had talked about my being a mother when we explored his feelings about becoming a parent. "If women involved with other women want to have children, it is so much less complicated than it is for men involved with men," he'd said. He liked it that I had knowledge and experience as a gay parent, and that I could understand much of what he may have been experiencing in making the decision to parent. He also felt, however, that my options were different from his, that going to a sperm bank bore no similarity to finding a surrogate. He had not wanted to use a surrogate, and he imagined that lesbians had less difficulty adopting a baby than gay men. How might the world respond to the idea of two gay men raising a baby? That would most certainly stir up a different reaction than the idea of two women raising a baby. As I explored Adam's feelings about the difference in our experiences, it was a moment of mutual recognition that, as Benjamin describes, "implies that we actually have a need to recognize the other as like us yet distinct" (1988). In our work, Adam and I had found a place in which sameness and difference were able to coexist. As parents, there were areas of great connection between us as well as areas of distance.

Breast-feeding, however, was something we had never discussed. One would assume that I knew the benefits it carried and the sacred place it held for many mothers. Breast-feeding, along with drug-free, fully natural childbirth, has been elevated to a sacrosanct place by many of the mothers of the twenty-first century. Among new mothers, there are often subtle, competitive interactions regarding which mother had the most natural birth and which did not, who is nursing and who is not. It is hard not to wonder, however, whether the value placed on breast-feeding is not only about the immunity and bonding it provides, both of which are clearly important, but a loud and clear indication that the mother who nurses is the real mother, trumping the adoptive mother, the nonbiological lesbian mother, and most definitely, the gay father.

What did it mean when Jennifer offered to nurse Adam's baby? Was it a moment of competition? Was it reflective of a dissociated feeling of Jennifer's that Adam and Nathan could not provide all that a child would need? Was it a moment of homophobia? Perhaps it was a moment of discomfort with adoption, with the idea that this child was going to lose her biological mother. Or perhaps it was simply a gesture of love, friendship, and selflessness in offering to help to provide all that a new baby needs. Regardless of what the answers might be to these questions, the feelings it stirred up for Adam embodied much of what it meant for him to become a father.

Buried just beneath the surface of Jennifer's offer, whether she intended it or not, was the implication that Adam and Nathan were lacking something their baby needed, something that would make her grow up healthy, strong, and able to fend off the toxins of the world. After all, what is the greatest value in breast milk aside from bonding? Immunity. And to be a gay parent in a heterosexual world, immunity is necessary. The child, as well as the parents, needs to feel secure and confident enough about the family they have formed to be, in a sense, immune to the responses of the world that carry within them the potential to contaminate the health of the family.

We live in a culture that values parenting relationships in a strange hierarchy. First and foremost is biology, hence the reference to the baby's "real" mother or father, be that in the context of adoption, or in that of gay and lesbian parenting when the nonbiological mother or father is given second-class status in contrast to the biological mother or father. Second is the legal relationship: if you have a legal tie to the child, you are given recognition regardless of the nature of your relationship to that child. And third is the emotional connection, which means the most to the child and provides the greatest sustenance, but often seems to be the one that is taken for granted.

As our session continued, Adam began to sort out what it was about Jennifer's offer that felt so disturbing to him. She was a close friend, and one he had relied upon as he went through the ups and downs of finding a birth mother who would want to give her baby to Adam and Nathan. Adam knew that breast milk was considered more nutritious for a baby than formula. Prior to Jennifer's offer, formula had been the only option for Adam and Nathan's baby, and it was an option about which that they had felt perfectly fine. Adam now found himself in an awkward spot. What did it mean that he and Nathan had decided to say no to something that was good for his baby's health? Did this say something about what kind of parents they would be? Was he putting his needs and his comfort ahead of his baby's needs? Why did he feel so adamant about it, so angry?

It became clear that Jennifer's offer of breast milk made Adam uncomfortably aware of his own fear that he would not have everything his baby might need. One thing that Adam and Nathan didn't have was the ability to nurse a baby. But there were also other things they didn't have, things the culture in which we live considers imperative for a child. Their child would not have a mother in the literal or traditional sense of the word. But that did not mean that she would not be mothered. If a child is raised by two fathers, then is someone missing? Is a mother *missing*? Or, is Adam and Nathan's family a different kind of family, with its own set of strengths and weaknesses?

It was important for Adam, as he entered the world of parenthood, to rec ognize that not only would it be impossible to give his child everything, but also that what he did have to give was, in the words of Winnicott, good enough. Adam realized that his reaction to Jennifer's offer was, in part, so strong because he already felt protective and nurturing toward his child and because he did not want anyone or anything to interfere with him and his partner bonding with their baby. The priority for Adam and Nathan in their first weeks and months as new parents would be to bond with their baby, and breast milk had nothing to do with that.

When Adam and Nathan's daughter, whom they named Rachel, was born, the two new fathers were at the hospital. They were awaiting the baby's birth when a nurse came out of the delivery room. She told them that the birth mother wanted them to be in the adjacent room so that they could hold the baby as soon as she was born and bond with her right away. This was an extraordinary moment for both men as well as for the birth mother, who clearly wanted the best for her child and felt that she was placing her in the hands of two wonderful parents.

For adopted children as well as for children from donor insemination families, there are the parents who are raising the children as well as the "shadow parents" (Schwartz 2004) to whom the children are biologically related. These shadow parents are present in various ways and at various times, consciously or unconsciously. They hold different types of meaning at different times in a child's life, and this is dependent upon many factors including the child, the family, and the community. The difference in the donor insemination family is that the child may not feel a sense of abandonment or rejection in the same way as an adoptive child sometimes feels (Schwartz 2004). In either family, however, how the child comes to think of his or her family, and whether they perceive their family as missing a mother or a father, has a great deal to do with the parents' feelings about the family and about how they created it.

Ehrensaft (2000), in her writing on donor insemination families, has noted that denial, not of the fact of the biological parent, but of the importance of that fact, may creep into the lesbian-parented donor insemination family. This can also be true in the two-mom or two-dad adoptive family. The fact that the child does not have a father (or mother in the case of the two-dad family) is acknowledged, but the significance of that fact is often either reduced or overemphasized. For example, the fact that your preschool daughter is singing "Someday my prince will come" does not mean that she is longing for a father or needs reassurance that it is okay that she does not have one. On the other hand, if she is wondering about not having a dad as opposed to most of her friends who do have one, quickly brushing away the topic by saying something like "But you have a grandfather" may give her the impression that this topic is sensitive and perhaps shameful, and that she should not talk or think about it too much. There are no answers as to how it should be talked about or when. However, if the parents in the two-mom or two-dad family do not feel their family is missing a mother or father but rather feel theirs is a different kind of family with its own set of strengths and weaknesses, then there will be more space for the child to think and talk about and imagine the biological parents while still feeling secure about the family the child has.

Whether the parents of a family are two men or two women, the social experience of not being perceived as a real family can have ramifications for every member of the family. When a woman and her toddler are sitting in a café together, playing and chatting, they are assumed to be mother and child. But when the other mother arrives to join them, they are now perceived as mother, friend, and child, or mother, sister, and child, or perhaps even mother, babysitter, and child. The same is true for the two-dad family when, almost always, one man is assumed to be the father and the other is, in a sense, demoted to the position of friend. How the parents handle these moments, whether or not they bother to correct those who assume there is only one true mother or father, and how they then speak to their child about experiences such as these, has a direct impact on the child's experience of his or her family.

There are more questions than answers when it comes to the issues that might arise for the adoptive gay or lesbian parented family. It is yet to be discovered just how Gus and Rachel will feel about their families at the various stages of their lives. It is clear, however, that the experience of adopting a child when the parents are gay or lesbian may evoke profound feelings of loss, inadequacy, or shame in the parents. If those feelings and any others that may accompany the process are not explored, they will have long-lasting effects for every member of the family. As clinicians, it is our responsibility to help parents to face those areas of loss and shame involved in the adoption process while also recognizing the parents' courage, determination, and success in creating strong families.

REFERENCES

Aron, L. 1996. *A Meeting of Minds*. Hillsdale, NJ: Analytic Press.

Benjamin, J. 1988. *The Bonds of Love: Psychoanalysis, Feminism, and the Problem of Domination*. New York: Pantheon.

Bononvitz, C. 2004. "Unconcious Communication and the Transmission of Loss." *Journal of Infant, Child, and Adolescent Psychotherapy* 3(1): 1–27.

Buell, C. 2001. "Legal Issues Affecting Alternative Families: A Therapist's Primer." *Journal of Lesbian and Gay Psychotherapy* 4 (3/4): 75–90.

Crespi, L. 1995. "Some Thoughts on the Role of Mourning in the Development of a Positive Lesbian Identity." In *Disorienting Sexuality: Psychoanalytic Reappraisals of Sexual Identities*. Ed. T. Domenici and R. Lesser. New York: Routledge.

Ehrensaft, D. 2000. "Alternatives to the Stork: Fatherhood Fantasies in Alternative Insemination Families." *Studies in Gender and Sexuality* 1: 371–99.

Glazer, D. 1998. "Lesbian Mothers: A Foot in Two Worlds." *Psychoanalysis and Psychotherapy* 16: 142–51.

Green, J. 1999. *The Velveteen Father: An Unexpected Journey to Parenthood*. New York: Villard.

Magee, M., and D. Miller. 1997. *Lesbian Lives: Psychoanalytic Narratives Old and New*. Hillsdale, NJ: Analytic Press.

Mitchell, S. 1988. *Relational Concepts in Psychoanalysis*. Cambridge, MA: Harvard University Press.

Savage, D. 1999. *The Kid: What Happened after My Boyfriend and I Decided to Go and Get Pregnant*. New York: Dutton.

Schwartz, A. 1998. *Sexual Subjects: Lesbians, Gender, and Psychoanalysis*. New York: Routledge.

Schwartz, A. 2004. "Ozzie and Harriet Are Dead: New Family Narratives in a Postmodern World." In *Uncoupling Convention: Psychoanalytic Approaches to Same-Sex Couples and Families*. Ed. Ann D'Ercole and Jack Drescher. Hillsdale, NJ: Analytic Press.

Chapter Six

Losing Each Other in the Wake of Loss

Failed Dialogues in Adoptive Families

Susan C. Warshaw

While children who have been adopted are brought for therapy because of a wide range of clinical concerns, many whom I see in treatment present with symptoms that evolve around experiences of loss and trauma within their adoptive families. Some of these children seem to be heir primarily to unresolved loss and trauma in the life histories of their adoptive parents. In others, symptoms have emerged subsequent to recent events such as the severe illness or death of an adoptive parent or close grandparent, or the separation of parents due to divorce. Though it is obvious that children who have not been adopted are also referred to treatment subsequent to similar life tragedies, it is possible to speculate that adoptees may be particularly vulnerable due to their early histories of loss, and in some cases, overt trauma. While in no way suggesting that all adoptees will develop pathological outcomes, Nickman (1985) asserts that within the normal course of their lives, adopted children must integrate both overt and covert losses that are a consequence of their earliest life experiences and adopted status. He also believes that these experiences, and the meaning made of them, profoundly affect personality development. Overt losses, which include the disruption of earliest attachment relationships, and covert losses, which include such issues as the effect on self-esteem of the knowledge of having been relinquished, lack of knowledge about one's original parents, and ambiguities of status in society, may be considered risk factors for the development of psychopathology. Nickman suggests that a primary preventive intervention is the development of a healthy dialogue between parents and child around adoption-related losses. He advocates the development of a sensitive awareness in parents to the needs for such dialogue, needs that occur at opportune moments over the lifespan when concerns regarding those losses and traumas are particularly stimulated. A capacity to engage in such healthy dialogue presumes a parent's emotional availability, including a reasonably nondefensive sensitivity to the adoption-related meanings stimulated by historic or current events and developmental concerns. This chapter is about the complexities involved in the development of these dialogues when old as well as contemporary loss and trauma permeate the lives of both parents and their adopted children, interfering with affective communicative openness. I will discuss two sorts of situations in which traumatic loss may compromise the parent-child dialogue. The first, more frequently discussed in the literature, involves the impact of traumatic and unresolved loss experienced by one or both parents, which is proximal to the child's adoption. The second involves the experience of traumatic loss within the adoptive family, at a time somewhat later in the child's development. Specifically, I will discuss loss and trauma in relation to death and divorce within the adoptive family.

Psychoanalysts, as well as contemporary attachment researchers, have contributed in significant ways to our understanding of parents' roles in helping their children process difficult, if not overtly traumatic, experiences. Within most schools of clinical thought, it is a strongly held belief that the ability of the parents to "grasp," know, bear, and formulate an understanding of the child's experience contributes in important ways to the child's ability to process and bear what might otherwise be considered unthinkable. Parents have various abilities to tolerate the affects and cognitively process the experiences of trauma and loss, both within themselves and as they affect their children. Prior histories filled with loss and trauma, as well as recent traumatic life events, integrate with overall personality organization to hinder or facilitate the parents' abilities in this regard.

Psychoanalysts have long recognized that unresolved conflicts from the parents' past significantly impact the parents' perceptions of their own children and powerfully affect their parenting behaviors (Fraiberg, Adelson, and Shapiro 1975; Lieberman 1999). Contemporary attachment research documents an association between parents' failures to resolve loss and trauma and the presence of disorganized attachment patterns in their young children, as well as the subsequent onset of psychopathology in older children, adolescents, and adults (Main and Hesse 1990; Hesse and van IJzendoorn 1998; Liotti, Intreccialagi, and Cecere 1991). Liotti, Intreccialagi, and Cecere, for example, report that in an adult psychiatric population, patients presenting with dissociative symptoms as compared with those without dissociative symptoms were disproportionately more likely to have had a parent who sustained a loss through death within two years of their birth. Lack of resolution of loss or trauma experienced by a parent frequently leads to a wide range of maladaptive defenses that contribute to problematic parental fantasies about the child, support misperceptions that lead to failures of attunement and recognition, and may preoccupy the parent to the extent that he or she may be less than optimally available to the child. Recent research (Schuengel, Bakermans-Kranenburg, and van IJzendoorn 1999) finds that parents who have unresolved losses and trauma engage in interaction with their infants that, while not necessarily abusive, may be frightening and disorganizing in subtle ways. For example, facial expressions may be lacking appropriate affect or may appear frozen, as in cases where depressive affect or frank dissociation is prominent in the parent. Contemporary psychoanalytic clinicians and attachment theorists have speculated that a parent's maladaptive responses and emotional processing failures, including dissociative symptoms, stimulated by unresolved losses and trauma, may be significant factors contributing to the child's symptoms.

As a group, adoptive parents are described in the literature as having experienced a significant amount of loss and damage when the decision to adopt is related to infertility. Many such losses are proximal in time to the actual arrival of the adopted child in the home. Thus it is quite possible to consider those adoptive parents who are unresolved about such losses as a subset of the parents described in the attachment literature referenced above. Within the adoption literature, the loss of both the wished-for birth child and intergenerational connectedness, as well as the damage to the parents' sense of wholeness and efficacy, has been suggested as leading to defensive processes in the parent that may be implicated in the adopted child's symptoms (Blum 1983; Bonovitz 2004; D. Brodzinsky, Smith, and A. Brodzinsky 1998; Glenn 1974; Schechter 1970). The parents' experiences of both infertility and the negative experiences often generated by the adoption process itself contribute to parental feelings of damage. Bonovitz (2004) notes the multiplicity of losses experienced by adoptive parents and adopted children, positing a "common ground of loss" that is shared by both parents and child. Thus, personal experiences of loss may serve as sources of distortion as well as points of identification for parents and child. Bonovitz suggests that parents' failure to mourn their lack of fertility and associated self-esteem losses may be significant contributing factors to a child's difficulties, and he advocates the facilitation of mourning in parent work. His thesis appears to be that facilitation of parental mourning may then set the stage for healthy mourning of losses on the part of the child, thus opening up room for positive identifications and a healthy connection between child and parents. Bonovitz's focus is primarily on infertility and adoption-related issues.

While infertility undoubtedly constitutes a profound loss for many adoptive parents, other losses and traumatic experiences may impact the adoptive parent's capacity to reflect in a meaningful way upon the child's affective experiences and prior losses. These losses may also serve as points of identification

with the child, that is, as a sense that while each of them mourns a different individual, they share the experience of having lost a most precious person. In
some cases, a parent's experience of loss may serve as a primary stimulus for
the decision to adopt. For example, the adopted child may fill the void of
parental loss (loss of the adoptive parent's parent), loss through death of another child, marital lack, or loss of the possibility of biologically creating a
family (a loss seen in single-parent adoptions). The powerful needs and fantasies, both conscious and unconscious, that underlie and surround these complicated reasons for adoption may also set the stage for formulations, projections, and preoccupations that impact significantly upon the parent's
attunement to the child's experiences. These may then complicate the resolution of adoption-related losses for the child, and if occurring early enough in
the child's development, they may impact the development of the child's core
experiences of self and other. The following vignette is illustrative of one such
situation.

ANGELS AND DEMONS: WHEN MOTHER
HAS LOST HER PARENTS

Carlos, the youngest child in a recently relocated professional family with
two older female siblings, was adopted in the year following the death of his
maternal grandfather. His maternal grandmother had died many years earlier.
The death of the grandfather was particularly traumatic for Carlos's mother
because the grandfather was her sole surviving parent, and his death had occurred suddenly in her distant homeland. Because of academic opportunities,
she and her family had left South America some two years prior to her father's death. One year later they adopted Carlos from their native country.
When they brought Carlos to a therapist at the age of six, his parents described Carlos as having severe difficulties with peer relations, as well as
poor school performance. Diagnosed with attention deficit disorder (ADD)
and subtle learning problems, Carlos had significant difficulty with the interpretation of social situations. His relationships within his family were problematic as well, with his mother in particular describing an inability to connect with her youngest and most desperately desired son. She described
Carlos as having been exceedingly close to her, in fact quite clingy, until
about the age of three, when he became prone to severe tantrums concomitant
with his belief that the house had become inhabited by an evil monster, perhaps the devil. While it is not unusual for three-year-olds to have fears of
monsters and devils, neither parent seemed able to unequivocally assure their
son that there was in fact nothing to fear.

The parents' religious beliefs were an integral aspect of the story of Carlos's adoption. Carlos's parents shared with their son the story that the recently deceased grandfather had made arrangements from heaven for Carlos to be sent to them. This newly arrived grandson was presented as a divine gift who would forever maintain the intergenerational connection between himself, his mother, and his grandfather. In this instance, the mother's attempts to maintain a connection and thus resolve the loss of her own father, as well as the loss of her homeland, had resulted in an urgent desire to have another child, in particular a son. This desire, at this stage in her life, was to be filled through adoption. While loss of her fertility was no doubt of some significance to this woman (and her husband), the need to mitigate the pain of the loss of her father through Carlos's adoption seemed to have primacy as a motivation. She also seemed eager to give her husband the male child whom he had longed for.

Of particular relevance to many of Carlos's subsequent difficulties was the above story of his heaven-arranged adoption, which was shared with the child as a bedtime story throughout his early childhood. Essentially obliterating the existence of his birth parents, Carlos's parents presented this imaginative and idealized version of his arrival into the family, and yet were mystified when at the time of referral for therapy, Carlos had not grasped the idea that he was adopted. Not surprisingly, Carlos entered treatment unable to tolerate any allusion to his adoption, the mere reference to which would evoke immediate withdrawal, which seemed to mask unbearable feelings of panic. His preoccupation with saviors and evildoers reflected self- and other representations that appeared in metaphor and were enacted in interpersonal relationships. The "evil" birth parents, with whom he felt himself to be identified, were described subsequently by his adoptive parents as people they hoped their son would never meet. The birth parents' behavior, which had resulted in pregnancy, was deemed immoral and deeply at odds with his adoptive parents' upbringing and personal values. It seemed that this desperately desired son needed to be separated from this contaminating source, thus denying the possibility of any positive formulation of his origins. While themes of saviors and evildoers have been previously described as components of adoption-related scenarios (Weider 1977), particularly as seen in the fantasy life of the adoptee, they are more typically formulated as constructions of the child. In this situation, the adoptive parents' conscious beliefs about and fears of the birth parents, as well as their need to see themselves as their child's saviors, contributed in significant ways to this youngster's fantasy formulations.

All of this was compounded by the mother's enormous guilt over not having been with her own father at the time of his death in their native country. She thus felt herself to be an abandoner, or in this instance, an evil daughter.

Such a preoccupation with evilness, loss, abandonment, and attendant guilt clearly impacted this mother's interaction with her young child. She profoundly feared the loss of her son, which created a desperate need for connection with her child. And both parents, unconsciously fearing that their son was born of evil stock, colluded in ignoring the actual origins of their child, elevating him to the status of an all-good angel, and lowering his birth parents to the status of evil sinners and abandoners.

In addition, there appeared to be ways in which the parents' early interactions with their son set the stage for behaviors usually described as correlated with anxious ambivalent as well as disorganized attachment. Presuming he would not have had much but for them, each parent was at times overly solicitous, showering him with attention and gifts. However, their expectations of what was to be given in return, that is, loving appreciation as well as excellence in achievement, were not answered. This in turn led to profound disillusionment, and despair followed by withdrawal, alternating with outbursts of anger at Carlos's noncompliance.

Carlos's presenting symptoms, which included tantrums, clinginess and excessively controlling behavior, and a subtle incapacity to interpret social cues, may be understood as reflecting early and ongoing disorganized attachment in relation to his parents. Particularly worrisome was his difficulty with perception of social interactions, which seemed to correlate with his parents' difficulties in making sense of him. That is, from the perspective of contemporary attachment theory (Fonagy 2002), parental difficulties in making sense of the son's emotional states, and interferences with accurately comprehending his developing psychological self, including his intentions, contributed to the son's developmental weaknesses in understanding the emotional states and intentionality of others.

While parental experiences of loss and trauma that complicate the motivations for and circumstances of adoption may contribute to the early onset of developmental difficulties in a child, one can speculate that loss, either through death or divorce within the adoptive family, may further complicate the lives of parents as well as adoptive children who are already working through adoption-related losses. Many sensitively attuned parents of adopted children have brought their child to treatment, worrying about the impact on their child's development of the compounding of losses. More than once I have heard parents identify with the pain their child must be experiencing and have encountered the intense guilt that parents feel for their failure to protect their child from once again suffering life's cruelties. Beleaguered and bereft, these parents intuitively know that they may have particular difficulty in being available for their child when consumed by their own grief. In some situations, parents may bring their child to treatment while in a state of emotional retreat themselves. Alternatively, in some families there is an extreme need for connection with the child, with whom there is a profound bonding in shared grief. I don't believe one can unequivocally say that the experience of such losses, or the parental reactions to these losses, is worse for the adopted child than for any other child, but as the following vignettes indicate, the child's attempts to come to terms with his experience of contemporary loss and trauma within the family will reflect his experiences of prior loss, will bring to mind and shape thoughts about adoption and its meaning to his life, and may stimulate an emotional search for an idealized safe haven that may very well include fantasies about birth parents and old homelands. I believe that it is the parents' ability to recognize and help their child make sense of this most difficult of circumstances that provides the best possibility of a healthy resolution.

THE DEATH OF AN ADOPTIVE MOTHER: FATHER'S WITHDRAWAL

Lisa was brought to therapy at the age of ten, two years after the death of her adoptive mother. An only child and adopted shortly after birth by affluent, older parents, she was prone to sudden temper outbursts that caused her to get into occasional trouble at school. Her mother, with whom she had reportedly been extremely close, had been painfully ill with a terminal illness for three years prior to her death. The last six months Lisa's mother had been bedridden, changing completely in appearance from a stunningly attractive and robust woman to a shriveled shell of her former self. Overcome with their own grief and exquisitely mindful of the abandonment their daughter would once again experience, neither parent could bear to prepare Lisa for the impending death of her mother. Lisa's father reported the enormity of the shock she experienced when told of her mother's death, and then her withdrawal into a vivid, imaginative world of fantasy readings and videotaped movies. Lisa particularly loved to watch *E.T.*, a film she and her parents had often seen together as a family while her mother was homebound. Her father guiltily confessed that he was somewhat relieved that she could occupy herself so thoroughly, as he was struggling profoundly with his own experiences of loss. He felt deeply sorry that Lisa had lost the mother who could truly comfort her, and he felt odd and uncomfortable with the physical closeness his sexually maturing daughter craved. He wanted her to have a female therapist because he didn't feel capable of addressing the many issues that her entrance into puberty would bring. He and Lisa, while coexisting, were becoming more detached during this mourning process.

The stories with which Lisa was most intrigued involved long, arduous, and heroic journeys, often to long-lost homelands, during which the hero or heroine survived a variety of near-death experiences. She also loved reading the Harry Potter books by J. K. Rowling. It should be noted that Harry, the protagonist in the Harry Potter books, is an orphan whose parents are witches with magical powers. Two stories written by Lisa in response to school assignments are of particular note. One involved the rescue from certain death of an endangered child whose distraught parents send her away with a kindly journalist, as they fear none of them will survive the war in Iraq. In the second, Lisa developed the tale of a lady-in-waiting, intensely rivalrous for the affections of the king, who has to flee the castle after having cast a deadly evil spell on the queen. The lady-in-waiting undertakes a long and dangerous journey as she seeks some haven of safety, trying to find her way to her homeland that she left years before. Lisa describes the woman's desperate attempt to escape from the irate king who, in a twist of fate, now appears not to desire her, preferring his now-deceased queen. The king's retaliatory, murderous wrath leads to the lady-in-waiting's death. What most characterized Lisa's fantasy world was a confusing mixture of themes: an explanatory adoption story, murderous wishes toward a queen, relatively normative Oedipal guilt and fear, attempts at resolution through escape to a hopefully safe homeland, trickery, and encounters with kindly and well-meaning saviors. Her stories were elaborate, and presented confused and confusing family romance fantasies. Notably lacking was any overt mourning for the profound loss she had experienced.

Assuming responsibility for the death of two mothers, and believing her father's withdrawal to be covering his retaliatory rage, Lisa confessed to her therapist that she feared she was violent, that her evil thoughts were capable of killing, and that this was quite evident to her. Also notable among her story themes had been the sense that the people and places that were to have provided a safe refuge could turn unsafe, and that murderous wishes could be actualized. I have previously described compensatory fantasies developed by children and adolescents in response to the premature destruction of an illusion of safety as a consequence of the death of a parent (Warshaw 1996). The search for a replacement for the truly needed parent of childhood, as well as the desperate attempt to reinstitute a context of safety, can be found in the fantasies and enacted relationships of children, adolescents, and adults who have experienced early loss. In Lisa's case, as reflected in her tales, a profound sense of guilt, wariness, and deep cynicism permeated her feelings about parent caregivers and safe havens. The reality of the death of Lisa's adoptive mother and her adoptive father's emotional withdrawal were the primary impetus for her fantasized searches. Fortunately, well-meaning saviors were also present in Lisa's tales, and people with benign intent were available as potential mentors. This cynicism mixed with guilt, and a desperate and hopeful wish for reconnection in the context of a secure base, were also notable in the emotional life of the following vignette's subject, Luke, who entered treatment at the age of nine, subsequent to his parents' divorce.

WHAT A TERRIBLE MISTAKE

Barely able to contain his excitement, nine-year-old Luke brought to his therapist's office his "adoption storybook," written for him by his birth mother and kept safely tucked away in his desk drawer. Recently he had been looking at it more, and he had been reading it the previous night while visiting with his father and his father's new fiancée. The adoption storybook told of his birth mother's search to find just the right parents for him, and her wish that he would love these people she had specially picked for him, knowing they would provide a life that she was not able to. "What a terrible mistake she made," quipped Luke, aptly describing his disillusionment with not just one, but two sets of parents.

His adoptive parents had gone through an emotionally wrenching divorce, first separating when he was seven years old. Though they believed he had not been aware of their constant late-night fighting, during which time his mother would threaten to leave, it was quite evident from observing his play that Luke had overheard his parents' intense arguments from his listening post in his bedroom. Now two years later, and once again hopeful that a new home was about to be established, Luke was becoming excited about the possibility of having a new mother, while simultaneously becoming dismissive of his adoptive mother who had primary residential custody, and with whom he was particularly furious. Luke wished to move in full time with his dad and another new mom.

Luke's play during the beginning phase of treatment was quite disorganized, with any narrative theme being particularly difficult to grasp. The chaos of his play seemed to be a metaphoric representation of his inner chaos, chaos fueled by the intense anxiety that his disrupted world generated. Terrible events happened suddenly and inexplicably, danger lurked everywhere, and people were tricksters. He was trapped, initially in a box, then in a jail cell from which there was no hope of escape. Other children tried to come to his rescue, bringing toys, clothes, and even a hacksaw, but then they would turn on him and withdraw all that they had offered. Successful attempts at escape led to recapture and return to a lifetime of imprisonment. His extraordinary crime was in fact quite trivial and involved breaking a very minor rule.

Things shifted, however, when hope was rekindled with the possibility of the establishment of a new family. Rather than initiating an elaborate fantasy search for an old homeland, Luke pinned all his hopes on his soon-to-be new mom. His play became more organized and easier to follow, but gradually a new theme emerged in which some inadequate person was always being left out or cruelly banished. At times the denigrated one appeared to be his adoptive mom and at other times his fantasized birth mother, but most poignantly it seemed to be himself who was deemed inadequate. An elaborate Oedipal scenario began to evolve as Luke came to the realization that he was not to be "numero uno."

In an attempt to grasp and formulate the meaning of Luke's experience, many questions emerged for the therapist. Was jealousy over the real relationship Luke's dad was developing with the new woman exacerbating long-standing fears that Luke was not good enough to belong? In what way was Luke's experience of inadequacy potentiated by his adoptive status? Was he doomed to be the one who did not fit in, reliving his fate as the one cast out? Would there be room for multiple loves, and multiple moms and dads? How was the therapist (and Luke) to understand the role played by Luke's life history of early adoption in his experience of himself and his family in this current life event, as well as the fantasy elaborations of such events? Similarly, as many contemporary theorists suggest (Cohler and Freeman 1993), was it not possible that Luke's life narrative was being rewritten, as inevitably understood through the lens of the present? We might ask similar questions regarding both Carlos's and Lisa's responses to and fantasy constructions of their life experiences as they sought security and connection.

AN INTERPERSONAL PERSPECTIVE

Our understanding of how the child constructs meaning out of real-life events may differ depending upon the theoretical traditions we embrace. This will be no less true for the child who is adopted than for the child born into his or her current family. Interpersonal psychoanalysts have tended to view fantasy as reflective of the child's attempts to construct meaning out of real experience, and in particular, to come to terms with realities that are hard-to-understand or mystified, rather than, instinctually derived, endogenously unfolding, and normatively present in specific forms at specific life stages (Levenson 1989).

Interpersonal theory has had as its bedrock a constructivist view of self. From this perspective, the psychological self has always been understood to be constructed within an interactional matrix that involves parents and child (Mitchell 1988; Stern 1985, 1995), as well as the larger social context. Perhaps reflective of the relational turn in psychoanalysis, most contemporary schools of thought echo this perspective (Skolnick and Warshaw 1992), with a growing consensus that the parents are integral to the development of the child's sense of self and other.

Relational analytic approaches contextualize the making of meaning, viewing personal meanings as coconstructed in the interplay of selves with others, and inextricable from the surround. Thus, when we consider the extent to which a circumstance such as parental death or divorce impacts adopted children differently than nonadopted children, we must consider conscious and unconscious parental and environmental beliefs about adoption, as well as responses to the reality of a child's having been adopted. Similarly we must understand parents' psychological adaptation to the contemporary trauma or loss and the impact of that upon their capacity to support their child through the process of mourning and beyond. Brinich (1995) exhorts analysts when involved in clinical work to be as mindful as the child is of the intrapsychic world of the adoptive parents. In particular, he contends that the understanding of symptomatic behavior in adopted children and adolescents is enhanced when we are sensitive to the inner experiences (conscious as well as unconscious) of both parents and child. Bonovitz (2004) approaches his work with adopted children and parents with this type of sensitivity to the inevitable interpenetration of the intrapsychic and interpersonal worlds of parents and child. It is in this context that he advocates an approach to treatment that involves a great deal of collateral work with parents, and as noted earlier, the facilitation of a mourning process for the parents' unresolved adoption-related losses. In both Brinich's and Bonovitz's formulations, the presumption is that the parents' capacity to see, hear, truly know, and meaningfully respond to their child's experience is interfered with by the parents' own distortions and personal preoccupations, which are sometimes consciously, and at other times not consciously, experienced. I would suggest that it is in the parents' failure to appropriately know and hold in mind their child's experience that the seeds are sown for the experiences of isolation, failures of comprehension, and mystification that lead to the child's compensatory fantasies and symptomatic solutions.

The extent to which parents are able to create a secure base in the face of awful life circumstances, and the extent to which they will be able to grasp the essence of their child's experience and to facilitate the cocreation of a coherent narrative of those circumstances, will, I believe, have a greater impact upon the outcome than the birth status of their child. When parents, whether they be adoptive or birth parents, are able to maintain emotional connection and to mutually share trauma and loss in ways that neither retreat from nor project into the relationship perceptions that are derived from needs that are primarily parental in origin, the outcome is most likely to be more fortunate than not.

REFERENCES

Blum, H. P. 1983. "Adoptive Parents: Generative Conflict and Generational Continuity." *Psychoanalytic Study of the Child* 23:141–63.

Bonovitz, C. 2004. "Unconscious Communication and the Transmission of Loss." *Journal of Infant, Child, and Adolescent Psychotherapy* 3:1–27.

Brinich, P. 1995. "Psychoanalytic Perspectives on Adoption and Ambivalence." *Psychoanalytic Psychology* 12:181–99.

Brodzinsky, D. M., D. W. Smith, and A. B. Brodzinsky. 1998. *Children's Adjustment to Adoption: Developmental and Clinical Issues*. London: Sage.

Cohler, B., and M. Freeman. 1993. "Psychoanalysis and the Developmental Narrative." In *Early Adulthood*. Vol. 5 of *The Course of Life*. Ed. G. H. Pollock and S. Greenspan. Madison, CT: International Universities Press, 99–178.

Fonagy, P. 2002. *Attachment Theory and Psychoanalysis*. New York: Other Press.

Fraiberg, S. H., E. Adelson, and V. Shapiro. 1975. "Ghosts in the Nursery: A Psychoanalytic Approach to the Problem of Impaired Infant-Mother Relationships." *Journal of the American Academy of Child Psychiatry* 14:387–422.

Glenn, J. 1974. "The Adoption Theme in Edward Albee's *Tiny Alice* and the *American Dream*." *Psychoanalytic Study of the Child* 29:413–29.

Hesse, E., and M. van IJzendoorn. 1998. "Parental Loss of Close Family Members and Propensities towards Absorption in Offspring." *Developmental Science* 1:299–305.

Levenson, E. 1989. "Whatever Happened to the Cat?—Interpersonal Perspectives on the Self." *Contemporary Psychoanalysis* 25:537–53.

Lieberman, A. 1999. "Negative Maternal Attributions: Effects on Toddlers' Sense of Self." In *Attachment Research and Psychoanalysis: Part 2: Clinical Implications*. Psychoanalytic Inquiry. Ed. D. Diamond and S. Blatt. Hillsdale, NJ: Analytic Press.

Liotti, G., B. Intreccialagi, and F. Cecere. 1991. "Esperienza di lutto nella madre e facilitazione dello sviluppo di disturbi dissociativi nella prole: Un studio caso controllo." [Unresolved mourning in mothers and vulnerability to dissociative disorders in children: A case control study]. *Rivista di Psichiatria* 26:283–91.

Main, M., and E. Hesse. 1990. "Parent's Unresolved Traumatic Experiences Are Related to Infant Disorganized Attachment Status: Is Frightened and/or Frightening Parental Behavior the Linking Mechanism?" In *Attachment in the Preschool Years: Theory, Research, and Intervention*. Ed. Mark T. Greenberg, Dante Cicchetti, and E. Mark Cummings. Chicago: University of Chicago Press.

Mitchell, S. 1988. *Relational Concepts in Psychoanalysis*. Cambridge, MA: Harvard University Press.

Nickman, S. 1985. "Losses in Adoption." *Psychoanalytic Study of the Child* 40:365–98.

Schechter, M. D. 1970. "About Adoptive Parents." In *Parenthood: Its Psychology and Psychopathology*. Ed. E. J. Anthony and T. Benedek. Boston: Little, Brown.

Schuengel, C., M. J. Bakermans-Kranenburg, and M. H. van IJzendoorn. 1999. "Frightening Maternal Behavior Linking Unresolved Loss and Disorganized Infant Attachment." *Journal of Consulting and Clinical Psychology* 67:54–63.

Skolnick, N., and S. C. Warshaw. 1992. Introduction. In *Relational Perspectives in Psychoanalysis*. Ed. N. Skolnick and S. C. Warshaw. Hillsdale, NJ: Analytic Press.

Stern, D. 1985. *The Interpersonal World of the Infant*. New York: Basic Books.

———. 1995. *The Motherhood Constellation*. New York: Basic Books.

Warshaw, S. C. 1996. "The Loss of My Father in Adolescence: The Impact on My Work as a Psychoanalyst." In *Therapist as a Person*. Ed. B. Gerson. Hillsdale, NJ: Analytic Press.

Weider, H. 1977. "On Being Told of Adoption." *Psychoanalytic Quarterly* 46:1–21.

Chapter Seven

The Adoption of Foster Children Who Suffered Early Trauma and Object Loss

Implications for Practice

Vivian B. Shapiro and Janet R. Shapiro

In terms of the emotional life of the child, one of the most significant developmental lines is the emerging capacity for human relationships (Fraiberg 1987a). While the genesis of the child's capacity for human relationships is dependent on both nature and nurture, it is the human context of the developing child's earliest experiences that is most critical. The attuned quality of the psychological relationship between parent and child remains central in helping the child to master successive maturational phases of development. Indeed, it is because of this special attachment relationship between parent and child that the parent is often referred to as the *transformative object* (Bollas 1987). These primary human relationships continue to change and evolve throughout infancy, toddlerhood, latency, and adolescence as the child's development continues to evolve in multiple spheres (Freud 1965).

Winnicott (1965a) describes the early caregiver-child relationship as a "holding environment" that provides the basis for a healthy psychic infrastructure of the child and the development of an internal sense of security and trust. Infants and young children rely on primary caregivers for the modulation of anxiety and other states of emotional and physiological arousal. However, children who have experienced traumatic early caregiving or repeated disruptions of parental care are at risk for developmental disturbances. Traumatic separations and precipitous object loss, and in extreme cases, child abuse and neglect, may interfere with the formation of a sense of "felt security" (Schore 1994).

In addition, research in the cognitive neurosciences describes the processes by which the sustained experience of early trauma can precipitate neurochemical and organizational changes in the developing brain that may predispose the child to further vulnerability over time. In fact, if internal, unabated stress exists for a long period of time, states of arousal can include unproductive patterns of emotional responses to stress, and these states can become habitual traits (Perry et al. 1995; Applegate and Shapiro 2005). This concept of emotional vulnerability is referred to by Balint as a "basic fault wherein a crisis that occurs long after the earlier trauma can trigger strong emotional reactions such as depression or unabated anxiety" (1968).

Thus, infants and young children who cannot rely on primary caregivers to help them cope with anxiety and other states of emotional and physiological distress often develop coping styles, or adaptations, that may interfere both with the mastery of developmental goals and the ability to establish trusting attachment relationships with others. When children who have experienced multiple foster placements are ultimately adopted, they may have significant problems in their transition as they bring their internal history with them to their new adoptive home.

This chapter will address the difficulties that can occur in what we refer to as *complex adoptions*, wherein children have been adopted following traumatic disruptions in their early attachment relationships (V. Shapiro, J. Shapiro, and Paret 2001). Specifically, we explore the experience of children who are adopted following multiple experiences of traumatic early care and precipitous object loss. Reflecting an infant mental health perspective, our work is informed by a conceptual framework that integrates developmental research, ego psychology, psychoanalytic theory, emerging understanding of brain development in early life, and an awareness of the child's ecological and cultural surround.

Through the use of case vignettes, we explore the reverberations of early trauma and attachment disruptions in the child's internal world and the long-term adjustment following late adoptions. In particular, we focus on how the child and adoptive parents alike need time and experience to form attachments to each other and eventually to form a coherent sense of family identity. The availability of a more positive and stable parent-child relationship can help the child gain a more solid internal sense of security and, relatedly, a more optimistic sense of self.

AN INTRODUCTION TO COMPLEX ADOPTIONS

In traditional adoptions, often referred to as "adoptions at birth," many children have the benefit of access to secure, consistent, and contingently responsive parental care from the first months of life. In such cases, most adoptive children and parents can, and do, form close bonds of attachment that serve to meet the developmental needs of the child and support the formation of a coherent and secure sense of family identity. Even so, it is important for clinicians to understand that the experience of traditional adoption may have special symbolic meanings for the adoptive parents and child. The symbolic meaning may change over time as the child matures and new questions are raised for both the child and parents. Over time, children usually gain increasingly sophisticated cognitive and linguistic capacities with which to consider the meaning of adoption, and they often want to know more about their families of origin and the reasons for adoption (Brinich 1990; D. Brodzinsky, Smith, and A. Brodzinsky 1998).

Complex adoption, as defined in this chapter, involves the adoption of children from foster placement. These children may be in the developmental phase of late infancy, toddlerhood, preschool, or latency. They may be adopted by their foster parent, by an unknown adoptive parent, or by grand-parental-kinship caregivers. It is generally thought that the age of a child at the time of adoption and the quality of his or her early care, including any history of early neglect, abuse, or multiple attachment disruptions, can have a profound impact on the overall developmental status of the child at the time of adoption (V. Shapiro, J. Shapiro, and Paret 2001).

The adoptive parents must be prepared for a prolonged period of social and emotional adaptation as the child transitions into the adoptive family. Initially, the child and the adoptive parents may be "out of sync" with each other in their readiness to claim each other. The child may have a great degree of internal fragility and a narrow view of the meaning of family. The family may be eager and ready to provide love, care, and an empathically attuned holding environment. Yet the child, having experienced a sense of "family limbo," may have begun to internalize a relational model that leads the child to continue to expect precipitous separations and loss.

From the parents' point of view, it is often hoped that the stability of their family will assuage the child's anxiety, but clinical cases reveal that even such external stability does not quickly resolve the internal fragility of the child. Children who have spent years in foster care without a sense of permanency, who have had multiple experiences of loss, and who may have had little control over what happened to them need time and understanding to experience a sense of permanency and belonging.

Many adoptive parents, whether adopting children from the United States or abroad, may not be aware of the extensiveness of the medical, neurological, and emotional history of their child. They may not realize the full impact this history may have had on their child's overall development. They do not anticipate, therefore, the potential difficulty of establishing a secure post-adoption relationship with their child. The hope of quickly becoming a close family is often deflated as the parents come to realize that they cannot easily help their child overcome his or her internal fragility. The establishment of a secure parent-child relationship will be a long journey, and often professional support, guidance, and treatment are needed to understand the internal view of the child and to help the child return to a more normal course along developmental lines. Indeed, young children who could not rely on their caregiver to assuage their anxiety may have withdrawn into themselves and may not expect or spontaneously seek comfort from available others. Thus, when previous attachment relationships were insecure, the child's initial stance toward the adoptive parents may be one of ambivalence, mistrust, and withdrawal (Fraiberg 1987b).

On the surface, the child may initially be compliant, but the child's inner feelings may be more complicated. Under the stress of a transition from one family to another, the child may reveal infantile coping mechanisms that were used to deal with the fears and anxiety of inadequate responses to the child's overall physical and emotional needs in the past. Where the child has not developed a protective bond of love with any primary object, the emerging bond with the adoptive parents may take extensive time, and may require significant efforts by the adoptive parents. When feelings of frustration and neediness occur, the child may express their feelings in withdrawal from or anger at their parents, without any expectation that their adoptive parents can help them calm down (Fraiberg 1987a). It may be that the child needs time to experience a new, more stable, and predictable parental relationship in order to begin to trust the parents of the present, and to internalize the new parental model. The adoptive parents may be puzzled and disturbed by the initial negative transference to them. If there are too many such relational disappointments, the parents may feel rejected, and their self-esteem and growing parental identity may be threatened (Benedek 1959).

For the child adopted following early experiences of trauma, many questions of assessment need to be considered to evaluate the child's developmental status and to develop an appropriate treatment plan. Each child will be different in that they will have had a specific history with different impacts on their development. Some of the many factors that need to be understood in the assessment process include:

- the child's prenatal, neonatal, and postnatal medical history
- the age of the child at first separation from the birth parents
- the number of years spent in kinship or foster care
- the number of moves made within the foster-care system
- the quality and context of care in various family homes
- the child's age at the time of adoption
- the emotional and social experience of the transition to permanent family care (V. Shapiro, J. Shapiro, and Paret 2001)

The reason that the birth parents had to give up the child is important to understand. Often, the first separation from the family of origin is associated with a breakdown in the birth family's ability to provide emotional or physical safety for the child. Family poverty, mental or physical illness, drug abuse, lack of social support, or impaired ego functioning of the parent may have put the child at risk. The immediate removal of the child from the family of origin is often precipitous, and once in the foster-care system, the child enters a new realm of uncertainty, particularly with regard to separations from attachment figures. Often the child is placed in numerous foster homes until the final legal decisions are made regarding permanency planning. The child may have experienced different models of care in a number of foster-placement situations. While many foster caregivers may have provided concerned and empathic care, others may have had greater difficulty in forming an emotional bond with their foster child. On the other hand, where the child has become attached to the caregiver, the loss upon separation may have added to the child's accumulative fragility.

Another important consideration in the assessment process is the structure of the adoptive family. Currently, because of the great need for adoptive parents for children with disrupted backgrounds, there is increasing openness to a greater diversity of adoptive parents including single older parents, gay and lesbian parents, grandparents, extended kinship-family parents, foster parents, interracial and multiracial parents, and open-adoption parents. Each family structure has its own dynamics, and each family has its own particular psychological history and resources and needs. Thus the narrative history and social and cultural considerations of the family context are also complex and need to be understood. In developing a working alliance with parents, it is helpful for the therapist to examine how the parents' pathway to adoption occurred and the nature of the symbolic meaning of parenthood to them. Often the parents' initial dream about the child they adopt is modulated by the reality of the adjustments that both the child and parents experience in the initial transitional phase of adoption.

NEW INSIGHTS FROM RECENT RESEARCH: SEQUELAE OF EARLY TRAUMA AND OBJECT LOSS

An integration of developmental research and neurobiological and psychoanalytic theory is needed to inform clinical work with populations of vulnerable children and families. Consideration of these perspectives serves to increase our understanding of the *processes* by which children develop and to highlight factors associated with patterns of *risk and resiliency*. A clinical, developmental framework can be especially valuable in helping practitioners to address the gap that may exist between normal, expected developmental trajectories, or outcomes, and the difficulties a child who has had serious early trauma may experience in the spheres of social, emotional, cognitive, and physical growth and development.

Over time, the study of human development has also broadened to include more diverse populations of children and families, and also to include the study of special populations of children at risk for a variety of negative developmental outcomes. This work has shown that *multiple* pathways to developmental well-being are possible, and that the particular social ecology, or cultural milieu, of a child combines with individual and familial characteristics to influence important outcomes. This perspective is very important because it addresses the wide range of individual differences that exist *within* diverse populations of children and families — an important conceptual framework for more nuanced assessment and treatment planning (Lamb 1999).

The adoption of children who have experienced traumatic early beginnings raises a distinct set of questions, most of which have been the subject of study in psychological and neurobiological research (Applegate and Shapiro 2005). These questions address the role of early experience in development, the child's capacity to recover from exposure to trauma and adverse early experience, the complexity of the recursive interaction between nature and nurture, and the centrality of primary attachments or caregiving relationships. Clinicians who work with children who have experienced early trauma and attachment disruption must always balance an awareness of the effects of such early experience with hope for change and growth via altered situational characteristics and early intervention efforts.

Among the earliest scholarly works describing the importance of stable and continuous attachment relationships were the descriptive clinical reports of Spitz and Wolf (1946) and Freud and Burlingham (1944), and the early descriptive research of John Bowlby (1953). These reports carefully described the grief-stricken reaction of children separated from their primary caretakers under conditions of stress such as war-related violence and unexpected childhood hospitalization, or in the terms of our focus, the experience of children exposed to early trauma, neglect, and multiple disruptions of early family care.

Current research on attachment conceptualizes the early attachment relationship as a regulatory system organized to achieve for the child the dual developmental goals of felt security and a capacity to explore the external environment of objects and people (Main 1999; Cassidy and Shaver 1999; Schore 1994; Siegel 1999). During the first years of life, children are thought to develop internal representations, or internal working models, of their important attachment relationships. The development of a secure sense of the other and of the self supports the child's capacity to make and sustain psychological investments in the external world of objects and people.

Infants and young children who are deemed to be securely attached are able to seek and utilize proximity to the caregiver when distressed, to modulate emotional arousal, and to see the caregiver as a secure base from which to explore and gain mastery over the external world. Conversely, insecurely attached infants are understood to represent caregiver-child dyads that are not organized to consistently achieve the dual goals of emotional modulation and exploration. Classified as *insecure/avoidant, insecure/resistant*, or *disorganized*, these attachment patterns are associated with a range of suboptimal developmental outcomes. (Main 1999) Infants classified as disorganized show the greatest insecurity in that their attachment behavior is observed to be confused and inconsistent. This pattern of attachment is overrepresented among groups of infants and young children who have experienced chronic abuse and neglect.

In general, however, children who have lacked access to consistent and responsive early care may exhibit a range of problems that can be understood as relating to one or more of the following dimensions:

1. The ways in which the child experiences, modulates, or expresses affect. Generally, as children develop over the first years of life, their capacity to experience emotion broadens as does their ability to differentiate various affective states such as anger, sadness, and feelings of love and happiness (S. Greenspan and N. Greenspan 1991). The internal experience of emotion broadens as does the child's capacity to verbalize feelings and to modulate states of affective arousal. Each of these developmental achievements rests upon the auxiliary support of trusted caregivers.

2. Problems in the capacity to mentalize, or reflect upon, the emotional and mental states of other people (Fonagy and Target 1998). While early experiences of deprivation may differ in kind or degree, a common element that may exist across varying experiences of environmental deprivation is a lack of access to interactions that are contingently responsive. It is in the context of contingently responsive care that children begin to acquire the ability to mentalize their own emotional states as well as the motivations and affects of other people. Children who have caregivers who are able to mentalize about the internal state of the child are more likely to develop a capacity to reflect on their own feeling states and to be able to identify and understand the internal states of other people. Children whose internal feelings have not been responded to are less able to mentalize, may misinterpret social cues, and may have difficulty in discerning ambiguous

social contexts and situations. As children move into broader social worlds, such as those found in the school environment, one of the relational demands made on them is their need to decipher the social cues of multiple people (teachers and peers) in multiple contexts (classroom, playground, neighborhood).

3. Difficulties in the formation of close and secure interpersonal relationships (Cassidy and Shaver 1999). In the context of consistent and empathically attuned early care, children develop close attachments to primary caregivers and an internalized view of relations as trusting and pleasurable. In the absence of such care, children may withdraw from these kinds of connections because intimacy and closeness may not be associated with felt security and pleasure but with negative affective states such as anxiety, anger, frustration, and despair.

4. Deficits in exploration of the environment, mastery, motivation, and "readiness to learn." Young children may first come to the attention of practitioners when they come up against difficulties in the broader social environment such as day care or school. To succeed in this environment, children need the capacity to experience, share, and modulate emotional experiences as well as the capacity to regulate attention and behavior. Difficulties in the regulation of affect may contribute to children feeling overwhelmed in the classroom as they become preoccupied with their own internal states and unable to adequately decode aspects of new relational environments.

Research in the cognitive neurosciences provides an additional empirical base for the importance of attachment relationships to the developmental well-being of the child. Siegel (1999) refers to such caregiving as being provided by caregivers who have "mindsight," or the capacity to understand the mind of the other. In addition, researchers have identified the ways in which a sensitive and empathically attuned caregiving environment supports the child's ability to experience both positive and negative states of emotional arousal while still being able to return to a state of homeostasis.

These findings thus suggest that the early lack of stability and the erratic early holding environment of many of these children create the potential for serious risk that is evident at the time of adoption, as well as ongoing developmental vulnerability. While adoption creates a new relational context, and presents an opportunity to support the resiliency of the child for broad developmental growth, the impact of less positive early experiences requires that the adoptive parents be sensitive to the residual sequela of their child's early traumatic experiences. It is here that adoptive parents often need clinical assistance.

The cases presented below illustrate the developmental crises of children at three different phases of growth: infancy, toddlerhood, and latency. All of the children were exposed to trauma and parental separations and were placed in foster care, and all were eventually adopted. The clinical examples reveal the significance of chronological age, attachment history, and the developmental status of the child in understanding clinical assessment and treatment needs. The clinician's task is complex in addressing both the family needs and the child's need for help in a number of spheres. The importance of creating a therapeutic holding environment for the parents cannot be overstated, as the parents need much support to deal with their own internal feelings regarding the difficulties they may encounter.

CASE VIGNETTE 1: A SIX-MONTH-OLD AT DEVELOPMENTAL RISK—AN UNCERTAIN FUTURE FOR SANDRA

This case presents an example of the developmental vulnerability that may ensue, even for an infant, when the early relational environment is characterized by trauma and object loss. Sandra was referred to protective services for evaluation at the age of six months by a public health nurse assigned to the family. After visiting the home many times, the nurse assessed Sandra to be at severe risk for medical and psychological neglect. Sandra's mother, Ms. D, was a single parent who was addicted to alcohol and drugs, and showed signs of mental illness. She was unable to focus on the needs of her three children or to provide even minimal care and safety for them. Sandra had been hospitalized for nonorganic failure to thrive and multiple episodes of pneumonia. During the hospital stays her condition improved, but upon returning home her weight loss resumed and her general health deteriorated. This pattern of illness at home and recovery in the hospital indicated a pattern of serious neglect (Gizynski and Shapiro 1989).

The nurse observed that at home Sandra was most often left alone on a couch, undressed in the winter and unattended to. When she whimpered, Ms. D directed the two older children, ages four and six, to care for her. The mother seemed to be in her own world, the house was chaotic, and evidence of serious neglect was apparent. Ms. D needed therapeutic assessment and treatment but would not accept the offer of a mental health specialist. While the visiting nurse tried to establish a working alliance with the mother, Ms. D barely seemed to remember her on subsequent visits, let alone to understand the seriousness of Sandra's failing health. Ms. D was in serious difficulty with symptoms of depression, being lethargic and distant. She also seemed disoriented. The family lived in a shadowy world where strangers drifted in and out. Ms. D refused a consultation with mental health services, and the baby continued to regress.

Sandra was a passive, unresponsive baby who seemed indifferent to the approach of others. She had a narrow range of affect and was essentially mute, with few vocalizations and muted, weak cries. She was lethargic and limp and did not show the normal sensory-motor development of a six-month-old. Her interest in the social world was limited. At six months of age, most babies can anticipate parental actions, express joy in relationships, engage in baby games, and show joy, surprise, fear, and disappointment.

Sandra's withdrawal revealed the developmental signs of too much aloneness, and her regressed behavior indicated a lack of experience with a responsive other. Developmentally, she was far behind her chronological age in sensory-motor development, expressive affect, state modulation, and cognitive development. The usual reciprocity between child and parent, as seen through anticipatory behavior, mirroring activity, and recognition of a special attachment relationship, was missing. Her affect was somber and restricted.

Consider how developmental theory can contribute to our understanding of Sandra's poor developmental status. How do we understand the etiology of Sandra's situation? Is it because of organic deficits, poor care, or both? Children who experience long-term effects from poor nutrition, failure to thrive, or untreated medical illness often present in hospital with symptoms of lethargy and developmental delays. With immediate treatment and good nursing care, they can regain some inner strength and begin to respond to the social effort of caregivers. Some infants have the resiliency to take hold of a more positive human environment (as we saw when Sandra was in the hospital), but their health is compromised when they return home to a depressed or ill primary attachment figure.

Our previous view of the newborn child as a tabula rasa, or blank state, has been replaced with an understanding of the many adaptive capacities possessed by the neonate. The sensory capacity to hear, to see, and to regulate states of alertness supports the neonate's capacity to engage in mutually regulatory relationships with caregivers from the moment of birth. As Stern (1985) has indicated, the infant is actually capable of responsive interaction from birth, but it is the parental caregiver who provides the responsive structure of infant care.

Within the context of a predictable and stable relationship, the child is eventually able to internalize a coherent view of the external world, which forms the secure base from which ego structure and exploration of the world proceeds. In Sandra's case, the world around her was unresponsive to her needs for holding, for comfort, for food, and for social relatedness. Without empathic caring or mirroring by the other, Sandra sank into a state of withdrawal and passivity. Sandra adapted to this emptiness, but her development was flattened out by a muted awareness of even her own states of hunger and affect (Bollas 1987).

Sandra was at psychological and medical risk for neglect, and observations showed that she was already at risk for illness and psychological development. When a supportive, caregiving environment does not exist and the attachment relationship has been disrupted, or not even begun, the infant may experience severe stress and develop behavioral mechanisms for coping with poorly regulated interactive experiences, including parental withdrawal and erratic care. Fraiberg (1987a; 1987b) describes the emergence of infant defenses such as gaze aversion, severe withdrawal, aggression against the self, hyperactivity, and extreme separation anxiety. These defenses may help the infant to manage states of unrelenting anxiety, but in the long run, the developmental costs of these defenses will impair social development.

In Sandra's situation, the nurse recommended that Sandra be referred to child welfare for evaluation and placement until the psychological status of her mother could indicate the treatment possibilities. However, it continued to be difficult to engage Sandra's mother in a working alliance, and she continued to refuse mental health treatment. With Sandra's well-being at risk, medically and psychologically, time was of the essence, and Sandra was removed to foster care. Given the uncertainty of her mother's recovery, Sandra's voyage in the foster-care system would take time before a permanent plan could be determined by the courts. Thus began Sandra's journey into the system of foster care with its long route of hope, loss, and turmoil.

Even in the best of circumstances, the relationship between a foster parent and the foster child is complex, as the prospect of separation is inherent in many cases. Sandra needed a therapeutic foster-care home where an experienced foster-care mother could help her recover from her profound withdrawal. The foster parent would need guidance and support to help woo Sandra into an interactive and responsive relationship, a relationship wherein the parental figure could provide attuned, empathic care. Further, the foster parent would need to pace her efforts to engage Sandra in relating because initially Sandra's social development lagged behind her chronological age. As Winnicott (1965a) has suggested, the parent-child relationship is at the center of the therapeutic endeavor, and it is within the parent-child relationship that the process of recovery from the internal scars of disturbances in attachment relationship can begin.

We can anticipate that once she has connected to an attachment figure, Sandra may become highly needy of her caregiver, and if she is moved either back home or to another caregiver, she will experience this loss deeply and will lose ground developmentally. This vulnerability to loss may remain with Sandra, and in Balint's words, the experience of loss may become a "basic fault" (1968). We can expect that future separations from attachment figures may lead to anxiety and depression for Sandra, and loss of the other may become a sensitive tipping force in her life. Treatment may be required at various phases of her development as Sandra may remain vulnerable to attachment and relational disruption.

CASE VIGNETTE 2: TODDLERS OF DRUG-ADDICTED MOTHERS AND GRANDPARENT ADOPTION

We now address the difficult issues that may arise for children whose pre-adoptive life has been clouded by parental drug abuse and chaotic home environments (Minkler and Roe 1993). The pre-adoptive risk history of these children often starts in utero when the fetus is exposed to teratogenic agents such as drugs or alcohol, poor nutrition, and inadequate medical care. Many are born prematurely, small for their gestational age, and with pronounced difficulties in the capacity for physiological state regulation. At birth they may show excessive irritability, frequent tremors, acute startle reactions, poor eating, disturbed sleep patterns, and poor muscle tone. In the service of keeping adoptive children in the broader family, and because of new state and federal efforts to find adoptive parents more quickly, many grandmothers are now able to become permanent legal guardians of these children (V. Shapiro, J. Shapiro, and Paret 2001). These grandmothers themselves are often in situations of great stress, and the burden of caring for the children is high because many live in economic poverty. As adoptive parents, these grandmothers have multiple tasks in developing a holding environment that can contain the children's anxiety and deal with the residual emotional sequela of the children's early experience.

As we mentioned earlier, infants have few defenses for modulating overwhelming states of anxiety and other affects. When parental help is available, they can generally use the auxiliary ego of the caregiving adult, who can help them calm down and recover a state of homeostasis. Where an important, responsive caregiving relationship does not exist, the growing child uses primitive defenses to handle their feelings, and may release their internal turmoil through aggression against the self or the other, withdrawal from social interaction, or the expression or development of symptoms such as acute separation anxiety, freezing, or hypervigilance (Fraiberg 1987b). As the child gets older, one sign of insecure attachment is the relative inability of the child to utilize the assurances of a caregiver to regain a state of affective balance following a state of dysregulation, such as an extreme loss of control.

When toddlers are adopted following neglect, trauma, or caregiving disruptions, their behavior is often volatile and seemingly without relationship to the circumstances. Because these children experienced emotional neglect in their first years, they are often unable to read the intention of others. The insecure toddler, without a sense of trust or attachment to the other, may at times strike out because of chaotic internal feelings of despair, anger, or extreme anxiety. While needing comfort and relief from the parental figure, they are unable to be comforted because they have in a sense transferred negative feelings of anxiety and anger from the past to the emotionally "unknown" adoptive parent. These unmodulated feelings of the child can be a great hardship for the adoptive parent, who may not initially understand the meaning of the child's behavior.

These conflicted and uncontrolled feelings of toddlers were observed in a study of a group of grandparents caring for the children of their cocaine-addicted daughters (Minkler and Roe 1993). The grandmothers revealed the heavy burden of caring for their emotionally needy grandchildren. Ms. H, for example, a sixty-two-year-old grandmother, described the extreme separation anxiety of her grandson Hank, who was three years old.

> When he first came he used to just scream. Every time I'd start getting dressed, he'd think I was going to leave him. He'd say, "Don't leave me!—He'd stand rigidly in the door till I got back even when I went to the washroom. (163)

Another grandmother in the study described the lack of trust of her grandson and his extreme separation anxiety.

> It feels like he doesn't trust you. He has his eyes on you at all times, the minute he hears you walk . . . he screams. I guess he lived in fear so long this is what he had to live with, with all the drug people in the house. It's fear, pure fear. (163)

In yet another study family, Ms. James, a forty-three-year-old grandmother, was hardworking and poor, had many medical problems, and suffered from depression and physical exhaustion. She became the permanent caretaker of Micky, aged two, and Max, aged three. Their drug-addicted mother had been sentenced to jail for stealing, and Ms. James wanted to keep the family together. But Micky and Max were out of control, emotionally unstable, and unresponsive to Ms. James's efforts to soothe them or set limits on their behavior. They were hyperactive, running all the time, and she had to struggle to physically handle them, and to feed, clothe, diaper, and bathe them. They engaged in dangerous play, such as jumping off furniture, running in the street, and destroying various objects. They clogged her toilet, colored her walls, and smashed the wood panels of her dresser. At times they flew into hour-long rages at her, and Max, the elder toddler, rammed his head against the wall. Ms. James's story describes the interactive problems and heavy burden of grandparent adoptive care, the children's psychological state, her own health needs, and the poverty and isolation of her situation (Minkler and Roe 1993).

The behavior of Micky and Max represents the children's attempts at coping with their past chaotic external world and their resultant anxious and impaired internal world. Without a safety net around them, and without a safe base of parental protection, Micky and Max developed primitive early defenses of hypervigilance, aggression, and intense motor activity in an effort to ward off overwhelming states of anxiety (Fraiberg 1987b). While these defenses may function to temporarily relieve internal anxiety states, they clearly limited the toddlers' opportunities for establishment of new relationships of trust with others, exploration and independent growth, and experiencing and modulating affect sufficiently.

The adaptive reaction of Micky and Max to their chaotic family situation is not unusual for children left in chaotic circumstances at too early an age. Evidence of insecure and disorganized attachment behaviors is revealed in the primitive coping mechanisms of the child (Main 1999). Ms. James soon sought psychiatric care because she was at her wit's end, was increasingly depressed, and had difficulties with high blood pressure.

A therapeutic approach needs to begin with the consideration of the larger holding environment, which includes the adoptive parent as well as the children. The patients in Ms. James's family system were of three generations: the grandmother, who had lost her own daughter to drugs and was overwhelmed by the tasks of parenting; the toddlers suffering emotional and developmental impairment; and the daughter in prison, a psychological part of the family, if not present. It is important to recognize that this was, in fact, an open adoption, because the children's mother, while not their legal mother, was in and out of contact with her family.

An important first step in this situation would be to begin to establish a working alliance with the adoptive grandparent and to consider her needs, concerns, and feelings about her situation and her perception of the children. Developing a working alliance with the adoptive parent is a necessary step because a relationship based on a sense of trust is essential where so many painful issues are at hand. But there is no easy or simple pathway to resolving so many complex needs at so many different levels. A primary objective in such a crisis situation at the time of adjustment would be to help stabilize the family situation. This might require the therapist to reach out to other community resources such as medical, preschool, and supportive services, while undertaking a broad assessment of the child's status and needs.

As clinicians, our primary focus is to articulate how we may be able to help the adoptive parent understand the mind-set of the child. Observations of the child's state at the time of adoption can help us understand the internal world of the child. Micky and Max, for example, and the other toddlers reviewed above, carried their internal anxiety and frightened view of the human world with them into their adoptive relationships with their caregivers. They showed the sequelae of children left on their own at too early an age, with resultant problems in attachment relationships, an inability to regulate their feelings and to seek relief through reliance on others, and a difficulty in reading the reality of the external world. They may have come to the adoptive family without a sense of basic trust, and with behavioral volatility related to precipitous feelings of anxiety, anger, and despair.

In the initial period, the therapist can offer insight and guidance to the adoptive parent. The therapist's understanding and empathy may help contain the caregiver's and the child's extreme feelings of loss, confusion, and helplessness, thereby supporting the stability of the holding environment. The clinician has both a therapeutic and an educational role, fulfilled by both listening with compassion to the worries expressed and interpreting the child's incomprehensible behavior as an outcome of past losses, and not simply a rejection of the caregiver's efforts to provide the child with a home.

The developmentally informed therapist can give advice about the ways the caregiver can help contain the emotional anxiety of the child, and can introduce ideas about the needs of the child for limits, stability, reassurance, comfort, and acceptance. It is hard to anticipate the level of resiliency of any child whose early years have been devoid of safety and empathic care. However, the opportunity to experience a sensitive and responsive holding environment may give the child a chance to develop a better sense of trust with respect to the outside world, and a more internal sense of safety, which might enable the child to integrate the building blocks of emotional development.

CASE VIGNETTE 3: A PROLONGED ADOPTION PROCESS AND A DESPAIRING VIEW OF THE WORLD DURING LATENCY

Antonio was first removed from his mother, Ms. Rivers, at the age of six weeks when she was arrested for drug use. He was returned the next day, and was again removed at the age of thirteen months when his mother entered a drug treatment center. At that time he was placed with a foster parent, Ms. Smith, who noted that Antonio was a quiet baby who cried silent tears when she started to feed him. He improved over the two months in Ms. Smith's care, and by the end of that time, he was affectionate, smiled, and could say, "Bye-bye." At fifteen months he was returned to his birth mother, whose mental health had deteriorated. Antonio's mother had not completed her drug treatment program, and when Antonio was eighteen months old and found to be suffering from an iron burn, he was returned to Ms. Smith's care. At this point, it was more difficult for Ms. Smith to make a connection with him. Ms. Smith was an empathic mother, and Antonio required extraordinary care under very difficult circumstances.

During a long court case, Antonio was mandated to continue to visit with his birth mother. Each of these contacts created deep upset and dysregulation for Antonio. He often left these visits sobbing and in great internal distress. For the next five years Antonio was in a state of family limbo as he was transferred back and forth between birth mother and foster mother. His emotional and behavioral states expressed fear, anxiety, anger, and at times depressive symptoms. At the age of four, Antonio began treatment with a psychologist. On his first visit Antonio said, "I don't want to go back and forth," a sad refrain that lasted until he was adopted by Ms. Smith at the age of seven (Paret and Shapiro 1998).

The therapeutic work became very important to Antonio, and he was able to use the therapeutic relationship to help him with his anxiety, anger, and internal pain. At six years of age he began to dictate stories to the therapist, and he expressed a view of the world that was lonely and dangerous, a world that was invisible to others but was real to him. He related a story of woe about a mournful pumpkin that escaped danger and searched for a friend to live with. In other stories he wove tales of children who were attacked by others and who did not know whom to trust. Danger was everywhere.

The therapist put into words Antonio's grief as well as his wish to live and go forward. Often these interpretations were followed by his clarification of his memories of early terror and abuse, and as he put his feelings into words, Antonio was beginning to have the capacity to differentiate between past and present. His internal view of the external world was that of a world requiring fear and distrust, and his internal view of himself was that of a child needing protection. At the same time he expressed a sense of loneliness and a wish for friendship (V. Shapiro, J. Shapiro, and Paret 2001).

After his formal adoption at age seven, Antonio was euphoric about the permanence of his life with his adoptive mother. However, soon he felt a sense of guilt about leaving his birth mother and elder brother. In school he began to have behavioral problems and was seen as oppositional. He felt left out and told his therapist that he was not like other boys because he was Hispanic and adopted. His hyperactivity increased, and he could not concentrate on his work. A psychiatric assessment resulted in medications to help him cope with his anxiety and ability to function in school. The threats he experienced as an infant and toddler and his infantile coping mechanisms had a continuing impact on his developmental growth. Indeed, his adaptive states had become traits (Perry et al. 1995).

As Antonio was about to enter puberty, his internal view of the world continued to be marked by his fear of danger, even within the school yard. He identified with soldiers in war and assumed a defensive readiness to fight the perceived dangers that surrounded him. He felt himself to be on the outside of normal relationships at school. His "false self" was presented by a blustery front to others, but his "true self" was frightened, and he was uneasy about moving beyond the family (Winnicott 1965b). For Antonio, his sense of unseen danger and lack of trust in people were internalized, and he continued to feel a lack of safety.

As Antonio approached adolescence, old themes of abandonment, confusion, loss, and fear reemerged. At times Antonio resisted therapy, but he continued with it. He used the therapeutic relationship as a place of safety in which to reveal his feelings of anxiety and fear, sometimes through words, sometimes through his behavior, and sometimes through his drawings or by bringing in rap music. The therapist listened to Antonio's internal worries and to his real difficulties at home and at school. She communicated her understanding of his anger and his fears, and recognized how hard it was for him to attend to the present. Although help was given to him related to achievement at school, his internal turmoil was overwhelming.

The normative tasks and achievements of adolescence—which include the growth of autonomy, an ability to tolerate anxiety, and a capacity to form new relationships—were difficult for Antonio. In elementary school, external structure is built into the learning environment. In middle school, however, children are expected to have the ego capacities needed to sustain the anxiety that may be associated with more difficult, abstract, and prolonged learning tasks. Antonio's impaired sense of efficacy and the general concerns he had about growing up interfered with his self-esteem and his functioning. Despite his high IQ, he was resistant to doing his homework, and concentration was difficult for him. In high school his cooperation was so poor that he was placed in a remedial school. Antonio's sense of agency was impaired.

Antonio also struggled with the process of identity formation. He partially identified with the world of his birth mother and also with that of his very different adoptive mother, who came from a totally different cultural background. He was uncertain that he would ever be accepted and successful in his adoptive mother's middle-class world. He had fears about separation from his adoptive mother and was unsure he could ever be independent as a young adult, and this may have had an impact on his unwillingness to move ahead at school. He was a gifted artist and story teller, and had more academic capacity than he would acknowledge to himself or his teachers. Eventually he entered a school program that was flexible and more attuned to his own learning style. The therapeutic holding environment continued to be a safe place wherein he worked through his struggles to begin to integrate a coherent sense of identity.

Antonio's adoptive mother was involved in the therapeutic work when he first started therapy. Antonio's relationship with his adoptive mother was often in a push-pull dynamic, in which extreme dependency alternated with rejection of his mother's efforts to provide discipline and limits. In developing a working alliance with Ms. Smith, the therapist provided a supportive milieu in which Ms. Smith could understand more about Antonio's behavior and deal with her own emotional responses to the slowness of Antonio's emotional growth. This dynamic was very difficult for Antonio's adoptive mother, but the stability of the therapeutic relationship helped her respond as best she could to the difficulties that Antonio faced as he completed high school. Despite the back and forth of progress, Antonio's development was within the realm of safety. He did not act out in a way that would lead to juvenile delinquency, and there was evidence of growing maturity. At sixteen, he was beginning to have the sense of a positive future, albeit knowing that he might need continuing support to deal with his ongoing vulnerabilities.

IMPLICATIONS FOR PRACTICE

For children who have experienced early attachment disruptions, loss, and trauma, patterns of vulnerability to stress and concerns about abandonment often reoccur at later phases of development. Each new developmental phase is associated with psychosocial tasks, such as the formation of new relationships and increasing demands for autonomous functioning. Often, unexpectedly, these new developmental steps are frightening because earlier developmental steps were associated with overwhelming states of anxiety, fear, anger, and loss.

Those professionals working to support the developmental well-being of these children need to understand that the child's early adaptations to overwhelming experiences of separation, loss, and anxiety may interfere with the child's ability to utilize more developmentally appropriate defenses when confronting age-related experiences of change and separation. Teachers, therapists, physicians, and parents can be helped to think about emergent behavior problems as potentially reflective of the child's relative inability to regulate affect in ways that support developmental well-being. This presents a difficult differential diagnostic question, because symptoms such as cognitive inattention, withdrawal from others, difficulties in the regulation of sleep and eating, inability to control impulses, and difficulties with the delay of gratification overlap with other diagnostic entities such as attention deficit disorder (ADD) and depression.

The assessment and treatment of children who have experienced early attachment disruptions, loss, and trauma require a broad developmental focus. In particular, it is important that the child's attachment history, especially the number and type of losses and disruptions that have occurred, are incorporated into our understanding of the child's needs. For example, if the very young child could not count on the auxiliary ego of the parent, the child may not be able to use support offered by new relational objects (Bollas 1987). A broad assessment of the child would include an understanding of the child's psychological, neurological, medical, and emotional developmental status.

When we see a child who is having great difficulty following an adoption, we must determine whether the child's behavioral adjustment is related to the stress of the transition, or related more to the child's past history of developmental disturbance. Given the fact that adoption itself is a disruption and a loss of previous caregivers, the assessment must distinguish between the child's current response to yet a new environmental and relational change and the child's more chronic and internal vulnerabilities.

The initial tasks in assessment and treatment planning are complex because we must address the crisis phases of treatment to help stabilize the adoptive family while also gathering an understanding of the dynamic issues that may lie ahead in long-term treatment planning. In terms of assessment and treatment, we must consider the clinical implications of the child's past *and* present functioning, and evaluate the degree of risk for his or her future developmental well-being. It is especially important, however, to focus not only on the child's vulnerabilities, but on factors associated with the possibility of the capacity for resiliency as well. If we can identify some internal strengths of the child, we can begin to support their internal capacity for resiliency, which can help shore up a self-esteem that has often been seriously damaged.

Therapeutic work with the child can be very helpful in the process of their recovery and development. The therapist can offer the child an opportunity to engage in a new and more positive object relationship: a real relationship where the child can experience stability, safety, understanding, and attuned attention to realities that come up (Hurry 1998). Therapeutically, the child needs to feel safe in being able to represent feelings from the past and the present. The younger child can express their internal view of themselves and the world through activity, representational play, and the use of the therapeutic milieu and the therapeutic relationship. As the child gets older, however, they may be more able to use language to represent their feelings, but they may also use actions to represent their unresolved conflicts, and the therapist must be able to understand the conflicts underlying the defensive use of acting out. The therapist must also be able to gauge the developmental status of the child in terms of establishing a relationship with the child at the level at which the child can feel a sense of safety in the therapeutic milieu.

Often, adoptive parents in complex adoptions have great anxiety about the short-term adjustment of their child and the long-term developmental outcomes. We as therapists can help them to understand that there are no easy or pat answers when helping repair the internal vulnerability of the child, but that acceptance of the child's needs for responsive care will set a framework that will support development. Often a team approach is needed as children may have specific problems, such as cognitive development delays, or medical problems that have not been attended to. This can place a great burden on parents' time and resources. The parents need to understand that the adjustment of the child to the family will take time and patience, and is often a process of the child going forward or sometimes regressing to the past.

It is important for the therapist to keep in mind that each parent has their own unique feelings about adoption, their own psychological and family history, their own defenses, and their own structural and cultural approach to child rearing (V. Shapiro, J. Shapiro, and Paret 2001; Siskind 1997). Cultivating an empathetic but realistic working alliance is essential in helping the parent endure the lengthy efforts involved.

As therapists, we can be sure that our initial relationship with the parents is an important context for establishing a positive and empathic working alliance. Developing a strong working alliance with the parents is critical because they are facing an emotional journey as they work to form a relationship built on trust with their child, and as they help the child recover from a traumatic pre-adoption history. Within the context of a positive working alliance, parents can begin to express their true worries, their doubts, their hopes, and their sense of loss of the idealized child they may have hoped to have and of the idealized process of attachment they had been expecting to occur. Their view of their child will often reflect some aspect of their own personal history, and the therapist can help them distinguish between their own experience as a child and the very different experiences and characteristics of the child who has come into their life. As with more traditional adoptions, parents in complex adoptions often have to come to terms with the innate nature of their child, and eventually have to be able to accept the unique internal core of the child's sense of self.

CONCLUSION

In this chapter we have emphasized how clinicians can utilize a developmentally informed approach to assist adoptive parents in establishing an empathically attuned understanding of the child who has suffered from early trauma, chaos, and relational disruptions. In particular, a developmental approach can help the parents to recognize difficult early adjustment reactions of the child, to understand that relational progress in development may alternate with periods of regression, and also to understand that patience and support are needed. It is important for the therapist to engage the parents as primary therapeutic partners who develop an expanded sense of the child, and who begin to see the child through a reflective lens. This is essential because the child's internal working model of relationships may represent not current, available attachment partnerships, but a sense of expectancy that reflects the child's past, and especially conditions of intense aloneness and stress.

Reflecting on the story of Micky and Max, for example, we can see that when they were adopted, their aggressive behavior and inability to be soothed were incomprehensible to their grandmother, who had believed she could help them recover. She had not anticipated that the fear and anger they expressed in her care were feelings from their difficult past that were now projected onto her, even though she was trying to build a safer family context.

The process of internal change for such children as these is slow, and is related to their age and ability to understand new realities. They may feel relief at being permanently adopted, but may also feel guilty at having left their family of origin, especially their siblings. In some situations, such as kinship adoption, the child may see the parents or parent who gave them up for adoption, and conflicts of loyalty may develop between their birth mother and their kinship parents (V. Shapiro, J. Shapiro, and Paret 2001). As the child enters adolescence, they may struggle to integrate aspects of both past and present parental objects in their own identity formation (D. Brodzinsky, Smith, and A. Brodzinsky 1998). This may be frightening for the adoptive parents, who may require therapeutic support in order to realize that this does not signify a rejection of them, but a partial identification with their birth parents.

Children of all ages who have been adopted from foster placement often find it difficult to tell their life story to others. This often becomes evident when they are asked in elementary school to write about their birth story or family. Even when these children are adults, an unexpressed, existential feeling of insecurity and loss can remain. They may never fully understand what has happened to them and may continue to feel responsible for having been sent away. They may remember the times when they belonged to no one, and the feelings they had of not being attached to a parental figure.

The following words from a study of adults who had been adopted after years of foster placement reflect the loneliness of fostering and the changes in the adults' emotional lives following adoption (Triseliotis and Hill 1999). The memories of fostering these adults carried were of "temporariness" and "moving on," and they conveyed the adults' feelings of anxiety, uncertainty, and lack of control over their lives. On the other hand, memories of their adoption evoked more positive images for the adults because it gave them a sense of "being part of the family," "not feeling left out," and "having a family for life."

These reflections suggest that adoption following foster placement can create an opportunity for the child to experience a more positive and powerful new relational model, wherein they can experience what had not been available to them. The permanence of adoption and the possibility of empathic care can help these children go forward on the developmental track. Despite initial difficulties in the transition to adoption, they may eventually respond to parents who can understand them as children, who will support their progress and development over time, and who will help them create a stronger sense of self based on the feeling that they can trust their parents to care about them forever. Even if the child remains with some sequelae of the earlier trauma, he or she can begin to internalize a sense of being wanted and worthwhile. The adoptive family can provide an empathic and trustworthy holding environment that can help change the child's internal view of self and help the child develop a capacity for meaningful human relationships.

REFERENCES

Applegate, J., and J. R. Shapiro. 2005. *Neurobiology for Clinical Social Work: Theory and Practice.* New York: W. W. Norton.

Balint, M. 1968. *The Basic Fault.* London: Tavistock.

Benedek, T. 1959. "Parenthood as a Developmental Phase: A Contribution to Libido Theory." *Journal of the American Psychoanalytic Association* 7:389–417.

Bollas, C. 1987. *Shadow of the Object: Psychoanalysis of the Unsought Known.* London: Free Association Books, 13–29.

Bowlby, J. 1953. "Some Pathological Processes Set in Train by Early Mother-Child Separation." *Journal of Mental Science* 99: 265–72.

Bowlby, J. 1973. *Separation Anxiety and Anger*. Vol. 2 of *Attachment and Loss*. New York: Basic Books.

Brinich, P. M. 1990. "Adoption from the Inside Out." In *The Psychology of Adoption*. Ed. D. Brodzinsky and M. Schechter. New York: Oxford University Press.

Brodzinsky, D. M., D. W. Smith, and A. B. Brodzinsky. 1998. *Children's Adjustment to Adoption: Developmental and Clinical Issues*. Thousand Oaks, CA: Sage.

Cassidy, J., and P. Shaver, eds. 1999. *Handbook of Attachment: Theory, Research, and Clinical Implications*. New York: Guilford.

Fonagy, P., and J. Target. 1998. "Mentalization and the Changing Aims of Child Psychoanalysis." *Psychoanalytic Dialogues* 8, no. 1: 87–114.

Fraiberg, S. H. 1980. *Clinical Studies in Infant Mental Health*. London: Tavistock.

———. 1987a. "The Origin of Human Bonds." In *Selected Writings of Selma Fraiberg*. Ed. L. Fraiberg. Columbus: Ohio State University Press, 3–27.

———. 1987b. Pathological Defenses in Infancy, 397–21.

Fraiberg, S. H., E. Adelson, and V. B. Shapiro. 1975. "Ghosts in the Nursery: A Psychoanalytic Approach to the Problem of Impaired Infant-Mother Relationships." *Journal of the American Academy of Child Psychiatry* 14, no. 3: 386–422.

Freud, A. 1965. *Normality and Pathology in Childhood*. New York: International Universities Press.

Freud, A., and D. T. Burlingham. 1944. *Infants without Families: The Case For and Against Residential Nurseries*. New York: International Universities Press.

Gizynski, M., and V. Shapiro. 1989. "Ghosts in the Nursery Revisited." *Child and Adolescent Social Work Journal* 6, no. 1: 18–37.

Greenspan, S., and N. T. Greenspan. 1991. *The Clinical Interview of the Child*. 2nd ed. Washington, D.C.: American Psychiatric Press.

Hurry, A., ed. 1998. *Psychoanalysis and Development Therapy*. London: Karmac Books.

Lamb, M. E., ed. 1999. *Parenting in Child Development in Non-traditional Families*. Mahwah, NJ: Erlbaum.

Main, M. 1999. "Attachment Theory: Eighteen Points with Suggestions for Future Studies. In *Handbook of Attachment*. Ed. J. Cassidy and P. R. Shaver. New York: Guilford.

Minkler, M., and K. M. Roe. 1993. *Grandmothers as Caregivers: Raising Children of the Crack Cocaine Epidemic*. Newbury Park, CA: Sage.

Paret, I., and V. Shapiro. 1998. "The Splintered Holding Environment and the Vulnerable Ego: A Case Study." *Psychoanalytic Study of the Child* 53:300–324.

Perry, B. D., R. A. Pollard, T. L. Blakely, W. L. Baker, and D. Vigilante. 1995. "Childhood Trauma: The Neurobiology of Adaptation, and Use-Dependent Development of the Brain: How States Become Traits." *Infant Mental Health Journal* 16, no. 4: 271–89.

Schore, A. 1994. *Affect Regulation and the Origin of the Self: The Neurobiology of Emotional Development*. Hillsdale, NJ: Erlbaum.

Shapiro, V. B., J. R. Shapiro, and I. H. Paret. 2001. *Complex Adoption and Assisted Reproductive Technology: A Developmental Approach to Clinical Practice*. New York: Guilford.

Siegel, D. J. 1999. *The Developing Mind: Toward a Neurobiology of Interpersonal Experience*. New York: Guilford.

Siskind, D. 1997. *Working with Parents: Establishing the Essential Alliance in Child Psychotherapy and Consultation*. Northvale, NJ: Jason Aronson.

Spitz, R. A., and K. Wolf. 1946. "Anaclitic Depression: An Inquiry into the Genesis of Psychiatric Conditions in Early Childhood: II." *Psychoanalytic Study of the Child* 2:313–42.

Stern, D. N. 1985. *The Interpersonal World of the Infant: A View from Psychoanalysis and Developmental Psychology*. New York: Basic Books.

Triseliotis, J., and M. Hill. 1990. "Contrasting Adoption, Foster Care, and Residential Rearing." In *The Psychology of Adoption Rearing*. Ed. D. Brodzinsky and M. Schechter. New York: Oxford University Press, 107–21.

Winnicott, D. W. 1965a. "The Theory of the Parent-Infant Relationship." In *The Maturational Processes and the Facilitating Environment: Studies in the Theory of Emotional Development*. Madison, CT: International Universities Press, 37–56.

———. 1965b. "Ego Distortion in Terms of True and False Self." In *The Maturational Processes and the Facilitating Environment: Studies in the Theory of Emotional Development*. Madison, CT: International Universities Press, 140–52.

Chapter Eight

Secrecy in the Psychotherapy of a Severely Traumatized Adopted Child

Jerrold R. Brandell

The experience of adoption in childhood, even when embarked upon in a thoughtful and well-planned manner and handled with the utmost sensitivity, must always embody dynamic meanings that differentiate it from the more usual course of human development. This is not to say that adopted children must on that account suffer from a disproportionately high incidence of emotional and behavioral problems, although that claim has often been advanced (Kernberg 1986; Brodzinsky 1987). Some clinicians believe that a pattern of externalizing psychopathology—involving disorders of conduct, acting out, antisocial behavior, or antisocial personality—is characteristic of adopted children who present with psychological problems (Kernberg 1986; Offord, Aponte, and Cross 1969; Taichert and Harvin 1975). Other authors believe that early developmental traumata are likely to coalesce into disorders of attachment and, particularly among older-placed children, may explain the rather vast range of emotional and behavioral difficulties presented by this population (Howe and Fearnley 2003). Still others believe there is little evidence to suggest the emotional and behavioral difficulties of adopted children take a particular clinical form or are clearly associated with a specific clinical diagnosis (Brinich 1980). Nevertheless, when such children and adolescents are referred for psychological help, the theme of adoption seems to figure prominently, often playing a rather significant role in the etiology of their problems (e.g., Barnes 1953; Berger and Hodges 1982; Brinich 1980; Davidson 1985; Hodges et al. 1985; Kernberg 1986; Sherick 1983; Wieder 1978). Undoubtedly, the picture has been further complicated by the differing mandates of social agencies arranging the adoption (i.e., whether the process is "open" or "traditional") and the often-conflicting advice that adoptive parents have received as to when and how (or whether) children should be provided with information about their adoption. Historically, many psychoanalytic clinicians have raised cautions against revealing the fact of adoption to children before they have negotiated the developmental hurdles of early and mid-childhood, and are more or less well ensconced in early latency. The developmental wisdom underlying this admonition is that knowledge of adoption is likely to cause a psychological injury, one for which younger children are inadequately prepared, by virtue of not having developed the inner emotional and cognitive resources that become available to children as they enter the latency period.

Berger (1979) has suggested that all adopted children struggle with two fundamental questions they ruminatively pose to themselves as well as to the adoptive parents and to others: "Who were my parents" and "Why did they give me up?" In the pages that follow, an unusual case involving an adolescent child whose adoption was complicated by a closely guarded family secret is examined in detail. In this instance, as the clinical material will underscore, *two additional questions* must be added to this list. Equally as fundamental, they are "What secret is being kept from me?" and "Who or what am I?"

CLINICAL ILLUSTRATION: THE CASE OF BRUCE

At the time of referral, Bruce, aged fourteen, resided with his adoptive parents and an eleven-year-old biological sibling, Valerie. His adoptive parents were especially concerned about Bruce's apparent disregard for authority and a pattern of increasingly serious antisocial behavior. For some time, household items had seemed to disappear without explanation, but now, one of Bruce's teachers had reported her suspicion that he had stolen twenty dollars from her purse. Confrontations yielded little aside from massive denial, pathological lies, and externalizations. It was always someone else's fault, the teacher or Bruce's parents were simply in error, he was being treated unfairly, and so forth. However, there were other problems as well.

As early as the first grade, Bruce had been referred for a psychoeducational assessment when his teacher and other school personnel expressed concern about his difficulty in acquiring basic language skills, compounded by impulsive classroom behaviors that had often proved disruptive. Testing at that time revealed weaknesses in language-mediated tasks, although the examiner believed Bruce's problems to be the result of a "disadvantaged and tumultuous" infancy and early childhood rather than lack of ability. In large measure owing to this pattern of distractibility, impulsivity, and disorganized behavior both at school and at home, Bruce's family physician acceded to parental requests for a trial of Ritalin. The results, however, were mixed, and Bruce's problems persisted. With the increasing intellectual and organizational challenges of middle school, Bruce's academic performance suffered, and in the first term, he brought home failing grades in several subjects. Teachers noted that his behavior at school seemed to fluctuate dramatically from one day to the next, although bad days now seemed to outnumber good ones. Rarely was he able to complete work at school; he became increasingly restless, uncooperative, and at times defiant. Retesting revealed a specific learning disability, with auditory memory problems, poor sound/symbol associations, attentional deficits, difficulty in task completion, impaired reading and writing skills, and compromised understanding of cause-effect relationships. The second examiner also observed that Bruce's self-esteem seemed almost mercurial, and hypothesized that it was as much a consequence of repeated academic failures as it was of socioemotional problems. Special classroom placement was recommended.

PERTINENT HISTORY

Although little was known of Bruce's early history, he reportedly suffered severe neglect and physical abuse in early childhood. When he was approximately two and one-half, Bruce's birth mother, overwhelmed with his care and pregnant with her second child, had him placed in a foster home. He may actually have been in as many as three different homes during the next eighteen months, although his final placement was with a family that belonged to a very strict fundamentalist Christian sect. In this home, he was often severely punished for any perceived misbehavior, and on at least several occasions, locked in a closet. In keeping with the sect's child-rearing philosophy, he was essentially treated as property; he was instructed not to speak unless spoken to, and his psychological as well as material needs were often neglected or withheld as punishment. Some months after Bruce was placed in this foster-care home, his birth mother, Rebecca, also relinquished custody of Bruce's younger sister to county social services. Valerie, barely a year old at this time, was subsequently placed in foster care with her older brother. It is perhaps noteworthy that Bruce became very protective of Valerie from this time onward, although he was not able to shield her from the sadistic-like punishments of their foster parents. Rebecca gradually became aware of this situation, however, and it caused her great anguish. Although she had by now given up any fantasy of having her children returned to her, neither did she wish them to become casualties of the foster-care system.

This is where Bruce's story becomes far more interesting. As it happens, Rebecca had an older stepbrother, Ron, who had been married for just over a year. She knew that medical complications arising from a previous surgery had rendered Teri, Ron's wife, infertile; and furthermore, she knew that the young couple had begun to consider the possibility of adoption. She contacted them to ask them whether they would consider adopting both her children. After lengthy discussions, Ron and Teri agreed, although by mutual consent, they and Rebecca decided that her real relationship to the children would remain a secret. Concerns were raised regarding the children's birth father, and Rebecca explained that Bruce and Valerie were actually half-siblings; furthermore, neither birth father had maintained an ongoing relationship with Rebecca, nor did their names even appear on the birth certificates. Adoption papers were signed. Bruce, now four, and Valerie, just one and one-half, arrived shortly thereafter at their new home.

Although Bruce's adoptive parents kept their promise to Rebecca, the fact that both children had been adopted was openly discussed with the children early on. Ron and Teri observed that both children accepted the story of their adoption rather well, though Bruce's development, owing to the emotional sequelae of the severe abuse he had suffered, had never been as smooth as Valerie's. I recall wondering whether this family's secret was as well kept as Ron and Teri believed it to be. After all, everyone else in the extended family knew the true story, and there were of course periodic visits with the birth mother (whom the children knew as their Aunt Rebecca). And, even assuming that Bruce and Valerie really had no idea, were their needs or those of the adoptive parents well served by this rather awkward pretense? Nevertheless, since no real parental alliance existed at this early juncture in treatment, I decided to wait until I felt our relationship to be on surer footing before bringing the matter up with Ron and Teri.

BRUCE'S TREATMENT BEGINS

Bruce was a tall, rather ungainly adolescent who entered my office in a sort of rush, almost as though he had arrived late for his appointment (he hadn't). I'm not certain how comfortable he felt talking with me in that first hour, though he did convey a good deal of information about himself and his troubles. He described having a "fairly close" relationship with his father, essentially because "we're both men." He usually got along with Valerie, though with the usual sibling disagreements. His relationship with his mother was somewhat like that with his sister, "because ladies can't understand stuff that men and boys are into." He confessed to having very few early memories, but did recall once lying in bed with his sister when both were very small, and a rooster came to the window and crowed, "Cock-a-doodle-do." I then introduced the topic of dreams. Bruce at first claimed not to have dreams, but then remembered a dream fragment from one or two nights before our meeting, in which he dreamed of "fighting a dragon and then slaying it." This was offered without associations. His three wishes were to (1) be able to draw anything, (2) own a Lamborghini sports car, and (3) have fabulous wealth so that he could purchase anything he wished for his mother, father, and sister. Bruce enjoyed sports, but didn't play on any teams. He had been studying karate for a couple of years, and took lessons twice weekly. He took pleasure in drawing freehand, and had a special affinity for the Hardy Boys mysteries, which his adoptive father had originally introduced to him.

I noted that Bruce seemed slightly anxious, and that his speech was a bit choppy. He was, however, relatively easy to engage, and agreeable. I was struck by his immaturity, relative not only to his interests and sensibilities, but also to the manner in which he presented himself. With many adolescents of Bruce's age, psychotherapy more closely resembles the sort of work one does with adult patients; indeed, with such patients, games, drawing, storytelling, and so forth would simply be out of the question. I quickly learned, however, that Bruce was far more comfortable when he could participate in such activities. Toward the end of the first hour, I asked Bruce if he could tell me a made up (i.e., an autogenic, or stimulus-independent) story, a technique that I and several generations of child therapists have used to advantage with countless young patients. In the early 1960s, child developmentalists Evelyn Pitcher and Ernst Prelinger (1963) described children's autogenic stories as the product of an interplay of forces bearing striking phenomenological similarity to the structure of dreams—and, in essence, furnishing the clinician with a "dream on demand":

> These forces consist on the one hand of unconscious wishes striving for expression and fulfillment, and on the other of forces aiming to disguise these wishes and to produce a story that is reasonably conforming to the standards of realism and social acceptability. Each story thus represents a compromise solution to a conflict. (216–17)

The essential idea is that the story doesn't consciously borrow from lived experience, television, movies, or other sources; that it contains some structure (a beginning, a middle, an end, and perhaps, a moral); and that the characters are not named or consciously modeled after real individuals.[1] Bruce told the following story:

The Snake That Came Out of the Hole

The snake started coming out of his hole when he saw a rabbit. Then he went back in and then he thought he could have some juicy meat if he killed the

---

1. This technique is elaborated in detail by Jerrold Brandell (2004, 257–91).

rabbit. He went out and killed the rabbit and went back in and fed it to his family. The end.

Moral: Snakes can kill people.

While such a story may be usefully approached from multiple vantage points, I was particularly impressed by several elements. One was the use of aggression and stealth in the service of procuring oral supplies. Assuming that the snake represents Bruce, here is a slippery, untrustworthy reptile that pounces heartlessly on a defenseless rabbit. Interestingly, however, the snake appears to have a sense of duty to family, certainly out of keeping with what herpetologists have led us to believe about these creatures. Little if any affect is conveyed here, and the moral is curiously dysynchronous with the story's content. (After all, weren't we talking about snakes and rabbits?) Another thought that I had was in connection with the snake's emerging (and reemerging) from the hole. Might this in some way represent birth and rebirth? Perhaps the "snake" perceived that its family—in this case, the birth mother—desperately required their *own* oral supplies. Thus, the snake/baby emerges from the womb in order to bring back the necessary sustenance for a mother (and later, a baby sister) too ill to gather this for herself. Along somewhat more classical lines, the snake emerging from the hole adds further dimension to Bruce's earlier comments regarding the common interests of boys and men—who have penises—and those of girls and women, who do not. And then too, this snake comes out of the hole *twice*, which I believe might signify Bruce's two families: birth and adoptive. Finally, we might also consider the distinct possibility that the *rabbit* serves as Bruce's personal representative in the story. Bruce, like the rabbit in the story, was treated as a piece of "juicy meat" by the foster-care system, and cruelly mistreated by his last foster family. It is also possible that Bruce has represented parts of himself in *both* characters, inasmuch as identification with an aggressor constitutes one well-established means of defending against the experience of victimization.

One or two sessions later, Bruce began what was to be an epic adventure story dictated to me in installments. The story involved two explorers from a dying village no longer able to provide water or food to its inhabitants. The two explorers are charged with the task of locating a new land where game is plentiful and fresh water is in abundant supply. Not long after beginning their journey through the wilderness, the explorers encounter a seemingly impenetrable wall. After many hours, they finally discover a way in: a tiny door that is barely big enough for them to fit through. Inside the great wall is a sizable village with nearly one hundred buildings. There is evidence of a very recent carnage, one so complete that it has claimed the lives of every single inhabitant of the village, all of whom have been either "stabbed or sliced with swords." The two explorers reason, "If we cleaned everything up around here and got rid of all the bodies, this would become a neat place to live." One and one-half days are spent on the cleanup, after which time the explorers make the journey back to their own village. When they arrive, lack of food and water has claimed the lives of many of their fellow townspeople; only one hundred villagers are left alive, thirty of whom die even before the villagers can make preparations to leave. In the next few installments of this story, the villagers are led to their new land by the explorers, encountering dragons, tribal warriors, and other mortal threats on the way—each of which is overcome. Once the villagers arrive at their final destination, quarrels erupt over which villagers are entitled to live in the houses, although this problem is peaceably resolved. With wild animals and unfriendly tribes on every side, the villagers realize they must protect themselves, and a great amount of collective energy is expended in constructing yet another massive wall to protect the villagers from the dangers that lie beyond the village. The men, the storyteller advises, are permitted to explore and to hunt for buffalo, deer, birds, and other game, and the women are not. Instead, the women must busy themselves with household chores.

DISCUSSION

This adventure story, which Bruce narrated excitedly, represents an elaboration of themes introduced in the far less detailed snake story. The principal theme appears to be that of the unavailability of oral supplies, a problem that is so severe that it threatens the very survival of an entire village. Two explorers are hastily dispatched to locate a new land—which may symbolize Bruce's new family—where food and water are in abundant supply. Although the explorers are successful in their quest, many dangers remain, both outside as well as within the great wall that surrounds the village. In fact, although the explorers find the great wall nearly impenetrable, this barrier had evidently offered little protection against the demonic forces that earlier overran and destroyed the entire village. If the great wall is understood to symbolize the very first "great wall"—that of the mother's body—it helps us make sense of the fact that there is only one way in or out, and it involves a struggle through a very small opening. Just as the snake in the first story has returned to its hole (i.e., the womb) with fresh kill, the explorers may be seen as retreating to a primal locus of security and satiety, what some writers have referred to as the "ur-mother." However, behind the great wall, there is no real safety, to which the scene of carnage readily attests. Furthermore, though there is water behind the wall and game is plentiful, one can never rely on others there for physical (or emotional) sustenance.

In his portrayal of these threats, Bruce revealed a great deal regarding his intrapsychic life. There is rather palpable evidence of his rage, which in the story is defended against via a combination of projection and symbolization. However, the original targets were undoubtedly the birth mother who abandoned and rejected him, and the foster-care system that treated him so inhumanely. Indeed, death, often violent, is everywhere, though it evokes neither sadness nor any other recognizable affects. Little is said of the carnage that has occurred just prior to the explorers' arrival; bloody and dismembered bodies barely recognizable as human are treated as a sort of detritus, and are simply a part of the cleanup operation to prepare the village for its new residents. In a sense, the attitude of the two explorers suggests Bruce's belated identification with his caregivers, as well as the original traumata, that is, the massive neglect and profound abuse Bruce had experienced following his placement in the foster-care system. Certainly, as they were recounted to me, these experiences were dehumanizing ones.

Bruce's explorers, for that matter, may also bear a certain resemblance to the adults in whose care he spent his first four years. These were individuals who, whether by reason of social immaturity, profound environmental stress, psychological deficits, or character pathology, were either incapable or simply uninterested in making an enduring emotional investment in Bruce. The explorers are focused exclusively on the goal of physical survival, although their actions portray what amounts to a parody of orientation to task. Not only are inner experiences involving grief, sadness, and love not recognized; practically speaking, they do not exist.

Finally, and somewhat more hopefully, it is possible that Bruce was also representing a nascent therapeutic alliance by creating *two* explorers, rather than a single one. Richard Gardner, a child psychiatrist who was very interested in children's story metaphors (e.g., Gardner 1973, 1993), understood such story elements as the child's way of symbolizing the process of treatment, and more particularly, the relationship with the therapist. Therapy is undoubtedly about the process of intrapsychic exploration, and such terrain is not easily negotiated. It is filled with hurdles to surmount, traumatic events to be remembered and worked through, painful losses that must be mourned, and frightening affects that must be fully unearthed and finally understood.

Over the next few months, Bruce seemed to become more comfortable with the process of treatment, and a therapeutic alliance began to develop between us. He had never learned how to play chess, and asked if I would teach him this game. I was at first reluctant, since experience has taught me that the therapeutic yield of certain board games, such as chess and Monopoly, is disproportionately low relative to how much time is typically expended on them, and further, such activities are often used in the service of resistance. However, this isn't invariably true. In Bruce's case, I considered his request to signify a deepening interest in his treatment, as well as an important indication as to the direction of his transference attachment, which seemed to contain both *partnering* and *mirroring* aspects (Kohut 1971, 1977). I believed that such an activity might furnish Bruce with a unique structure through which such transference wishes and fantasies might take root. I also saw chess as an opportunity to help Bruce anticipate the consequences of his actions and develop a somewhat greater capacity for tolerating disappointments and frustration, as well as a greater capacity for the containment of disruptive affects. Put in somewhat more general language, I hoped that learning and playing chess might offer Bruce a bridge from his internal experience, one dominated by primary process, to the developmentally more sophisticated world of secondary process experience.

It wasn't easy to teach Bruce chess, though he seemed determined to learn this game, which we played for a portion of every hour over the course of many weeks. At times, he would become extremely frustrated. Indeed, once, after I had captured several of his pieces in successive moves, he picked up the chess board and threw it across the room, scattering the pieces in the process. I must have appeared surprised, for he quickly apologized, picked up the pieces, and contritely asked whether we might begin a new game, a request to which I acceded. Gradually, Bruce developed a few good opening moves, and began to play more skillfully. He often correctly surmised my next move, and began to anticipate more complicated scenarios involving multiple moves. He also became harder to beat, and took great pleasure in posting a win against me (which, I might add, was earned). Aside from the sense of mastery that acquisition of these skills afforded Bruce, our game playing also gave him a chance to reflect on the difficulties he experienced in making and keeping friends, and on his feelings of social isolation from peers at school.

At the same time, the dehumanization theme seemed to grow in prominence. Gradually, as we returned to the storytelling Bruce had enjoyed earlier in the treatment, he composed a number of story-narratives in which the principal character was either a ghost or a person whose efforts to struggle with basic questions of self-identity were complicated by a sense of inner depletion and self-alienation. During one session, Bruce quickly turned a squiggle drawing of mine into a ghost with a head but no arms or legs. He spent a great deal of time drawing in the face, however, which bore a sinister, almost sadistic expression. As he finished the drawing, he added dark tears underneath one of the ghost's eyes, and then told the following story:

The Ghost with a Conscience

Once there was a ghost who lived in a huge mansion. He was always scaring people, and people said they weren't going to come around again. He went back to his family, and talked to his dad, and his dad asked him why he always scared people. He said, "Aren't ghosts supposed to scare people?" His dad said, "Ghosts aren't always supposed to scare people; they're supposed to be nice sometimes." He told his dad that he'd try to be nice to people. He went out, and saw a boy who was mad. He went up to the boy and asked, "Why are you mad?" The boy jumped up because he thought he was dreaming. The boy ran. The ghost called out, "I'm your friend." [The boy stopped and] the ghost sat down with him and asked him why he was mad. The boy said, "I always scared little kids and now they won't come near me." The ghost said, "You don't always have to be mean. . . . You can be nice sometimes." The boy and the ghost talked for a long time. The boy promised to try it and then to come back in a few weeks. He came back in a few weeks, and told the ghost, "What you told me works. I even have two girlfriends." The ghost said, "I tried it, too, and now people like me." They went out for lunch. Another boy comes up to the first boy and scares him. The first boy says, "You don't always have to scare people." The second boy says, "Thanks for the advice." Then he goes home and lives happily ever after. The end.

Although the solutions proposed in Bruce's story are magical ones that proceed from a faulty premise (i.e., that by behaving nicely to others, painful self-states and deeply entrenched conflicts may be permanently dispelled), the parallel with his experience of treatment is a relatively transparent one. Indeed, the ghost seems strongly identified with a quasi-therapeutic role, to the point of assisting another who presumably also struggles with containment and modulation of negative affects. Interestingly, the father, who appears to have a human form, seems relatively unconcerned with the fact that his son is a ghost. The father's suggestions, therefore, are not intended to help the ghost-son achieve a human form. Rather, employing a sort of absurd logic, they are designed to help him adapt to a world in which he will function more or less permanently as a shadow. We never learn the basis of the ghost's rage or why he experiences such great sadness or, for that matter, what the storyteller really has in mind in his titling of the story. What are the contents of this ghostly "conscience"?

Storytelling had long since become a reciprocal activity in Bruce's therapy, and I responded with the following therapeutic rendering of Bruce's version:

The Boy Who Felt Like a Ghost

Once there was a boy who lived in a large house. He was quite lonely and also deeply angry at his family because they didn't understand his loneliness, nor were they able to help him very much. Other children didn't like to play with him because he would try to scare them, or treat them badly. He talked to his dad, who said that he should try being nice. Although this sounded like good advice, the boy *still* felt like a ghost, plus he didn't feel like acting nice. He met some other kids who also felt lonely and had problems dealing with their anger. Sometimes, they played, although these friendships weren't that important to the boy. Finally, the boy decided to go to an exorcist—a person who casts out evil spirits. The exorcist tried a magic formula. It didn't work. He tried it a second time, slowly and clearly chanting the magic words. It still didn't work, and so the exorcist tried the formula one last time. When it didn't work for the third time, the exorcist told the boy that he wasn't able to help him. He said, "Your problem has to do with old, deep-seated feelings—not evil spirits. First you have to understand what these are, and only then will you be able to get rid of them."

Moral:

1. You can feel like a ghost if you are lonely and unhappy inside.
2. Usually problems like this start when you are little but they don't go away and sometimes get to be even bigger problems when you get older.
3. It's hard to act one way when you feel another way.
4. There is no magic when it comes to such problems, and they can only be solved over time and with hard work.

DISCUSSION

Bruce had not yet grasped an essential truth about the relationship between the traumata of his early childhood and his continuing difficulties, namely, that the "past persists into the present." In fairness, it must be said that he was hardly alone in this, since a good many adolescents and an impressive number of adult patients regularly reveal a similar difficulty. However, this lack of awareness cannot be satisfactorily explained as simply being due to psychological naïveté, nor in Bruce's case can it be attributed solely to faulty cognition. To be sure, Bruce's difficulties in learning were very real, and they contributed heavily to his social and emotional problems. However, there was a reservoir of psychic pain that I believe had much less to do with these disabilities and far more to do with traumatic infantile experiences, largely unresolved, that had been further compounded by the messages he continued to receive in his adoptive family. Act nice, the father in the ghost story admonishes his son, because even though you are a ghost, you aren't always supposed to be scary. Undoubtedly there was some distortion in the representation of the father here, though Bruce's father, much like the character in this story, appeared to rely on such defensive strategies as denial, concealment, and reaction-formation in his approach to Bruce and Bruce's problems. Not too surprisingly, however, these solutions hadn't worked very well, a fact of which both Bruce and his parents were painfully aware. With this knowledge in mind, I instead spoke to the inadequacy of such strategies; furthermore, by introducing an exorcist who fails in his attempts to remove the bad parts of this boy-ghost, I tried to dispel the infantile belief that intrapsychic change occurs effortlessly and spontaneously.

The ghost in Bruce's squiggle-completion drawing seemed to be express-ing affects that were frightening in both kind and intensity, and this theme re-asserted itself in other material, principally stories and drawings, that Bruce produced during this phase of his therapy. One example, which is reasonably representative, is reproduced in figure 8.1.

Figure 8.1.   The Tidal Wave
Source Drawing by Jerrold R. Bradell, re-creation of Bruce's drawing.

Bruce not only feared the breaking-through of his own affects, feelings that had been walled off for so long that they seemed unmanageable, but he also feared the counterreaction of his parents, whose own limits in tolerating Bruce's outbursts had been stretched beyond capacity. Both he *and* they were helpless, and though Bruce was not able to articulate this abject dread in a more direct form of verbal discourse, his drawings and stories revealed just how terrifying his inner experience was.

In my meeting with Bruce's parents at around this time, they reported a "mixed picture" of progress, which for them hinged almost exclusively on the degree to which Bruce was able to conform to his school's mandate for "pro-social behavior" and to accommodate at home to parental rules and proscriptions. I agreed with them that Bruce's rather clumsy efforts to purloin money or various objects from their bedroom shouldn't be overlooked, but also emphasized what I regarded as the symbolic meaning of these acts. I told them that Bruce was attempting to assuage a profound inner emptiness, and that he continued to believe that necessary psychic supplies could only be extracted via deception. It might be easier, I offered, to view this behavior as stemming partly from Bruce's desire to feel close to them. In effect, he was much more willing to risk being caught and punished than to take a chance that a request might not be honored, or a need refused. Further, because Bruce continued to view himself as inherently bad, the inevitable punishments may have afforded him a certain relief.

Interestingly, the very thing his parents complained most about—that he had no respect for the integrity of their personal space—they ignored completely when it came to Bruce's bedroom. Under the pretext of keeping his room clean, searching for lost items, and so forth, they regularly entered his room, alternately dismissing his protests offhandedly or responding to them with righteous indignation. Although Bruce's father didn't elaborate, he had once entered Bruce's bedroom without knocking and discovered his son lying nude on the bed. Both father and son were embarrassed by this, and it wasn't mentioned again. I pointed out that it was probably important for Bruce and his parents to respect each other's privacy, an idea that Ron and Teri initially resisted but later seemed more willing to consider. For his part, Bruce was almost gleeful when, in our regular individual session several days later, I informed him of the recommendation I had made to his parents.

I had also begun to advise Ron and Teri about the importance of telling Bruce the true story of his adoption. They were deeply ambivalent about this. Wouldn't this further complicate their relationship with Bruce and add to his negative feelings about them? Could such knowledge exacerbate his behavioral problems at school? What about his birth mother? As I noted earlier, Rebecca (the birth mother), Ron, and Teri had all agreed many years before to conceal the actual circumstances of the adoption—and Ron and Teri now felt concerned that Rebecca would be both hurt and angry at them for going back on this promise. I pointed out to Ron and Teri that there was rather compelling evidence that Bruce knew more about the adoption than he had revealed to his parents, though some of this knowledge was not fully conscious and was what might be termed an "unthought known" (Bollas 1987).

Indeed, Bruce knew just enough to feel both confusion and mistrust. Although he felt one thing in his gut, there had been no way to affirm these unsettling feelings, inasmuch as his parents and other family members had colluded to suppress and deny the truth of his adoption. I explained to Ron and Teri that at this juncture, I was not questioning their original rationale in making the decision so much as I was attempting to help them understand how continued denial and secrecy no longer served anyone's needs very well. Success in their son's struggle to consolidate his own self-identity could never be achieved, I submitted, unless Bruce knew *all* the parts of his story. I also believed that Valerie, now eleven, should be furnished with the same information, though the parents might wish, at least initially, to present this to their daughter separately. Of course, I reassured them that I would be as involved in supporting them through this process as they and Bruce wished me to be. However, Ron and Teri remained somewhat skeptical about the relationship between their suppression of the adoption story and Bruce's problems, and further, questioned the wisdom of making this revelation now, after so many years, to either of their two children. We revisited this topic several times in the remaining months of Bruce's treatment, though his parents remained unconvinced.

Despite Bruce's continuing interpersonal problems at school during this period, his teachers noted that he seemed to make a greater effort to control himself. His academic performance also improved slightly, despite the lack of alternatives for children with learning disabilities in Bruce's school, a small middle school located in a semirural community. One story Bruce told during this phase of his treatment involved a class clown who makes a conscious decision to become "smart and serious" after another youngster trips him in retaliation for a past slight. This decision is made spontaneously and without elaboration in the story, and it comes as a surprise not only to the student's classmates and teacher, but also and perhaps more notably, to his mother. Overnight, the reformed clown acquires a most serious demeanor, and soon makes the school's honor roll. Not yet recovered from her shock, his mother lavishes praise on him, and honors his every wish. When, at the story's conclusion, she wonders aloud what has motivated her son's dramatic transformation, he states simply, "I did it for you."

In this story, in contradistinction to earlier ones in which oral needs seem to predominate, the most fundamental desire is for recognition and affirmation of those skills, talents, or unique personality features that make Bruce who he is. A secondary theme hints at the special nature of the relationship between Bruce and his adoptive mother. The story suggests that one way of procuring such needed selfobject supplies, though not particularly adaptive, is by being a class clown. This was a pathway Bruce had often traversed, although one that had been less traveled in the recent past. This may have largely been on account of the negative sanctions such behavior brought, though I believe Bruce may also have recognized that such attention, while exciting, was fleeting, and merely a momentary distraction for his classmates. The story's conclusion suggests that a superior academic performance may also elicit such affirming responses from one's selfobjects, one's mother in particular. However, several important story elements are left out. For example, what inspires this remarkable decision? What did the protagonist gain from being a class clown in the first place? How is this decision actually implemented? And, what evidence is there of a struggle—are there no temptations to return to the old way of handling selfobject needs?

To be certain, there is a degree of therapeutic (and developmental) progress in this narrative, both because the protagonist is able to recognize an affect (dysphoria) and locate it within himself, and because there is an effort to take adaptive action. However, because important elements are not developed, the solution comes far too easily to the story's principal character, and closely parallels the magical resolutions operative in stories Bruce told at an earlier point in his therapy. One might argue, in fact, that such stories are best understood as products of resistance, a position that Gardner held (1973). It may well be that Bruce's story is a narrative of resistance, although it also incorporates new material—the significance of his adoptive mother as a source of selfobject supplies—that was far less central earlier in his treatment.

Shortly after telling me the class-clown story, Bruce arrived for a session looking far more tentative than usual. He had little to say about the week's events and after several rounds of squiggles, drew a picture of a bird (see figure 8.2) and then told me the following story:

The Bird That Never Laughed

Once there was a bird that never smiled or laughed. He was always sad, ornery, mad-looking. Once a guy (another bird) made a joke, and all the other birds thought it was funny, but this bird didn't even smile. The other birds asked why he wasn't laughing—didn't he think it was funny? So, they went to his mom and asked why her son never laughs. She said she didn't know, and she'd ask when he came home. So, he came home, and she asked. He said, because none of the jokes are good. She asked why all the other birds were laughing at the jokes. He said, because they thought it was funny. "It's like the joke you told last night—everyone but me found it funny." Anyway, the bird went [back] to school. The other birds were telling different jokes, and there was one that he

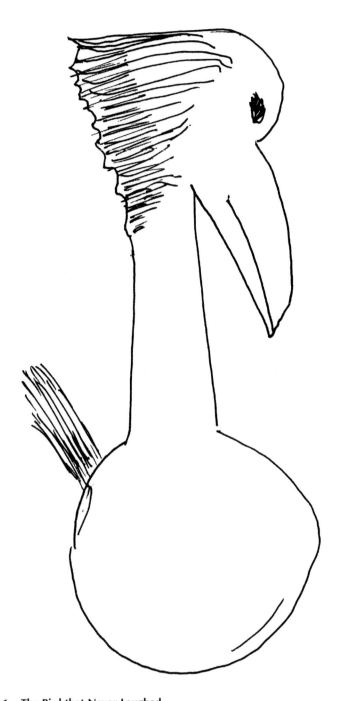

Figure 8.1   The Bird that Never Laughed

Source Drawing by Jerrold R. Brandell, re-creation of Bruce's drawing.

found amusing, so he laughed. He came home to his mom and told her that he'd laughed at a joke. She said, "Now you should laugh at jokes *other* people find funny, not just the ones you like." They lived happily ever after.

Moral: You don't have to laugh at the jokes you find funny, but you *should* laugh at the ones you *don't* think are funny.

DISCUSSION

This story proved to be one of the last Bruce told before the rather abrupt conclusion of his treatment. Its significance is severalfold. In the first place, never before had Bruce offered such compelling evidence that he not only recognized the powerful affects and conflict-laden wishes that drove much of his behavior but also that he could begin to acknowledge them as his own psychic property. His sense of inner depletion, which gave rise to feelings of orneriness, sadness, and anger, also appeared linked to the disavowal of important self-knowledge. I believe that it is in this story that Bruce actually lays out the impossible dilemma that perceived untruths about his adoption had created for him. When the principal character in the story confesses to feeling one way about the jokes, he is admonished to behave as if he felt a different way—as though this were a reasonable position. This position is, of course, nearly identical to that taken by the ghost's father in the story described earlier. There is further development of the centrality of the character's mother as an important source of selfobject supplies. In this particular instance, the principal character seems far more concerned with pleasing his mother and holding on to this relationship than he is with being true to his own feelings, however powerful these may be. Finally, the story offers an adaptation that, while in the service of maintaining self-object ties, is hardly likely to be enduring.

In this story, we also recognize an important basis for an earlier dynamic theme—that of dehumanization. For Bruce, in making a desperate effort to remain connected to the only reliable source of selfobject supplies—his adoptive mother—must relinquish a great deal of his selfhood. He must be consigned to a psychic existence in which his deepest feelings and fears are minimized, negated, and disbelieved, and in which abiding beliefs about his physical origins are suppressed. The combined effect of such messages on Bruce's sense of self and on his affective development, among other things, was pernicious.

The twin themes of loss of vital supplies and dehumanization continued to dominate the final two hours of Bruce's therapy. He told one story involving a climber who runs out of oxygen and is revived by a rescue crew that arrives just in the nick of time via helicopter. In another, he is a "punky" (i.e., petulant and rebellious) seahorse whose mother gradually gains weight and begins to act "strange" and withdrawn. It turns out that she is pregnant, although she had not intended to reveal this "secret" to her son. The seahorse-son drags the mother to a doctor in order to force his mother to reveal the truth to him. And, although mother and son "live happily ever after," there is little elaboration of the story's resolution, which is, at best, unsatisfying. In Bruce's final hour, he told a story about a ghost who wants to be a major-league ballplayer. Although the ghost is permitted to play, no one can figure out who he is. The moral of this story was "If no one recognizes you, then don't do something to make [them] recognize you. Just be your 'normal' self."

It is of considerable interest that the occasional presence of Bruce's birth mother seemed far more palpable in the final hours of treatment. I now believe that this material was very near the surface, as Bruce ever more closely approximated the true story of his adoption, the secret that had so complicated his development. Perhaps the doctor to whom the seahorse (Bruce) drags its mother in the story was in reality a representation of me—his therapist. For it is true that, in an important sense, I had been less than successful in helping Bruce in this important quest for personal knowledge, a theme that was also more generally related to my countertransference reactions throughout the life of this case.

COUNTERTRANSFERENCE
THEMES IN BRUCE'S TREATMENT

Though hardly less important than in the psychotherapy of adult patients, the child and adolescent clinician's countertransference has only recently begun to receive the attention it deserves (Brandell 1992). In Bruce's case, my countertransference was complex, and represented at least three distinct though intersecting themes. In the first place, Bruce's burgeoning interest in therapy was also a source of pleasure for me, and may have contributed to an unconsciously held belief that I could furnish him with emotional supplies that neither his birth mother nor his adoptive parents had been capable of providing him. Second, I recall feeling impatient with Ron and Teri, and at times I disapproved of their parenting decisions as well as of their apparent insensitivity to Bruce's emotional needs, which seemed so transparent from my point of view. Furthermore, like the rest of Bruce's extended family, I also possessed a critical piece of knowledge that he was not privy to— at least, not consciously. This had the effect of both undermining the authenticity of our treatment relationship and of placing me in a false alliance with his parents. One might argue that Bruce's stories in the last few hours of his treatment not only demonstrated how close he was to figuring out the family secret on his own, but that he suspected the therapist might be holding out on him as well.

CONCLUSION

Bruce's parents discontinued his treatment following this session, which occurred at the very end of the school year. Bruce had demonstrated modest gains in his academic performance, and seemed somewhat more in control both at school and at home, although I noted that his parents had seemed vaguely dissatisfied at the time of our last meeting together, just a few weeks earlier. Nevertheless, we had discussed the need for Bruce to continue his treatment over the summer, vacation schedules, and so forth. I then saw Bruce for another five sessions. A few days after the session in which Bruce told the story of the ghost ballplayer, Bruce's parents left a message canceling his next hour, and advising that they would be in touch to reschedule. When I didn't hear from them soon thereafter, I returned the phone call. Ron and Teri had decided to see how Bruce would do without treatment over the summer. If they felt he needed to return to therapy, they would contact me in the fall. I strongly advised against this plan, stressing the vital importance of continuing his therapy especially in light of the recent symptomatic improvement he had shown and the stable treatment alliance we had been able to forge. Teri repeated that she and Ron thought it was important to see how well Bruce would be able to do without therapy, and that summer vacation provided them with such an opportunity. Perhaps not surprisingly, I didn't hear from them again.

In retrospect, I now wonder to what extent Ron and Teri's decision, which led to the derailment of the treatment, had been codetermined by two variables. The first of these was of course their considerable discomfort with my recommendation that the family secret finally be revealed. Despite my caution in introducing the topic, it is entirely possible that my timing was not quite right, or that I appeared too invested in having them decide to go ahead in making this revelation which, in their view, would greatly complicate their lives and upset the fragile family equilibrium they had maintained for so many years. Bruce had also gradually become attached to me and experienced undisguised pleasure in the more permissive and tolerant ambience of therapy, a reaction of which his parents were painfully aware. As is often the case, Ron and Teri appeared to have experienced my deepening relationship with Bruce as a dangerously competitive one for them, to which they reacted with narcissistic injury, envy, and finally, defensive assertion. Ending Bruce's therapy may have deprived him of a much-needed opportunity to recover more fully from developmental traumata and to "re-rail" his arrested development, but continuing it required that a false family persona be given up completely or at least substantially modified.

I have wondered from time to time how Bruce is doing, and whether the seven months he spent in treatment with me were of any enduring value. It is possible that he continued to make a satisfactory adjustment at school, and that the antisocial behavior of which his teachers and parents had complained ceased to be a significant problem. In my last meeting with his parents, they had also noted modest improvement in their son's ability to tolerate minor frustrations, and said that he was getting along a bit better with his younger sister. Clearly, there had been some symptomatic improvement. Yet, I believe that the most troubling aspects of this case were not even close to being resolved. In an important sense, however, additional therapeutic progress for Bruce was contingent upon his parents' willingness to enter into an authentic dialogue with him in which the true circumstances of his adoption might finally be told. At least within the time I worked with Bruce, this goal, regrettably, was not yet within reach.

REFERENCES

Barnes, Marion. 1953. "The Working-Through Process in Dealing with Anxiety around Adoption." *American Journal of Orthopsychiatry* 23, no. 3 (October): 605–20.

Berger, Maria. 1979. "Preliminary Report of the Study Group on the Problems of Adopted Children." *Bulletin of the Hampstead Clinic* 2, no. 3 (October): 169–76.

Berger, Maria, and Jill Hodges. 1982. "Some Thoughts on the Question of When to Tell the Child That He Is Adopted." *Journal of Child Psychotherapy* 8, no. 1 (April): 67–88.

Bollas, Christopher. 1987. *The Shadow of the Object*. New York: Columbia University Press.

Brandell, Jerrold, ed. 1992. *Countertransference in Psychotherapy with Children and Adolescents*. Northvale, NJ: Jason Aronson.

———. 2004. *Psychodynamic Social Work*. New York: Columbia University Press.

Brinich, Paul. 1980. "Some Potential Effects of Adoption upon Self and Object Representations." *Psychoanalytic Study of the Child* 35:107–33.

Brodzinsky, David. 1987. "Adjustment to Adoption: A Psychosocial Perspective." *Clinical Psychology Review* 7, no. 1 (January): 25–47.

Davidson, Dorothy. 1985. "An Adolescent in Search of Her Identity." *Journal of Analytical Psychology* 30, no. 3 (July): 339–46.

Gardner, Richard. 1973. *Therapeutic Communication with Children: The Mutual Storytelling Technique*. New York: Science House.

———. 1993. *Storytelling in Psychotherapy with Children*. Northvale, NJ: Jason Aronson.

Hodges, Jill, Rosetta Bolletti, Frances Salo, and Rudolph Oldeschulte. 1985. "Remembering Is So Much Harder: A Report on Work in Progress from the Research Group on Adopted Children." *Bulletin of the Anna Freud Centre* 8, no. 3 (September): 169–79.

Howe, David, and Sheila Fearnley. 2003. "Disorders of Attachment in Adopted and Fostered Children: Recognition and Treatment." *Clinical Child Psychology and Psychiatry* 8, no. 3 (July): 369–87.

Kernberg, Paulina. 1986. "Child Analysis with a Severely Disturbed Adopted Child." *International Journal of Psychoanalytic Psychotherapy* 11:277–99.

Kohut, Heinz. 1971. *Analysis of the Self*. New York: International Universities Press.

———. 1977. *Restoration of the Self*. New York: International Universities Press.

Offord, David, Joseph Aponte, and L. A. Cross. 1969. "Presenting Symptomatology of Adopted Children." *Archives of General Psychiatry* 20, no. 1 (January): 110–16.

Pitcher, Evelyn, and Ernst Prelinger. 1963. *Children Tell Stories: An Analysis of Fantasy*. New York: International Universities Press.

Sherick, Ivan. 1983. "Adoption and Disturbed Narcissism: A Case Illustration of a Latency Boy." *Journal of the American Psychoanalytic Association* 31, no. 2 (April): 487–513.

Taichert, Louise, and Donya Harvin. 1975. "Adoption and Children with Learning and Behavior Problems." *Western Journal of Medicine* 122, no. 6 (June): 464–70.

Wieder, Herbert. 1978. "Special Problems in the Psychoanalysis of Adopted Children." In *Child Analysis and Therapy*. Ed. Jules Glenn. New York: Jason Aronson, 557–77.

Chapter Nine

Adoption Fantasy in the Treatment of Two Adolescent Girls

Jane Hanenberg

The development and exploration of one's identity is at the heart of adolescence. Since adoptees technically have two sets of parents, and may be of a different culture than their adoptive families, the course of their teenaged years is often challenging. Knowledge of one's family and culture are the basis for adolescent identity development (Erikson 1975). A sense of oneself within these contexts serves as the bedrock from which identity can be forged and then challenged as a necessary condition for ego development and character formation during the adolescent years. Adoptees must ask themselves the customary questions about who they are and who they will become, and at the same time must integrate parts of their biological heritage that have not been experienced and may not be known.

All children have fantasies about their parents. But adopted children are especially vulnerable to some of the troubling feelings these fantasies may arise from and engender. For many adopted children, even those with knowledge of or actual contact with their biological parents, ideas about their adoption are confusing. Elements of unconscious fantasy, blended with whatever knowledge has been imparted by adoptive parents, can become activated in new ways with the onset of puberty. Neither of the two patients discussed here reached adolescence with full information of her actual birth story, and each had many fantasies about the causes and circumstances of her adoption. Both had defensive narratives about the adoption that had worked sufficiently for them in their earlier years. However, the regressive experiences of early adolescence brought both girls to experience turmoil which neither they nor their families had expected or could understand.

In his work regarding character formation, Peter Blos (1968) comments that character development raises the question of what "*takes* form and what *gives* form" (244–45). In normal development, the vast physical and emotional upheavals of adolescence provide an opportunity for questioning one's identity, as well as enabling its evolution. A hallmark of successful separation is that earlier identifications are challenged and, often, some are repudiated. Blos asserts that it is these processes that give rise to a consolidation of identity in later adolescence. For the adoptees to be discussed here, the inevitable incompleteness of knowledge about "what *gives* form" to their lives was filled with troubling fantasies. The questions of what "*takes* form" were, in turn, met with apprehension generated by the lives they hadn't lived and families they hadn't known. As one of the girls commented, "Getting to be an adult is like jumping into a black hole."

Rejection by biological parents, coupled with the absence of lived experience of them, is part of what shapes the self-concepts of adopted children. In the unfocused longings of early childhood, children may imagine and wish for benign and optimistic solutions to their questions about adoption. Prior to their treatment, these two patients had opportunities to discuss fantasy material about their adoption. Their families had shared some knowledge of the girls' births and their birth families. The girls had peers and classmates who were adopted, and talk about adoption was welcomed at home and with their extended families. As one parent said, "We think of adoption as an issue, not a problem." However, by early adolescence, each girl had experienced an intensified resurgence of feelings of abandonment by her biological parents.

In all adolescents, separation is achieved with a certain degree of sadness. This event has been compared to the grief of mourning (Freud 1958; Wolfenstein 1966). Although the mourning is metaphorical, the grief is palpable. It is often observed in rapid shifts of mood and affiliation in young adolescents. After the onset of puberty, when parents no longer occupy a cherished and idealized position, the parents are "let go." A swap takes place, and the parents are exchanged for intimacies elsewhere. This loss allows for disillusionment, and the parents are devalued. Adopted children experience this grief twofold.

By early adolescence, each girl I will discuss had experienced an intensified resurgence of feelings of abandonment, and had reacted by withdrawal from her family. Adolescence proceeded in both cases with an intensity that neither the girls nor their families could have anticipated.

CASE 1

Jill was referred for psychotherapy at age thirteen by her parents. They were frightened by her anger, her impulsivity, and, as I later learned, by her potential for decompensation. There had been some testing in grade school to help understand Jill's emotional and educational development. These tests revealed that Jill had profound dyslexia, but no significant psychopathology. Jill received appropriate tutoring both inside and outside the classroom. As grade school progressed, Jill's affect had remained mildly unstable. Occasional rageful storms arrived quickly with great intensity, and then subsided with equally puzzling speed. Her parents reported holding Jill during tantrums through much of her grade-school years. Jill had been an active and oppositional toddler and preschooler. Her parents, who were both professionals in child-related fields, were each endowed with tolerance and a robust sense of humor. They loved Jill and accepted her idiosyncrasies. They explained that this was how Jill was "wired." But both had hoped, unrealistically, that Jill's behavior would "even out" before adolescence proper.

Jill was adopted in early infancy with the help of an agency that facilitated domestic adoptions. Her parents had married somewhat late in life and hoped to have a child. They had had rewarding experiences fostering several older children, and this influenced their decision to adopt an infant. The couple had been disappointed during a previous attempt at adoption when the birth mother had, at the last minute, decided to keep her child. The opportunity to adopt Jill came quickly, and only after the couple had feared that an adoption would never take place. Within a very few days of hearing about Jill, they had become her parents.

After this roller-coaster experience of hope and loss, Jill's parents were stunned and delighted when she arrived. She was, from the beginning, large, loud, and wild, and by the time she approached puberty, she outsized her peers in energy, hardiness, and girth. Jill worried that her hair was too thick and her voice too emphatic. In true counterphobic style, she dressed in the latest sexualized fashions with bright colors, platform shoes, and glittery eye shadow. In contrast, she sometimes sported more childlike clothing with images of cuddly animals. When Jill was impatient, she swore with malice and gusto. She also reflected, "You must think I could kill someone, but you know I'm really a puppy dog."

Despite her shifting moods, Jill was tremendously adept at the management of her environment. She could master a mechanical project, cook a meal, or clean up in record time. Throughout the treatment she drew and painted, fashioned jewelry and puppets, and organized the play materials. These projects were accomplished with a sense of purpose and finished quickly without any stated ambivalence about the results.

Even as an early adolescent, Jill knew there were tremendous incongruities between her powerful affects and her lagging emotional development. She discussed her confusion about her lack of control, and her guilt about wishing harm to people. Once, after a short but intense fistfight at school, Jill was remorseful. "He was a jerk, but I know he didn't deserve that." Jill relished her practical intelligence as an antidote to her learning difficulties, but her aggression puzzled her.

Jill viewed herself as a conundrum. With so many significant contradictions, Jill often felt out of step with her peers and with her family. Jill's mother understood her daughter's confusion. She once lamented, "Jill never feels very good about herself. The problem is that I can't cheer her up, since the things she is depressed about are all true." She viewed Jill's difficulties as a result of her genetic endowment, and feared that she could not help.

At age twelve, Jill had begun to wonder more openly about her birth family. Their presence was somewhat palpable, since she knew there were legal provisions for her to meet her biological mother when she became an adult. Since her birth mother had been single and no father was identified, Jill's fantasy was that her mother had been "screwed and dumped" by "some guy" who had disappeared after Jill's conception. The yearly Christmas and birthday gifts from her birth mother led Jill to assume that this mother knew nothing about kids, since the gifts did not match with Jill's interests. The yearly correspondences were met with overt disappointment. In tandem with these concerns, Jill's curiosity about the families of her older foster siblings began to develop, and she began to idealize these other unknown families. Their imagined good qualities temporarily quelled Jill's doubts about her own beginnings.

Jill attended treatment sessions grudgingly. She greeted me with glum resignation. Occasionally she asked for specific kinds of play or art materials, but rejected them when they appeared. At these moments, I must have seemed to her like her biological mother, whose attempts to connect were disappointing. Jill reassured me that her lack of engagement with me wasn't personal, but that she was attending sessions to assuage her mother. When I questioned why she might want to do this, Jill was saddened. She expressed remorse about her erratic behavior and "all I've put her [my mother] through." Jill seemed to feel that she was "too much" for me, for her birth mother, and for her well-meaning adoptive mother.

Jill's treatment gradually took shape as her art developed. After a series of pleasant drawings of soft, shaded, and empty landscapes, Jill drew a sports car. Some zippy action had appeared in the lifeless landscapes. This drawing seemed to foreshadow more engagement with the treatment, and the start of Jill crawling out of her "black hole." Jill then decided to focus her hours on fashioning a personal alphabet with corresponding pictographs. She dedicated herself to this for a number of sessions, portraying symbols for abstract concepts, the natural world, and people. All the symbols were thoughtfully developed, but the man and woman symbols were unique since they were each accompanied by a small companion. The man's offspring resembled his abstracted form, and the woman's mirrored hers. When I suggested that the drawings might be representative of her biological parents, Jill explained that she often looked for her biological mother, who "might be coming around the corner at any time." Jill imagined that she would recognize her immediately. This helped me to understand more of Jill's initial rejection of my offers of play materials. When I asked about this, she confirmed that she was merely waiting for the "right" gifts to arrive.

Soon after this discussion, Jill sculpted a series of figures that helped us understand the adoption fantasies of her younger years. These multicolored figures, fashioned of plastic clay, featured brilliant fluorescent colors, exaggerated hair, and piercing eyes. Bella, with chartreuse hair and clown-like features, appeared surprised. Billy Joe was a sinister character with a scar, nose ring, and unruly hair. And Bonnie Sue, less formed, more cartoon-like, and naïve, was presented as Jill's infant, pre-adopted self. In every scenario Jill played out with these characters, Billy Joe preyed on the frightened Bella. In what appeared to be a fantasized construction of Jill's birth, an assault had occurred, and the unformed Bonnie Sue was both helpless and responsible. As we began to talk about Jill's fear that she behaved like Billy Joe, her mother brought news that Jill's behavior in school had improved and her teachers had noted that Jill was trying to use some restraint. As Jill's identification with the aggressor was interpreted in the drawings, she seemed to fear her own aggression less.

Some aspects of this theme were played out in Jill's friendships. While earlier she had belonged to a stable group of loyal girlfriends, Jill's new, teenaged friendships were problematic. Jill was initially concerned about these friends' escapades with boys, alcohol, and freedom. She worried that the girls might suffer harm, like the innocent Bella. Then, inevitably, when her protests were ignored, Jill became enraged that her friends were putting themselves in danger. Rejected and angry, Jill assumed that they would encounter their just rewards since, like her imagined birth mother, they had been flaunting their sexuality. As Jill's sexuality emerged, she seemed concerned about her own impulses and the potentially destructive consequences.

As Jill was preparing to enter high school, there was a family crisis. There were a number of deaths in her parents' extended families, and Jill's mother became unemployed. Jill became convinced that her father had been behaving "inappropriately," since she had found adult magazines in his room. She was sure her father was a "pervert." Jill's father was calm and rational, but Jill was explicit about her rage. "I don't want to hear or see anything about him humping anyone. He's disgusting."

In several ensuing meetings, the family all spoke calmly and openly, and Jill's father was restored to her moderate good graces. Jill readily acknowledged that her desire to hurt him was reparation for the fantasized rape of her biological mother, and that when it came to men she was "not ready to forgive." Although Jill's attitudes about the character of men reflected unconscious fantasies about her biological father, I wondered later if this outburst also conveyed Jill's disappointments and longings for her adoptive father. In the adoption fantasy, Jill supposed herself to be the product of impulsive "humping." This may have produced shame, which may in turn have caused Jill to protect herself from her wishes to be close to her father at home.

The catastrophic fantasies that had come to define Jill's ideas of her birth and the causes for her adoption were complex. If her biological mother had been abused, she was not responsible for relinquishing Jill. The imagined violence of her biological father had been the cause for Jill's adoption, and Jill was spared anger at the mother she hoped she would find around the corner. In a discussion of these fantasies, Jill assured me, "If I had been around I would have protected her." This fantasy enabled Jill to keep her birth mother close, just as she was separating from her adoptive family.

In some ways, Jill's catastrophic fantasies paralleled those of her parents'. In a session with only Jill's parents, they explained that their high tolerance of their daughter's tantrums was probably derived from apprehension that Jill could become psychotic. They had worried from the beginning that Jill's birth mother had an undiagnosed psychosis that explained her affective instability and that Jill was destined to inherit. These reciprocal fantasies were elaborated by Jill, who had often worried that her idiosyncrasies meant that she might be crazy. She confessed that she felt out of step with her parents' orderly and thoughtful restraint. She described how, at age twelve, she had watched her body move without volition as she hit a classmate.

As we examined the layers of the whole family's adoption fantasies and their intermingling, everyone's anxiety increased. Jill seemed poised in an untenable position. She was less identified with her fantasized, violent birth father, and more comfortable with her adoptive father. She displaced her ambivalence onto me and onto her adoptive mother. Fueled by a desire to be a constant object, and to repair a splintered relationship with her own mother, Jill's adoptive mother stayed close. Through this era of devaluing and sometimes explosive behavior, Jill's adoptive mother maintained optimism. She brainstormed new summer plans, hosted parties for Jill's friends, and gave Jill a clothing allowance. During this time there was a collective family effort to reframe fears of craziness to realistic worries. Jill's losses, her parents' desires, and even those of the foster siblings began to seem more manageable. Ironically, Jill's lability seemed more appropriate to adolescence than it had earlier in her life, and her teachers were optimistic.

At one point Jill wondered what it had been like for her biological mother at the time of the adoption. At age fifteen, Jill decided to act on her curiosity about her birth. She penned a note to her biological mother and left it in a public spot at home for her adoptive parents to view. The note said that she was doing well in school and life, and had been adopted into a "great family." This note may have anticipated the meeting that could take place in a few years, and expressed Jill's desire to be known by her biological mother. As yet, the note is unsent.

Maturation has been good to Jill. As individuation and more nurturing, positive identifications of later adolescence have arrived, she feels less out of place among her peers. Jill seems to know herself better in the context of teachers, family, and friends, and a part of the "black hole" seems to have been filled. As Jill has made meaning of her fantasies and expressed them in the context of therapy and the family, her sense of self has expanded.

CASE 2

The custom of marking the body is prominent in many cultures. People mark themselves to claim membership in a group, and to identify themselves in public and private spheres. Some marks express aesthetic preferences and others express allegiances toward certain beliefs. But the mark one is born with is different. The next discussion is about a girl who felt and was marked in this way.

Sara, who was referred at age seventeen, was the youngest of three children, and the only adopted sibling. She had been adopted from Guatemala as an infant, after having been well tended in foster care for several months. Because they had experienced some secondary infertility, Sara's parents had been eager to adopt her. Sara's siblings were boys, and both parents had wanted a daughter.

Sara was referred for treatment after having fled a new boarding school during her first week in the dorms. Sara had had a tumultuous high-school career, which included reckless drinking, academic difficulties, and many angry confrontations with her parents. There had been a brief psychiatric hospitalization after Sara revealed that she had cut herself superficially in the midst of a family disagreement. Both Sara and her family were exhausted. At this point, Sara's parents were somewhat wary of seeking a psychotherapist for her because she had been in treatment several times before, and had made little progress. Sara had been compliant, but had shared little of herself.

Sara had always been extremely shy in school, but had functioned well within the family. Her parents, who were gregarious and well organized, were invested in providing Sara with experiences that would keep her affiliated with her country of origin. There had been adoption groups, language lessons, and during grade school, a trip back to Guatemala. Sara was enthralled with this visit, and recalled the comfort she felt there as a unique experience, and one that would have been unimaginable at home.

Looking back on her early adolescence, Sara professed surprise and embarrassment at the changes that had erupted so suddenly. She could not recognize the girl she had been who had so many angry and frightening confrontations with her family and friends. Her parents described this period as "somewhere between adolescence and mental illness." At times, they lost hope for Sara.

When Sara was in high school, the reserved girl vanished. She became rageful, and what Sara referred to as her "evil twin" appeared. Sara had a group of fast-paced, unruly friends, and often found herself observing them closely. When she did join in, tempers would flare, and Sara did many impulsive things that puzzled and shamed her. These events offered Sara a "foreign" view of herself. When Sara described these friends, whose first names all began with *J*, we considered the notion that her relationship with me, another *J*, might offer her new and different views of herself. However, she may have also feared that our work could intensify her angry feelings and cause her to act impulsively.

Sara was born with a *naevus flammus*, a red birthmark that encircled one arm, a shoulder, and a portion of her face. Its impact on her appearance was significant. The birthmark was rarely discussed when Sara was growing up because her parents wanted Sara to think that she was beautiful. Medical treatment had not yet been developed to treat the birthmark. Sara did not recall other people's reactions to the birthmark until she was in early adolescence, when her peers called her "half-face" or "two-face." Until we discussed the birthmark together regularly, Sara minimized its impact. She did not express discernable feelings as she related the many curious questions or cruel remarks she heard about it on a regular basis. Sara explained that though the taunts were painful, they reminded her of the reality that she had two kinds of faces. Later on in the treatment, Sara made the connection that the characteristics of her birthmark mirrored her internal splits. Sara felt she had two sets of feelings and two selves, as well as two families, two countries, and two faces.

In Nathaniel Hawthorne's story "The Birthmark," a scientist is obsessed by a mark on his wife's face. Though she is unconcerned, her husband tries to develop a cure that will remove the mark. He continues until he actually relieves her of both the birthmark and "the burden of life." Hawthorne's character could not tolerate his wife's imperfections. For Sara, her birthmark was an encumbrance that elicited surprise, concern, and distress from those around her. In some ways, she was puzzled. She would not be herself without the birthmark, so when medical treatment became available she was unsure she wanted to pursue it. If she altered her face, who would she be?

Sara also experienced herself as different from others because she was one of the few "nonwhite" people in the city where she lived. She poignantly recalled feeling completely "at home" during the visit to her country of origin. While there she looked around in a public place and had the novel experience of looking like everyone else. In her jobs, at school, or in any situation where she was not accompanied by her family, Sara felt invisible, separate, and at times, otherworldly. In her anxiety, she was often speechless. In a family meeting with me, her parents wondered if Sara "was excluding herself before others excluded her." Sara's experience was that she was both invisible and a conspicuous object of curiosity.

At the beginning of treatment, Sara and I were both concerned about her safety. She was relieved to be away from the social milieu of her school, but was still terrified that her turbulent feelings would reappear. She worried that the era of occasional suicidal thoughts and wild counterphobic behavior would return as if she were in "a revolving door and unable to get out." Her guilt about these experiences still overshadowed any opportunity to understand them. Sara's parents helped her by creating structure and clear expectations now that she was living at home. However, Sara really believed that it was her remorse that kept her from a setback. Still contrite, she remained in her room and away from the dangers of her old crowd.

Sara spent many sessions recalling and reworking the events of her traumatic years and her confusion about them. She seemed exhausted at the end of these hours. She never left the office without a polite "Thank you." At this time, her idealized transference seemed in keeping with her preadolescent relationship with her parents. She viewed me mainly as a benign authority who occasionally misspoke. Over time she became less afraid of speaking about these missteps. This began with Sara's feeling that I had overstated her negative affects. As we clarified these moments together, Sara discussed her feelings that I would view her as impolite if she was annoyed or disapproving. As she described these concerns, I wondered if they were indicative of abandonment fears related to her adoption, and if Sara might be afraid of losing me.

During this phase, Sara attended a local university and got a job. Progress came slowly, but Sara was determined. Each class assignment or car ride to a new destination was rehearsed. Then Sara discovered an opportunity to travel abroad with a church group. It was a success. Having mastered some challenges, Sara was now able to "retrace her steps" with a new peer group, and her ability to observe herself burgeoned. At her mother's suggestion, Sara began to pay for her treatment.

Sara deflected my queries about fantasies that her birthmark may have played a role in her adoption. When I persisted, her answer was surprising. In her continuing idealization of the birth parents, Sara had supposed that they were unlike Hawthorne's scientist. Her idea was that the birthmark had not repulsed her parents, but made it even more difficult for them to relinquish her, since she would need their protection. She assumed that these right-minded adults would have kept her but for their poverty. Although the world was frightened by her face, it was a mark of Sara's uniqueness, and a link to her birth family.

Sara had had information from the adoption agency that she had many siblings. She assumed that her birth parents were poor and had been unable to support another child. While discussions about her birth family were brief, they led to more candid discussions about her adoptive family. Prior idealizations softened, and Sara reported that disagreements and frustration had become more common. Sara noticed that for the first time in years, she had felt angry at home without feeling out of control. It heartened her that her mother was excited about this, and seemed to give her permission to feel and be oppositional. At the same time, Sara grew more candid about her fears. She had often spoken about her regret that she had been unable to tolerate separation from her family in her grade-school years. She had missed many of the pleasures of friendship and affiliation due to her anxiety.

Sara also explained that she felt she could not forgive herself for the pain she had caused her adoptive family. During her stormy years, Sara had feared that life at home would become untenable. Sara's articulated adoption fantasy was that her burdened birth parents had needed to protect themselves due to their lack of resources. Her adoptive family's concern that they could not deal with Sara's rages had then seemed to reenact this predicament. Sara's red birthmark was not only a link to her biological family, but also a symbol of her anger. She had withdrawn from the stares of strangers and the risks of new relationships and sought solace in protection at home. However, Sara's regression was mirrored by the force with which she turned away. For Sara, this time felt perilous since it seemed to threaten the loss of both families. Her adoptive parents' despair may have confirmed this for her. As a marked, but invisible child, Sara felt that being "seen" in the larger world placed her adoption in danger.

When Sara reached the age of consent, she wrote a long, imagined letter to her birth family. She was proud to be able to relate her successes, and was pleased that her parents were supportive of the plan. We explored Sara's hopes about reunion, and her fears that her birth parents might have died, or worse, would not respond. To her amazement, Sara received a return note praising her for her endeavors, proposing further contact, and apologizing for the "sin" of the adoption. This had great meaning for Sara, since she felt that her birth parents had been able to imagine her sense of loss and to express their remorse. Sara remained cautious about the next contacts she would have with her birth parents. However, the reward for her curiosity and initiative has been more success at home, at work, and with a few friends. With more positive maternal identifications, she has found more comfort in her world.

CONCLUSION

Despite both of their parents' love, Jill and Sara each, at times, felt they were unlovable. As the separation from their younger, more peaceable ties with their adoptive families began, both girls were faced with the tasks presented by the onset of adolescence. The adoption fantasies of their earlier years were experienced in a heightened, more disruptive fashion in keeping with their new physical and emotional changes. In the seesaw of early adolescence, turmoil ensued.

Jill's image of the black hole and Sara's birthmark were salient metaphors for their inchoate but powerful adoption fantasies. The black hole, usually a representation of emptiness, actually conveyed Jill's fears about violence and her family's worries about psychosis. Sara's birthmark symbolized the many ways she felt different and separate from others. Central to the adoption fantasy of each girl was considerable guilt. Jill felt that since she had failed to protect the well-being of her defenseless birth mother, she had to identify, instead, with her imagined, violent father. Sara, whose intense shyness was in part a defense against her anger, was certain that her birth had burdened her biological family.

Separation can be frightening when one's roots seem fragile and unknown, and loss is difficult when one has been abandoned, rejected, or "marked." The adoption fantasies described here came to characterize Jill's and Sara's internalized object connections. When adolescence arrived, each girl was faced with the enormous task of giving meaning to feelings that were unconscious and seemed immutable. With the help of their families, Jill and Sara could ask themselves who they were and who they might want to become in the context of the larger world.

REFERENCES

Blos, Peter. 1968. "Character Formation in Adolescence." *Psychoanalytic Study of the Child* 23:245–63.

Erikson, Erik. 1975. "The Concept of Ego Identity." In *The Psychology of Adolescence*. Ed. Aron Esman. New York: International Universities Press, 178–95.

Freud, Anna. 1958. "Adolescence." *Psychoanalytic Study of the Child* 13:255–78.

Hawthorne, Nathaniel. 1955. "The Birthmark." In *Hawthorne's Short Stories*. New York: Vintage, 147–64.

Wolfenstein, Martha. 1966. "How Is Mourning Possible?" *Psychoanalytic Study of the Child* 21:93–123.

Chapter Ten

Identity and Identification

Being Different and the Quest to Belong in an Adopted Young Adult

Susan B. Sherman

Being racially and culturally different from one's family is bound to evoke feelings of being an outsider, and internationally adopted children often report this experience. How these differences affect each child is dependent upon a variety of factors: for example, the circumstances of the adoption and how that story is transmitted to the child by the adoptive family; the composition of the adoptive family, that is, the presence of biological siblings or other adopted siblings in the family and the impact of their races and cultures; the parents' unique personalities and parenting styles; the manner in which the child's family of origin and its culture are acknowledged and presented to the child by the family and perceived and dealt with by the surrounding community; and the child's specific natural endowment, coping skills, and developmental process. I will discuss the case of one young adult patient, adopted as an infant, whose differentness and the ways in which it was managed in her family played a significant role in shaping her identity and personality organization. I will then discuss what I have learned from this patient and her experience that may be helpful to clinicians treating internationally adopted children. I will also raise as yet unanswered questions about these children, which require further observation and research.

CASE EXAMPLE

Alison came to me in a crisis about an urgent and conflictual career decision. She described having struggled throughout her life with a feeling of emptiness and not belonging, as well as with an inability to form a close attachment to her adoptive mother. When I met her, she seemed to be searching for her identity from without by embracing her birth culture in a variety of ways. Her search was externalized, intellectualized, and abstract.

Alison has African biological parents and was adopted when she was a few months old by an Irish-American couple. She has two brothers, one three years younger and one five years younger, both the biological children of her parents. The family resides in a suburban community outside a large Midwestern city where her adoptive dad is a professor of history at a local community college and her adoptive mother is a receptionist in a doctor's office. Her mother has multiple sclerosis, which had been in remission until shortly before Alison began seeing me. Mrs. C, her mother, had a relapse at that time that manifested primarily in difficulty ambulating. Alison sought treatment because she had become depressed while grappling with a major life decision: whether to teach abroad or continue working and living in the United States, whether to leave or to stay. Her dilemma was in part created and influenced by the fact that she had been adopted from another country. Her physical differences from her adoptive family and her natural, intellectual curiosity about her birth culture created a somewhat disguised form of search behavior; that is, while she did not want an actual reunion with her biological mother, she seemed to be seeking a way to connect with her through her native culture. Although our work was short term and not completed, it had an intensity that may shed light on the inner experience of an internationally adopted child. I worked with Alison twice weekly for six months, at which point she left a lucrative but unfulfilling job to teach in Africa. I saw her for two additional sessions a year later when she returned for a trip home.

Alison is a strikingly attractive young woman with a light brown complexion and features that identify her as being of African origin. Entering my office for the first time, she sat very close to me on the edge of the couch. She made intense eye contact, and her gaze was anxious and searching. She had volumes to say and did so in a rapid, express-train manner. However, her affect was quite flat. The only evidence of emotion was an occasional single tear, which she would allow to fall without wiping it away. In these moments, she seemed unable to acknowledge her sadness or comfort herself.

In the first session, Alison immediately offered the story of her adoption. At the time that her parents had been planning to start a family, her mother was diagnosed with multiple sclerosis. Mrs. C was advised not to become pregnant and so decided to adopt instead. Initially Mrs. C had difficulty being approved as an adoptive parent because of her physical disability. Alison's parents had ultimately been able to arrange the adoption through a network in Africa they had learned about from friends. They flew there when Alison was a few months old to gather her from an orphanage.

Alison told me at once that she had always felt different from her immediate family and in her community but had attempted to suppress this feeling. She could not tell her parents she felt different because she had tremendous gratitude and indebtedness toward them and believed they would be deeply hurt. Shortly before beginning treatment and perhaps as a prelude to it, she had finally shared with her mother her feeling of unlikeness. It was a brave and painful task for Alison, which was reflected in her mother's response: "I didn't know that; I feel terrible." In Alison's neighborhood, everyone was Caucasian. Her obvious physical differences were never addressed at home, and perhaps because she was both a gifted student and socially adept, she experienced no overt discrimination at school. She was a talented athlete, an exceptional artist, a member of every school club, and the girlfriend of the class president. She planned to study art in college, but when she realized she was "not the best," she stopped painting and never picked up a paintbrush again. As she related this part of her story, she said, "Isn't that sad?" But her affect belied her words. She stared at me, perhaps seeking for me to feel and express her unacknowledged emotions. She changed her major to sociology with a concentration in black studies, and participated in study programs in different African countries during her junior year abroad as well as for a year after graduating from college. She attended a large university in an urban setting that felt universes away because of its ethnic diversity. She said that upon arriving there, she "breathed a sigh of relief." For the first time, she had a sense of comfort and of belonging to a community and could only then acknowledge her past suffering and feelings of alienation.

Initially Alison seemed unaware of the multiple meanings of her dilemma: to stay in her job or to teach in Africa. She spoke of her motivation for working abroad as different from that of her peers who had decided to pursue the same career. They wished merely to "help people"; she wanted to be an "agent of change." She was aware that she was disappointing her parents in her desire to leave.

She was also in a relationship with Robert, the son of an African-American mother and a Caucasian father. He, too, was a person of two cultures, and felt that he could not be with a woman who was not, at least, part black. He said he could only love someone who looked like him. He said he wanted to marry Alison, but she distrusted him, feeling his love for her was selfish. He, too, could not empathize with her need to work abroad and offered marriage to keep her close. During the time we worked together, Alison ended their relationship. She wondered, with me, if she needed to "leave him sooner" to avoid the deeper pain of a later loss. Since her wish "to leave" had always been a part of her, she seemed to hold herself back in all her relationships, reflecting a general fear of intimacy.

During the time I saw her, Alison's father and brothers were not the focus of her attention. Nonetheless, they were portrayed as benign, and her relationships with them were described as essentially positive and nonconflictual. Like her mom, Alison's dad also did not want her to leave her job, but his reasons were pragmatic. Alison saw him as more objective, but nevertheless she did not seem influenced by him. Only the brother closest in age to Alison was supportive of her plan and seemed to intuitively understand that it had great meaning and importance for her. However, the general tone of her relationships with her father and brothers did not significantly emerge during the course of this short treatment.

Alison's relationship with her mother was her most intense relationship, and she was deeply conflicted about leaving her. She felt her mother was overly identified with her, calling Alison her "soul mate." Alison experienced herself as being quite special to her mother, her favorite. This feeling may have been Alison's wish or a reaction formation in both mother and daughter: for her mother, to protect herself from favoring her biological children; and for Alison, to protect herself from feeling different and rejected. Alison and her mother spent more time together than they did with other members of the family. Alison's mother confided in her like a friend, sometimes sharing personal information Alison wished not to know. Perhaps the degree of maternal distance was magnified because Alison was not her mother's biological child, creating a kind of peer relationship between them. At the same time, Alison's mother would often accuse Alison of being cold and selfish. I wondered whether Alison's beauty and accomplishments were both narcissistically gratifying to her mother and a cause for envy.

In contrast to her mother's feeling that Alison was her soul mate, Alison felt totally alien from mother. In temperament, she saw herself as rational and her mother as emotional. She felt her mother was extremely anxious; she could not imagine what it would be like to be her, so on edge, so volatile. Alison seemed oblivious to her own acute anxiety. She felt her mother was neither adventurous nor risk taking, neither ambitious nor aggressive intellectually. She felt they had almost nothing in common. Alison had intense ambivalence toward her mother, which is not unusual in late adolescence and early adulthood. Still I wondered if some of her alienation from her mother was based on their actual differences. They did not share the same genetic material: Alison seemed to have higher intelligence and greater drive, and she was more beautiful. If a daughter does not share some obvious, observable qualities of her mother, is their bond affected in some way? Does a child seek adults with like physical and emotional qualities with whom to identify? It is possible that Alison's mother felt inferior, and Alison felt guilty for surpassing her mother at an early age, creating a more highly charged Oedipal rivalry.

For many years Alison had been hoping and planning to teach abroad, and once she got the job, she had postponed her departure for two years because of her own ambivalence and her mother's protestations. But she now seemed eager to go. When her mother had a relapse just prior to her leaving, Alison was somewhat troubled and briefly considered staying home to help her but feared being exploited. She quickly determined that her mother's illness would not hold her back, and she continued to move forward with her plan. Possibly her mother's returning symptoms were more disturbing to Alison than she could consciously acknowledge and were a major precipitant for her seeking treatment. But Alison did not appear to react affectively. What most disturbed Alison was her mother's inability to share her excitement about her new job, and to admire her courage and determination. Her mother, who often attributed her own meanings to Alison's motives, causing Alison to further withdraw from her, suggested that Alison's sole reason for going to Africa was to find her biological mother. This suggestion infuriated Alison, who accused her of discovering this idea in a textbook. In fact, Alison had intentionally chosen African countries in which to work during college and at this time that were not her native country. Alison believed that if she searched for her biological mother, she would deeply wound her adoptive mother; moreover, she did not consciously experience a desire to meet her biological mother, perhaps defending against that wish. She spontaneously remarked in one session, "We should be talking in here about what's really important, the adoption . . . " but after trailing off, she associated immediately to Robert and how they had not talked about her leaving. She wondered, "Maybe I'm leaving him before he leaves me." Her mother had remarked to Alison that this was what Alison was doing to her: fighting to make their separation easier. Alison seemed unconsciously aware of a connection between her adoption and the idea of rejecting another before she was rejected, of reversing a painful part of her history. The sequence of Alison's associations also suggested that she had not discussed with her mother "what's really important": her adoption and her differentness from her family. This emerged in the following manner in our work.

Midway through the treatment, it became clear that Alison's decision to leave was firm but that she wanted to have a deeper understanding of its meanings. She began a session talking about one of her bosses. She didn't know this boss well and had recently informed her of her departure. Alison was surprised by her boss's genuine and spontaneous interest in her plans. Alison was always surprised when people took an interest in her. She then spoke about Robert, listing all the evidence supporting his lack of true devotion to her. She briefly considered whether she was making it so. She remarked, "He can't be close to anyone. He's caught between two worlds. He needs someone who he feels is a lot like him." I neglected to interpret what might be her need to be with someone who is like her. I reflected that perhaps she wished not to be important to anyone and that they not be important to her, allowing her to leave with no regrets. She responded immediately: "Do you think this is because I was adopted? My mother held me in her arms when I was an infant, but do you think there is something biological that doesn't allow me to attach or feel close?" and she burst into tears for the first time. She associated to people always thinking she was African, especially when she was in Africa. She asked, "Will this all affect my future relationships—my need and desire to live in my native country, my feelings of acceptance there?"

A year later she returned for a visit home and came to see me although there had been no contact in between, except for a payment and a note: "I'm fine—will write soon." She did not write. When she came to the session, she was happy to see me and spontaneously hugged me at our reunion. She talked about her continuing fears that she would somehow fail at her job, that she would be punished for leaving her mother. She began to examine what she called "self-sabotage": pushing others away by acting "elitist." She tended to socialize with African teachers and students, rather than with the American group with whom she came. She wondered if she especially rejected the white teachers because she, too, had always felt left out. She felt special, the only foreign teacher treated as a native. In some ways, it was the fulfillment of a dream, she said. She described a new romantic relationship with a young Caucasian man who was finishing his teaching commitment and returning to the United States. She wondered if once again she was reversing an abandonment: leaving him before he left her. "Am I trying to avoid mourning him?" she said. Her parents had grown increasingly accepting of her career choice because she had not lost touch, keeping in close contact through e-mail and a visit from them and to them. She felt they had a growing sense of pride in her accomplishment. At this point, increasingly self-observant, she questioned her motivations and feelings in a more active way as she continued to define herself and become more authentically herself.

DISCUSSION

Erikson (1956, 57) defines identity as a "persistent sameness within oneself . . . and a persistent sharing of some kind of essential characteristics with others." The formation of identity requires a process of identification with both parents to take place. Identity integrates the organization of the self and comprises multiple early identifications. Internalization (the process by which aspects of early relationships with primary objects are preserved by making them part of the self); identification (an unconscious process in which one "modifies his motives and behavior patterns and the self representations corresponding to them . . . to experience being like, the same as or merged with . . . one or more representations of that object" [Schafer 1990, 179]); and the establishment of identity (the ongoing experience of the self as a unique, coherent entity) are complex, if not impossible tasks for the adopted child who is both racially different from her adoptive parents and who was deprived of an ongoing actual relationship with her birth parents. How can one feel a "persistent sameness" when one feels so very different from one's family? Naturally, Alison's identifications with her adoptive parents were more highly developed than those with her birth parents because she was raised by them. She also worked consciously to create identifications with her birth parents in a number of ways, including through her studies and career choice. But one wonders if these identifications could be as strong and useful for her since she had not known her birth parents, and since identification is largely an unconscious process that evolves from early interactions with the primary objects. The internalization of both sets of parents, and therefore the formation of Alison's identity, remained fluid and in process, which was natural at this stage of her development and was also an expression of the unique developmental struggles posed by her adoption.

The identity dilemma Alison presented at the beginning of the treatment can be viewed as a compromise formation for the complex conflicts surrounding being given up by one mother and taken by another who is racially different from herself. It was the story of Alison's inability to attach to either mother. In an attempt to identify with her biological mother in fantasy, Alison had to internalize a mother who would give a child away; hence there was an aloofness, a coldness, a detachment, and a shallowness to her emotions. Alison had to temper her attachments and become someone who could reject, who could let both her mothers go. She reenacted what happened to her and attempted to dis-identify with her adoptive mother, for example, by not being too emotional. Her rationality was a defense against being too much like her adoptive mother, whose emotions were scary, but at the same time, she could hold on to the cold mother, her biological mother, who could give her child away. Alison might frame it: "I am not important to my biological mother; she gave me away. My adoptive mother holds on to me only out of her own needs; if I fail to fulfill them, perhaps she, too, could let me go."

In the literature on adoption, the family romance, as it is played out in adoptive children, has been addressed by many authors (see Weider 1977; Glenn 1985; Kernberg 1985; Brodzinsky 1987; Hodges 1989). Weider discusses how difficult it is for the adopted child to get angry at the adoptive parents because of

the child's extreme dependency and fear of retaliation through a second abandonment (198). Alison's holding back her feelings of being different and her
worry about going to Africa and wounding her parents are illustrative of this
point. Kernberg discusses the difficulties for an adopted child in trying to be simultaneously the child of two sets of parents. Many adopted children will employ splitting of the introjected parental images into the good and bad parent.
Glenn describes this phenomenon in some adopted children who feel they have
two sets of "deceivers" and "deserters" (1985, 311). Bertocci and Schechter
(1991, 187) warn that "splitting needs to be differentiated from attempts to reconcile dichotomies, dissonances, and contradictions that are inherent in the
adoptive experience." At different times, Alison seemed to have made each
mother the bad mother, depriving herself of someone with whom to identify. In
Alison, we perhaps observe a combination of the more pathological splitting described by Kernberg and the adaptive kind discussed by Bertocci and Schechter.
When adoptive parents are also racially different from their children, more formidable challenges exist for the child. Weider suggests that one of the adoptive
child's resolutions of the family romance is to "establish a fantasized blood tie
to the adoptive parents, erasing the humiliation adoption implies" (1977, 199).
But that option was not available to Alison because of her racial differences. In
a 1985 study, Stein and Hoopes found that adopted children racially different
from their adoptive parents who searched for their birth parents tended to perceive themselves as more dramatically physically mismatched with their parents
than subjects who were not "searchers." Physical differences often intensified
identity concerns and the desire to locate birth parents. Alison may have inflated
the importance of physical difference because it was a taboo subject in her family. She also seemed to overemphasize her emotional mismatch with her mother,
as discussed earlier. While Alison denied looking for her birth mother, she was
searching for her "roots," and I often wondered if this substitute search would
end in Alison's seeking out her biological mother.

What of the identifications of Alison's mother with Alison and the conflicts
surrounding them? What are some of the challenges for the adoptive mother
of a racially different child? And how did Alison's mother negotiate first, being prevented from having a biological child because of her illness, and second, the arduous adoption process, including being rejected because of her
handicap? When a child is not biologically one's own and does not live up to
one's ideal, one might say, "Well, the child's not really mine." If the child
does live up to one's ideal or surpasses it, as Alison seemed to have done, one
might still say, "The child's not really mine," which can be a serious narcissistic injury for a mother. Alison might have been idealized by her mother,
representing both a narcissistic gratification and a narcissistic wound. Physically, Alison's mother could not see herself in Alison, and similarly, Alison

could not see herself in her mom's reflection. Alison's mother wanted a biological child and may have felt she was "settling for" an adopted child, that is, a child who was only second best (see Kupferman 2003; Bonovitz 2004). Because of her narcissistic defenses, Alison's mother may have needed a child more similar to herself. Likewise, Alison seemed to have wished for a mother more similar to her, intellectually and physically, and her disappointment may have been felt by her mother as a deep rejection.

Some of Alison's narcissistic conflicts were demonstrated in her sense of being special, in her grandiosity and perfectionism. If she was not the best, she gave up. A sequela of her adoptive experience might have been a sense of defect, of feeling the opposite of perfect, and she might have used her perfectionism as a defense, shutting down before risking failure or disappointment. Or she might have feared the kind of success that could threaten her relationship to her mother by making her "better than" her mother. Alison saw her "mission" in Africa as superior to the motivations of others. She attempted to convert differences into uniqueness. Her view of herself as special masked the opposite: her feeling of being a child rejected by her mother as inferior, or worthless. Alison's narcissistic defenses served to protect her against feeling empty and not having a good maternal object.

Alison's dilemma was also enacted in the transference. I, too, am the Caucasian mother. Alison comes to me when she is leaving. She does not have to get close to me or become attached. She comes on the run, not stopping long enough to settle in to the work. She wonders if I, like her mom, will hold on or let go. At times she seems to want to make me a new mother who is different, who keeps her best interests in mind, who allows her to separate and individuate. She does not want to have to protect me or be angry at me; she wants a mother about whom she does not have to make a choice. Simultaneously, she comes toward me, then pushes me away. She almost sits on my lap, then becomes aloof and low-key. Two weeks before the end of our time together, she decides to go away for a week's vacation, distancing herself from both her mother and me, as if she must temper the intensity of our contact at this time. She leaves her jacket behind in my office; I suggest that this enactment reflects her mixed feelings about leaving. She is intrigued by this "slip," but because it is so early in the treatment process, she is not able to fully make use of this interpretation. In our last session, she tells me that she has given her mother a plane ticket to visit her while she is in Africa. I interpret this gesture as her wish to soften what she feels is her abandonment of her mother. Similarly with me, she tells me she will write and then come to see me when she returns in a year for a vacation. Her ambivalence is reflected in her need to both abandon and take care of us. It is also possible that these "gifts" express the wish for and beginning presence of an internal good mother.

My countertransference to Alison reflected her transference to me. I felt she was letting me go before "having" me; I felt as her mom and her boyfriend may have felt: abandoned before I abandoned her. I had a strong wish to help her "follow her heart," not be constricted by either mother, to separate, to be herself. I felt she sometimes induced in me a wish to be a better mother. I wanted to help her integrate and internalize her two mothers. I wanted to hear what was beneath her dilemma, to discover who she was inside. I felt frustrated by her thwarting my opportunity to help her complete the work she needed to do.

Exactly what part adoption played in this young woman's development is a complicated question. As I have suggested, Alison seemed unable to attach to either her adoptive or biological mother, resulting in a lack of depth in her intimate relationships. One wonders if some of these conflicts might have been alleviated had her adoptive parents confronted her differences early on and throughout her development. We observe some of the difficulties that can permeate a mother-child relationship when the mother is narcissistic, perhaps regardless of whether the child is biological or adopted. In Alison's situation, these conflicts may have been magnified because she was so unlike her mother. Neither saw the other in her own reflection; and neither could sufficiently identify with the other, creating narcissistic injury in both. Of course, physical and emotional mismatches can and do occur between biological mothers and children. However, both Alison and her mother seemed to feel a powerful sense of guilt about the fact of the adoption, creating a greater distance between them. The adoption was never discussed, and Alison's racial differences were denied. Alison's adoptive mother seemed threatened by the idea that Alison wished to find her biological mother; Alison felt she would betray her adoptive mother to do so. So much was not spoken. Alison continued to grapple with the separation-individuation process of adolescence and identity formation that appeared to be influenced, in part, by her adoption. How she used the facts of her adoption in her developing sense of self might have been a unique variation of a familiar journey. Her physical appearance labeled her as different from her family, signaling to the outside world that she was adopted. Additionally, she and her family denied her differences, so the process of solidifying her identity had been arduous. Alison's mission to embrace and internalize her two mothers was impressive. She discovered a means to identify with and feel close to her biological mother through embracing her native culture and appreciating her first home and the world of her mother. Hopefully, this move toward identification with her first mother will be gradually integrated with her internalization of her adoptive mother as Alison continues the journey of separation-individuation.

APPLICATION TO CLINICAL PRACTICE

While this treatment was brief and unfinished, it left a deep impression. The knowledge I had accumulated from years of working with children and young adults did not provide me with sufficient understanding of this young woman's experience of growing up "different." The experience was difficult to assess because it had happened in the past, and Alison was either unaware of it or could not remember much of it. Fortunately, she came to me at a time of transition, when I had a special opportunity through our work together to consider a part of the profound impact of the adoption process upon an individual racially and culturally different from her adoptive family. But the treatment raised more questions in my clinical work than it answered.

Having a child who is physically very different from the parents imposes conditions on both the child and the parents that need to be understood and addressed internally. We as clinicians need to find pathways for easing the potentially painful and complicated experiences of adoptive families. We need to help parents comprehend and appreciate their child's unique experiences. In addition, attention needs to be paid to acknowledging the child's place of origin and to some extent the culture of that place. The degree to which the child's background needs to be addressed is best decided through the parents' observations and understanding of what it may mean for their particular child. We have been taught to always listen to the child, to shape our responses and be guided by the child's individual needs, yet a great deal of the popular literature on adoption—books for both parents and children—tends to generalize, sometimes diluting complicated situations or giving formulaic advice, and it can gloss over what is painful about adoption.

For instance, parents of adopted children may encourage their children to find their birth parents, yet there is insufficient research demonstrating the wisdom of this endeavor in all cases. Motivations for these searches are complex and may not always be in the child's best interests. The reunions may be healing, disappointing, or even devastating. The parents' motivation for helping their child find her birth mother might be an attempt to erase the child's loss or their own. Some parents discourage such a search. In Alison's case, her mother read Alison's wish to teach in Africa as Alison's desire to find her birth mother, and she wanted to stop her. But this may have been a misreading or a premature and disruptive insight for Alison, and so it created dissonance between the two. Alison experienced her mother's idea as an intrusion and as a prohibition. It may have underscored her mother's sense of inferiority and heightened Alison's guilt. Alison's mother may have been responding to her own sense of loss in Alison's not having been a biological child, and to her feeling, perhaps, of not being "good enough" as a mother.

While Alison's "search" seems more disguised, she was in fact seeking to acquire an emotional connection to her birth mother. Still, what may have diluted her wish to actually locate her biological mother was her intense fear of hurting her adoptive mother and losing her love. Bertocci and Schechter (1991), in reviewing the literature about reunions with birth parents, found that the "searchers" were a self-selected group, usually Caucasian females whose relationships with their adoptive families seemed to improve when they had found their birth parents. For Alison, after so many years, to be able to share her feelings of isolation with her adoptive mother and to act upon her desire to work with people of her culture seemed to create a growing closeness and mutual understanding between her and her adoptive parents. It is important to note that Alison's search was self-motivated and not a product of parental intentions. Bertocci and Schechter discuss search behavior as representing the adopted child's becoming an "agent of change." Interestingly, Alison used that exact expression when she described her unique and different motivation for teaching abroad. Bertocci and Schechter believe that for some children, the search consolidates identity; it seems to have done this for Alison, enhancing her ability to separate and individuate.

But how can we as clinicians help parents and children who feel mismatched in physical and other traits to acknowledge both their differences and similarities and be attuned to one another? Alison's mother did not know that Alison felt different. Her sadness and remorse when Alison informed her that she had always felt different suggest this. Unconsciously, in order to feel closer to Alison and more alike, she may have needed to erase their differences. Perhaps her obliviousness to these differences also reflected her understandable maternal wish that Alison fit in and feel comfortable. In fact, on the surface Alison appeared to fit in beautifully: she was a star academically, socially, creatively. But a part of Alison lay dormant, and she longed to discover that part.

Alison's story raises other questions regarding the clinician's role in helping adoptive parents. We need to think carefully, observe, and discuss how and when to familiarize children with their native culture. We need humility in acknowledging our relative ignorance about what is best, and we need to try and find answers together with the parents about their unique child. We have all worked with parents who expose their child to the child's native culture on a regular basis by enrolling them in language and cultural programs from early childhood, going on visits to the child's country of origin, or having ongoing contact with their birth family. In contrast, there are parents like Alison's who tend to push the child's cultural heritage to the background, causing it to almost entirely disappear. What we know as clinicians working with parents and children is that a guiding principle in promoting development and growth is to encourage the parents to learn who their child really is in the child's uniqueness and specialness, and to help that child know their parents in a similar way. It's a formidable challenge for a parent to acknowledge a child's "roots" while simultaneously helping the child embrace the culture and community of the adoptive family. Our most important role as clinicians may be to help parents sort this out, that is, to somehow do both. We can accomplish this by encouraging parents to help their children be more in touch with their feelings about their differentness, rather than disavowing this important factor in their lives, and to help them incorporate these feelings into their self and object representations.

REFERENCES

Bertocci, Doris, and Marshall D. Schechter. 1991. "Adopted Adults' Perception of Their Need to Search: Implications for Clinical Practice." *Smith College Studies in Social Work* 61, no. 1 (March): 180–95.

Bonovitz, Christopher. 2004. "Unconscious Communication and the Transmission of Loss." *Journal of Infant, Child, and Adolescent Psychotherapy* 3, no. 1: 1–27.

Brodzinsky, David M. 1987. "Adjustment to Adoption: A Psychosocial Perspective." *Clinical Psychology Review* 7:25–47.

Erikson, Erik. 1956. "The Problem of Ego Identity." *Journal of the American Psychoanalytic Association* 4:121.

Glenn, Jules. 1985. "The Adopted Child's Self and Object Representations: Discussion of Dr. Kernberg's Paper." *International Journal of Psychoanalytic Psychotherapy* 11:309–13.

Hodges, Jill. 1989. "Aspects of the Relationship to Self and Objects in Early Maternal Deprivation and Adoption." *Bulletin of the Anna Freud Centre* 12:5–27.

Kernberg, Paulina. 1985. "Child Analysis with a Severely Disturbed Adopted Child." *International Journal of Psychoanalytic Psychotherapy* 11:277–99.

Kupferman, Kerstin. 2003. "'Empty Womb-Full Cradle': The Achievement of the Fullness of the Experience of Motherhood of the Adoptive Mother." In *The Inner World of the Mother*. Ed. Dale Mendell and Patsy Turrini. Madison, CT: Psychosocial Press, 227–43.

Schafer, Roy. 1990. *Aspects of Internalization*. Madison, CT: International Universities Press.

Stein, Leslie M., and Janet L. Hoopes. 1985. "Identity Formation in the Adopted Adolescent." New York: Child Welfare League of America.

Weider, Herbert. 1977. "The Family Romance Fantasies of Adoptees." *Psychoanalytic Quarterly* 46, no. 2: 1–22.

Chapter Eleven

The Plight of the Adoptee in Adult Life

A Case of Kinship Adoption

Cathy Siebold

More than a decade ago, James, a man in his midthirties, came to me for an initial consultation. Among the reasons he gave for wanting to begin psychotherapy was that he had just become a father. In that first interview, he expressed a fantasy that foreshadowed the central focus that adoption would take in our work together. He told me that until his child's conception, he had believed that he was unable to father a child. There was no physiological reason to think that he was sterile. Nevertheless, this was his belief. Now he was amazed, pleased, and worried by the birth of his child. Both he and I were curious about this conviction that he had held about his reproductive ability. There were many ways to understand his belief; for instance, James experienced himself as flawed. He came to believe that it was a way to identify with his adoptive parents, who had been unable to conceive. Moreover, he thought that it served as a connection with his adoptive father, who he felt had not loved or wanted him. For James, shame and blame were constant themes. He was flawed and could not be repaired. His being unable to create a child was one of the many beliefs that served to reinforce his feeling that, because he was adopted, he was damaged goods.

In therapy, James came to understand his early experience and the way that it influenced his feelings and behaviors as an adult. There were many factors that were significant to James's therapeutic course—issues that are similar even for many patients who are raised by their birth parents. Like all of us, James's affective development and defensive strategies were overdetermined. I will focus, however, on the constitutional and experiential factors related to his kinship adoption that influenced his capacity for affect regulation, and the false self that masked his shame and conflict about himself and his history. The transference and countertransference responses illuminate the transformative course of James's analytic experience.

163

ADULT ADOPTION AND SHAME: A LITERATURE REVIEW

Most psychoanalytic descriptions of patients who have been adopted are about children and adolescents. Few reports of adult analysands who have been adopted are available. Although the impact of adoption on an adult patient may be included in case descriptions focusing on other issues, a review of the psychoanalytic literature found only two reports emphasizing adoption as a factor in an adult patient's therapy. Similarly, kinship adoption has not received the attention of psychoanalytic writers. It is assumed that where adoption is within families, the adopted child may fare better (Nickman 2004). There is little published clinical evidence to support this notion. Additionally, some researchers suggest that the practice of kinship adoption has outpaced research on its benefits or limitations (Gleeson, O'Donnell, and Bonecutter 1997).

Ambrosio (2002) describes a kinship adoption where the oldest child of one sister was adopted by another sister because she was unable to conceive. Complicating this adopted woman's experience was the fact that both families continued to reside in the same building. Ambrosio suggests that in kinship adoption, Oedipal or triangular struggles may be impeded because of confusion about which family member the child belongs to. The patient in this case, Nina, seemed to be continually searching for a consistent attachment figure. Minerbo (2002), discussing this same case, suggests that the family secret of Nina's adoption further complicated the development of a cohesive self and object representation. Caparrotta (2003) presents a different adult adoption story. He describes a woman who at birth was given up for adoption. His patient left her hometown as a young adult, after giving up her own out-of-wedlock baby for adoption. Caparrotta sees the patient's actions as a continuing effort to escape her origins and to avoid developing a more realistic view of her birth mother and herself. The patient's transference reaction of wanting to terminate with him after his vacation was interpreted by Caparrotta as a repetition of the patient's wish to run away from knowing and being known. He suggests that his patient's efforts to avoid knowing that her analyst could not always be there for her, and that she could have angry feelings toward him, illustrated her wish to preserve an idealized view of herself and her birth mother.

These two case histories reflect the ways in which adoption may be a traumatic experience, resulting in distinct struggles for the adoptive child that may persist into adulthood. They are also consistent with the clinical literature about child analysis with adoptive children (Brinich 1980; Hodges 1989), which asserts that constitutional factors, the child's perceptions of adoption, and disruptions in caregivers during the adoptive process all stress the child's developmental course. Missing from the articles about adults who were adopted, yet relevant to the case I will present, is a discussion of the adoptive parents' impact. Adoptive parents may struggle to reconcile their feelings of inadequacy at being unable to conceive a child. The intrapsychic blow of being infertile and the repeated disappointment of attempting to conceive, if they are not in the conscious awareness of the adoptive couple, may impact their interactions with the adopted child (M. Schechter 1970).

Bonovitz (see chapter 2) notes the projective and asymmetrical influences of the adoptive parent on the child. He states that the adoptive parents' sense of loss related to an inability to conceive can be transmitted to the adopted child via the adoptive parents' projections and projective identifications. The adoptive parents' awareness of their response toward the birth parent is another way that the adoptive parents may affect the adopted child. Adoptive parents' capacity for empathy toward birth parents (Nickman 2004) and their ability to create an environment that allows children to come to know their origins have also been observed to influence adopted children's development (Brinich 1980).

Unlike the clinical literature, which understandably represents those adoptive children and parents who are struggling, the research literature about adoption's impact on adaptation is positive. Longitudinal studies of institutionalized children who were later adopted or returned to their birth parents (Hodges and Tizard 1989), and studies of twins separated at birth (Smyer et al. 1998), found that adopted children fare better in regard to education, employment, and in avoiding substance-abuse problems than do children in these cases who return to or remain with their birth families. Yet these same studies note increased emotional distress such as anxiety, depression, or alienation in children who are adopted. Researchers suggest that greater study of individuals who are adopted, and particularly their interpretation of meaning, might illuminate emotional difficulties associated with being adopted (Smyer et al. 1998).

As is demonstrated by this brief review of the literature about kinship and adult adoption and the response of the adoptive parent, the adopted child's fate is to some extent dependent upon constitutional factors and experiences before adoption. But, it is also dependent upon the capacity of the adoptive parents to become aware of their unconscious feelings and fantasies related to adoption. As with any trauma, it is the repetition of painful experience and the lack of any intervention that take a toll on the internal world of the developing child. Efforts to adapt often lead to future emotional and relational struggles (Russell 1998). Moreover, the real loss of and perceived or real rejection by the natural parents compound the experience with the adoptive parent, and serve as a potential source of devaluation of the self, or shame (Ambrosio 2002; Caparrotta 2003).

Because adoption can be a traumatic event and because adopted children and adults may perceive adoption as a stigma, or defect of the self, shame may be particularly relevant to understanding adoption. Shame has increasingly been identified as a significant affect in the psychoanalytic literature. Simply put, shame is a feeling directed toward who one is, whereas guilt is a feeling that is directed toward an act. Shame is a passive experience in response to rejection or external trauma, whereas guilt is an active effort to adapt to or compensate for conflicted desires. Like guilt, the underlying source of shame is unconscious. Lynd (1958) also suggests that shame may manifest itself as a state of "aimless anxiety."

Some psychoanalysts have emphasized shame as part of Oedipal development. Others have emphasized the impact of shame throughout development and as an important part of the analytic process. Caparrotta's (2003) account of an adopted adult emphasizes Oedipal shame, and is consistent with D. Schechter's (1979) and Lansky's (2003) view of shame as an affect associated with the *ego ideal*. The ego ideal is the idealized view of who one should be. It is further described as a component of the superego, the psychic structure that in classic theory develops during the Oedipal phase. Shame has been increasingly described as a significant affect that is not limited to one phase of development. Nor is it seen solely as an intrapsychic process. Lewis (1971), for example, suggests that shame is an unconscious response to feeling rejected, criticized, and abandoned by the self and others. She was among the first to assert that shame is a deeply hidden, but pervasive, emotion. More recently, Morrison (1986) suggests that shame is associated with a sense of defect about the *ideal self*. Although similar to the ego ideal, the ideal self is the subjective sense of who one wants to be that evolves during development. The experience of shame leads to defensive strategies to hide or camouflage one's sense of defect. In psychoanalysis, shame may be evidenced by the patient's efforts to hide information (Morrison 1986) or his or her attempts to become like the analyst (Caparrotta 2003).

Because adoptive parents have their own struggles with a sense of defect at having been unable to conceive and because they may have conflicted feelings toward the birth parents, adoptive parents may transmit their sense of shame or defect to their adopted children (see chapter 2). Adoptive parents who are unconscious of their own sense of defect may negatively impact the child's self and object representations. The adopted child is also vulnerable to responses from outside the nuclear family. The cultural attitudes and stigma that may be attributed to adoption (Lynd 1958) can also be internalized by the child as a defect or flaw.

What follows is a description of the decade-long treatment of James, and the way that shame and hiding were important aspects of the therapeutic action. Initially, the therapy was conducted once weekly, and face to face. After several years, there was a conversion to the couch. Although there are many ways to think about and understand James's struggles, I will focus on repetitions of experiences with parental figures and the secrecy surrounding James's kinship adoption. As James became aware of his pattern of repetition, he became increasingly aware of the false self that obscured or camouflaged his shame and fear of exposure.

THE CASE HISTORY

James entered treatment with me during his thirties because of continuing anxiety and unhappiness with his career and relationships. He also had concerns about his capacity to be a good parent. His birth mother's brother and sister-in-law had adopted him at age two and one-half. James's biological father was married and uninvolved in the birth or adoption process. James was not sure if his was a premature birth, but he knew that his birth weight was low. During infancy, James was placed in an orphanage twice. In his first stay, he was diagnosed with *mirasmus*, which he was told improved when he came home to his adoptive mother. *Mirasmus*, or failure to thrive, has been associated with anaclitic depression. James's response to being separated from his birth mother suggests a need for the object that was inadequately met in the orphanage. The second admission to the orphanage occurred after James had lived with his adoptive parents for about two years. He was placed in the orphanage the second time because his birth mother had doubts about relinquishing him for adoption.

According to James, his adoptive parents told him at a very early age that he was adopted. He thought he was about four. Although James was told that he was adopted, he was not told his birth mother's identity until after her death, at which time James was in his early twenties. He remembered his adoptive parents telling him that they had chosen him from all the other children at the orphanage. He was special and wanted by them. James did not think that as a child he had any idea that his birth mother was a member of his adoptive family. He also reported that his cousins, as children, were not told that he was adopted. James remembered worrying as a little boy. His adoptive father's response was to criticize or belittle him for worrying. His adoptive mother might listen, but she denied that he had anything to worry about. One source of concern that he remembered was his anxiety that his father did not like him. He described many experiences of asking to do things with his father and being told no. James felt that he was criticized for not being the son that his father wanted. He tried to share his father's interests, but he wasn't successful. When he tried to speak with his adoptive mother about his father, she responded by talking about her disappointment with her marriage, or denied James's perceptions of his father.

As James became older, his efforts to capture his adoptive father's attention turned to resentment. He never felt able to express these feelings directly. Instead, he would sit seething about something his father had said. When James was a teen, there were a few instances of getting into trouble, using drugs, for example, but his own sense of remorse and fear of what might happen to him helped contain his impulse to act out. His adoptive parents' response to his getting in trouble was to talk with him about the consequences of his behavior. As he remembered it, they seemed genuinely concerned about the effect of his actions on his future. They "grounded" him for using drugs, but the tone of their interaction was one of concern that he not ruin his life. James's school performance was average. He believed that he should be content to work in civil service as his adoptive father and uncles had. Upon completing college, he took a position as a civil servant in a state agency overseeing data analysis, and he rose to a supervisory position. He never enjoyed his job. James thought about pursuing an advanced degree, but he also thought that he could not succeed.

James believed that his adoptive father did not want him. He also believed that his extended adoptive family didn't want him. His was a fairly large, French-Canadian family. James felt that he was always trying to make friends with them, but was never welcomed. Because he did not know about the identity of his birth mother, he believed their response to him was because he was adopted and not a legitimate member of the family. His birth mother did not attend family events, even though most of them were with his adoptive father's family. Her absence may have been one way that the family was able to keep his birth mother's identity a secret from James. After his birth mother died and he was told her and his birth father's identity, James never contacted his birth father. Although James was curious about his birth father, he refrained from contacting him. James assumed, because of his birth father's lack of involvement, that he wouldn't want to be contacted.

When James was a young adult, his adoptive father died from complications associated with alcohol abuse. At that point in his life, James was living with a divorced woman, M, and her children. He did not remember grieving over his adoptive father's death. It had been a lengthy illness, and James had felt relieved for his adoptive mother. He continued to have phone contact with his adoptive mother, but never spent much time with his family after high school. At the time of his father's death, he was preoccupied with his relationship with M. He reported that he never felt that his relationship with M was "going anywhere." He finally ended the relationship with M and moved to another town. After that he had a series of confusing and disappointing relationships, and he decided to become a member of Alcoholics Anonymous (AA). At the time he started seeing me, he was married to H, and the couple had just had a child. H knew that James was adopted, but his friends and colleagues did not.

SECRETS: THEIR EMERGENCE
IN THE THERAPEUTIC PROCESS

As James told me his life story during the first year or two of therapy, it evoked many speculations about the impact of his adoption, and about the way that he may have reenacted the abandonments and secrets of his early history during his adult life. In those first years, there were few opportunities to explore the meaning of James's experience because of the continual crises that were occurring in his day-to-day life. I believed that these crises, such as having a negative interaction with a colleague, were ways James used to defend against knowing himself—a resistance to the therapeutic process. His continual anxiety also reminded me of his description of himself as a young boy, always worrying that something terrible was happening.

As Schafer (1983) notes, the transference is the repetition of something old, but it is also something new. The therapeutic process is transformative because the patient experiences old feelings and experiences with a new object who responds in new ways to the patient's distress. For example, learning that James when he was a young boy was always afraid something was wrong, and that his adoptive mother would always dismiss his concerns, led me to believe that it was important to listen to James's concerns rather than confront the defensive aspects of his behavior. Providing a holding environment in which James could experience someone who would tolerate his anxiety and listen empathically to his distress created a secure base from which we could begin to explore James's construction of his history and the transference-countertransference responses (Bowlby 1984; Siebold 1999).

Initially, James perceived his difficulties as being the result of his inability to mourn the death of his adoptive father. He had been in a previous therapy where this had been the focus of his and the therapist's attention. Despite their efforts, however, sadness about his adoptive father's death seemed elusive. In

those first years of therapy with me, James continued to talk about his difficulties with his father. He revealed numerous episodes where he felt rejected
by his adoptive father. One poignant story was of him hanging on to the door
asking his father not to go out. His father ignored him and kept going. There
were many other stories of experiences with his father and experiences with
children in his neighborhood, which all had a theme of James being attacked,
belittled, or abandoned. There was a disconnect, however, between the content of the stories and the affect with which James told them. The stories were
sad, pathetic. The tone in which they were told was intellectualized.

I wondered about James's absence of sadness regarding his adoptive father's death, and the lack of sadness for himself when talking about his childhood experiences. Although I might wonder aloud at the absence of affect, it
did not seem to help James or me to better understand him. James had always
thought that there was something wrong with him. He just didn't know what
it was. He also said that he didn't feel that he knew who he was or what he
wanted to be. He hoped that therapy would give him a better understanding
of himself. Talking about his adoptive father's death, however, did not allevi-
ate these concerns. As time went on, I wondered about the absence of any discussion of his adoptive mother. Periodically, I asked James questions about
his adoptive mother, but he rarely volunteered any information. When asked,
he would describe her as "needy." She wanted his attention and was very
present in his life, but was unsympathetic to his concerns. The absence of discussion about his adoptive mother seemed to me to be an important omission.
I also believed that pressing James to talk about her would reenact through
me his early experience of being with a woman who had her own agenda. I,
too, would then be ignoring his concerns about his relationship with his adoptive father. At that time, however, my thought was to stay empathic to his experience and wait for other opportunities to explore his feelings about, and
memories of, his adoptive mother, particularly as they might be manifested in
the transference.

Concomitant with James's stories about his early experiences were his efforts to see how I was responding to him. In our sessions, he would watch to
see my response and he would ask what I thought was wrong with him. My
countertransference response was to feel uncomfortable at his scrutiny. At
times I felt pushed away by his questions. It wasn't that I felt attacked, but
rather that I felt overwhelmed by his need. At the same time, I felt empathic
to his need for reassurance. Yet, I wasn't quite sure what response would be
helpful. How could I know who he was and what he wanted to be? I felt inadequate. Since I believed that my feelings told me something about myself
but also about James, at times I responded to James by reflecting his feeling
of being overwhelmed, helpless, and unable to make his life better. At other

times, I would offer to him that perhaps his anxiety about me was connected to the uncertainty of his early childhood experiences, particularly with his two mothers. It seemed to me that being adopted and the disruptions that had occurred during his early life were important experiences for James. I wondered aloud, "Might I abandon him in the way that his birth mother and adoptive mother had during the first thirty months of his life?" Alternatively, I said, "Might I deny his feelings and needs as his adoptive mother had?" James would agree that these were interesting ideas, but his agreement seemed more an effort to please me, a manifestation of the false self, rather than some conviction of his own. Similarly, my attempts to explore the discomfort he experienced in telling me his story were met with polite attention, even agreement, but little affective resonance.

It was through his descriptions of current extratransferential occurrences that James began to be able to talk about and experience the shame and self-loathing that were defended against by the false self that he presented to the world. One example of this was James's repeated attempts to gain his supervisor's praise. Despite many experiences of seeking approval and being "shot down" by his supervisor, he continued to try to get a different outcome. In one session, he spoke with me about asking his supervisor for a review of his performance. We explored his past experiences, and the likelihood that he would be disappointed in his efforts. When he came in with his report, he was visibly upset and had to review what the evaluation said, and what had transpired between him and his supervisor. As I heard him recite what was written, there actually were some positives. There were criticisms, but overall it was a balanced review of his work. This incident gave James and me an opportunity to examine his feelings and the strength of those feelings. He began to think about the way that first, he asked for help from someone who resented his request, and second, he heard only the negative aspects of the report. It was as if he expected to be "vilified" by anyone whose opinion he desired.

James had wanted his father's approval, but had felt rejected by him. Now his supervisor was another man whose approval he sought. He was being criticized, but in this contemporary situation, James began to recognize that he was also influencing the interactions. He was not just at the mercy of the other person. This insight was the first of many insights into the way that James anticipated and sometimes set himself up to be humiliated and criticized. The words he used to describe himself were ones such as *wretch* and *bastard*. And his use of words like *humiliated* and *shamed* to capture the feelings he conveyed to me resonated with him. It no longer sounded as if he were giving a lecture on the subject of supervisor-supervisee relations. As he was able to experience his shame in relation to others, James began to feel able to acknowledge his concerns about being criticized by me. He watched for it, but he could see no signs of it happening. But since he felt criticized by so many people, my not doing so must be deliberate. As James stated it, 'he assumed I didn't criticize him because telling him the truth wouldn't be therapeutic.'

James seemed to expect criticism even when it wasn't forthcoming. Reflecting on my countertransference at that time in the therapy, I recognized that I felt perplexed and concerned by rather than critical of James's needs. One way I used this understanding was to suggest that perhaps James's supervisor and his father had many feelings toward him. Some might be critical, but some might be concerned. Because keeping something from him would be consistent with his experience of secrecy in his adoptive family, I also offered to James the interpretation that given his experience, it was understandable that he would believe that I, too, was keeping secrets from him. The continuing exploration and experience of feelings with regard to James's supervisor and his father as well as James's increasing ability to share those feelings with me were one aspect of the transformative processes that occurred in therapy. James found himself feeling less anxious and less concerned about seeking approval from others. His interactions with me became more reflective and less concerned about how I thought he was doing. At this point, James asked about using the couch. He and I discussed his feelings about it, ultimately deciding to convert to the couch. This conversion seemed to facilitate James's ability to focus internally, and to encourage the emergence of new information and new ways of thinking.

As James was able to speak more freely, he was also better able to explore his transference responses. As I have already noted, in the first years of the treatment, James continually asked for reassurance, and scrutinized my reactions to him. When I explored his requests and reactions, he talked about his expectation that I would tell him he was too difficult, too unanalyzable, and too defective; like his father, I might criticize and reject him. James's expectation that I would criticize him was clear, and present from early in the therapy. There were also infrequent occasions when he would dismiss comments made by me that were intended to suggest a more balanced or benign view of his actions.

For example, there were times when he would berate himself for his past experiences with lovers. He expressed feeling that he had been cruel or mean to them. These relationships were complicated and seemed to repeat his experiences of feeling criticized by his adoptive father or unheard by his adoptive mother. But his response to me was also illuminating. In one discussion about an ex-lover, I offered to James that it seemed as if he had not always been kind to his lover, but he also did not seem to think that he might have had a right to leave her. It also seemed that he did not think that this woman might have had a part to play in what happened. His response to my intervention was to talk about how terrible he was, and that I was just being a nice social worker. His intonation was dismissive. As we explored responses such as this one, we became more cognizant of James's need to push away my efforts to be a good object. James was affirmed in his perception of badness. By discrediting my words, he sustained his perception of his badness. He was adopted and that meant he was flawed. Perhaps I, too, was flawed because I couldn't quite get how defective he was.

Preserving his sense of badness was one aspect of dismissing my words, but it also served to create distance from me. In my experience of having my words dismissed, I felt pushed away by James. Feeling pushed away caused me to wonder if his response might also be associated with a fear of intimacy. His action toward me was aggressive, but it also served to protect against connection. As we explored his reactions to me, James also began to examine his relationships with women. James had a pattern of becoming involved with women who pursued him. The women determined the course of the relationship. As James saw it, he was a passive participant. He would then become unhappy in these relationships, believing that his needs were not being met, or perceiving the women as being too critical. James's sentiments about his lovers were similar to those that he used to describe his experience with his adoptive mother. In the transference, James was potentially rejecting me for being too demanding, for asking him to explore more than he felt able to. But his rejection of me also served to protect him from intimacy and being known by me.

I pointed out to James the possible dual nature of his action. In rejecting my more benign view of his actions, he was dismissing my words—an assertive act. But he was also rejecting my effort to understand him—an avoidance of intimacy. Interpretations such as this one allowed James to talk about his fears of needing me or of letting me know his feelings toward me. Concomitantly, he began to explore his feelings about his two mothers. The initial loss of his birth mother was a traumatic event, leading to the *mirasmus*. It was his adoptive mother's love and attention that then alleviated his failure to thrive. Being abandoned by a woman, James had learned, could lead to near death. Being rescued by a woman could restore life. As we considered his early experience, it seemed to us that this dual perception might be frightening to him. Women were powerful. They could save you, but then they could reject and leave you. Certainly his contemporary reactions to me and to other women suggested a need to protect himself by re-creating an experience of disappointment by dismissing our importance to him.

Acknowledging his desire for intimacy, particularly in relation to me, and talking about his fears of connection to others seemed to help James become more receptive to letting me in as a good object. He also began reporting greater satisfaction with his marriage. As James became aware of his fears of women, his relationship with his adoptive mother also changed. He could acknowledge her commitment to him. His interactions with her became less argumentative. He felt grateful to her for what she did do, as he also recognized her need to focus on herself.

Within the context of this growing awareness of his thoughts and feelings about his adoptive parents and about me emerged an increasing ability to share secrets with me. One way James was able to recognize hidden, shameful aspects of himself was by examining his participation in AA. Initially, James reported that being a member of AA was helpful to him. Yet as he discussed his experiences in AA, they began to sound similar to his descriptions of his experiences with his extended family. He wanted to be part of the group, but he never felt accepted by them. The more he talked about his reasons for joining, the more he questioned his participation. He joined AA because he knew a number of people who attended. In some ways, it felt like a family to him. At the same time, James felt that he had to keep secrets from the other AA members. He revealed to me that although he drank, he never drank much. Listening to other members' stories led him to feel that his own stories were insignificant.

As he elaborated his thoughts and feelings about AA, James began to think about the way that he perpetuated feeling unimportant and small by being a member of AA. Their method of exposing a person's failings seemed to confirm his feeling of being flawed. At the same time, he realized that his participation in AA was complicated. It allowed him to protect himself from becoming like his father. It also served as a way to continue his connection with his father. And the rule of anonymity that he kept for other AA members reminded him of the secretive way that his adoptive family had dealt with his adoptive father's drinking and James's kinship adoption. As we continued to explore James's feelings and thoughts about participating in AA, he described feeling like a pretender in the group. He made up stories about binges that never occurred, and then felt ashamed for being dishonest. It was painful to pretend to be something that he was not, but he also did not feel that he knew who he was supposed to be. He recognized that he was always trying to be somebody, even if it felt like a false identity.

Although James was willing to let people think that he was an alcoholic, he told no one that he was adopted. As James became better able to acknowledge the false identity that he had taken on by being a member of AA, I interpreted to him that perhaps having a false identity was somehow safer than acknowledging his identity as an adopted child. This was another way that we began to talk about his sense of shame about being adopted and about his family. James felt flawed. His adoptive parents were also flawed because of alcoholism and financial struggles. He was a bastard, and his birth mother had been a pathetic person. Conveying his thoughts and shameful feelings to me seemed to encourage James to become more decisive about who he was. One way that this occurred was through his decision not to continue to participate in the club in which he had never been a member: he decreased and finally ended his attendance at AA meetings. Several years later, there was no evidence to suggest that drinking was or ever would be a problem.

Secrets and the shameful affect that they served to defend against continued to emerge. Episodically, James would take me by surprise. He would introduce new information as if it were a known fact. In his first few sessions with me, James had revealed that he was adopted and that it was a kinship adoption. It was not until five years later that he talked about his birth mother's continued interaction with him. In the middle of one session, James mentioned that his birth mother had lived upstairs from his future adoptive parents for the first few years of his life. My immediate response was that this was an important piece of information that I had never heard before. I felt surprised. Thinking about it in that moment, I felt sure that we had not talked about this before. It also seemed to me that this was not the first time that James had told me something that left me feeling surprised.

In that session, I told James that I did not believe that I had known about his birth mother living nearby during his early life. It came as a surprise to me, I said. James's response was curiosity about the fact that I had not known this. He could not remember telling me, but he could not remember not telling me. It also seemed to me that he experienced my questions about this new information as a critique, giving us another opportunity to talk about his perception that he was always in the wrong. In future sessions, we were able to continue to explore the meaning of this new information and the way that he had presented it to me. For example, we both suspected that his taking me by surprise might have been a re-creation of his own experience of surprise at learning his birth mother's identity.

Through a process of renovation (Edward 1986), James and I were able to think about the way that having his birth mother's identity kept secret from him seemed to have led to a repetition of this and other secrets about himself. It also provided additional ways to understand his conflicted relationships with women. James believed and had been told by his adoptive mother that she was the one who wanted to adopt him. James's birth mother had been reluctant to release him for adoption. When James first came to live in his future adoptive parents' home, his birth mother lived upstairs. She would come down to the apartment where James lived with his future adoptive parents, and take James upstairs. James's adoptive mother didn't feel that she could stop her sister-in-law because James wasn't legally hers.

It seems reasonable to assume that James's low birth weight and his lengthy absences from either his birth or his adoptive mother during infancy were contributing factors in James's feelings of anxiety. Thinking in terms of the transmission of unconscious conflict by the birth or adoptive parents that Bonovitz (see chapter 2) has identified, this suggests that James's capacity for affect regulation was further complicated by his early experience with these two mothers. For the first two and one-half years of his life, James's future adoptive mother was anxious about whether she would be allowed to keep him, and his birth mother was sad that she would be forced to relinquish him. James received intermittent attention and care from both these women. Through a process of projective identification, James may have taken on their feelings of anxiety and loss, which may have been another contributing factor in his inability to regulate his anxiety or feel good about himself. The unpredictability of James's relationships with these two women may also have fostered uncertainty in regard to his self and object representations.

James's extended family pressured his birth mother until she agreed to sign the documents that would release James to be adopted by her brother and sister-in-law. After the adoption, James's birth mother moved away and rarely saw him. Whether James had any reaction to her departure was unknown to him. We can only guess that it made his adoptive mother more important, and more dangerous. She was more important because she was there; she was more dangerous because she, too, could one day disappear. James could also associate these ideas to his experiences with lovers. He became involved with women who, like his adoptive mother, demonstrated that they wanted him. He avoided situations with women where he was unsure of their interest. Despite feeling wanted by the women he became involved with, he continued to be uncertain of their feelings for him and his feelings for them. Was he thus preserving with lovers his anxiety and uncertainty regarding who he was and who they were? Who wanted him, and who did he want?

Although kinship adoption is perceived as less damaging to the child, James's experience suggests that this is not always so. The benefit of being adopted by a family member, in this case, was obviated by the secrecy and shame surrounding the identity of James's birth mother and her continued presence in his life. As he and I reconstructed the story, James's birth mother never wanted to give him up. She was forced to do so by her French-Canadian family. Although James was not blamed directly for the circumstances of his birth, his being an out-of-wedlock child was probably culturally perceived by his extended family, and perhaps by his adoptive father, as a shameful event and a stigma.

As James pursued his perceptions of his birth mother's story and internalized my empathic view of her (Brinich 1980), he began to express the belief that being forced to give him up had been a continuing source of sadness for his birth mother. He remembered visits to his birth mother, where she seemed to be watching him. He described the experience of being watched as seeming odd, but he did not remember feeling uncomfortable. His birth mother could be thought of as an ambiguous figure—her intentions uncertain. As he thought about his experience of being watched, however, James reconstructed it to mean that his birth mother had loved him and never wanted to give him up. As he reconstructed his adoption story, there was a concomitant emergence of his true self.

Instead of asking me how he would ever know what he wanted from life, James began to make decisions and do things that he enjoyed. For example, he finally took a painting class. James also began to experience greater enjoyment in being a husband and parent. Rather than worrying that he would fail his son, he tried to recognize negative feelings that he was vulnerable to projecting onto his son. He used such insights to change his behavior toward his son. Further transformations were evidenced by changes in his interactions with his family and friends. When James first began therapy, his activities focused on work or AA meetings. Over the years, his behavior changed. He expressed, and acted on, a greater desire to be with his family. He shared with some friends the fact that he was adopted. Learning to tolerate the sadness of what could never be and the uncertainty of what could never be known—as he recognized what his adoptive mother attempted to provide—allowed James to experience and express his feelings of love to those who provided him with emotional connection: his family, friends, and analyst.

CONCLUSION

The plight of the adopted child as an adult has received limited attention in the psychoanalytic literature. Researchers suggest that adoption is less of a developmental stressor than other factors (i.e., Hodges and Tizard 1989; Smyer et al. 1998). Yet, these same studies also suggest that anxiety, depression, relationship difficulties, and identity conflict are more likely to affect adopted children and adults. In this chapter, we have explored the therapeutic course of an adult male who, as he became conscious of the shame and disavowal of his adoption, was able to experience a reduction in anxiety and a greater integration in his sense of self. Moreover, he became less isolated from others and invested himself in relationships with family and friends. James's therapeutic experience raises questions about the lack of attention to the long-term difficulties of adopted adults.

In particular, James's kinship adoption and the secrecy surrounding it led to a repetition of that secrecy when James became an adult. Secrets such as the one James's family kept are not anomalies, however, and they continue to negatively impact children in contemporary society (see chapter 8). In James's case, his adoptive parents protected the secret of his origins until he was an adult. It also appears that they had little empathy for his birth mother. It seems reasonable to assume that adopted adult patients in analytic therapies may experience unconscious shame that leads to hiding and disguising aspects of the self. Acknowledging the significance of adoption in such patients' emotional development, and exploring their possibly unconscious sense of defect and shame about the self, is one way that therapists might mitigate the long-term plight of the adult adoptee.

For James, the therapeutic process of being listened to with curiosity and empathy in regard to his perceptions that he was flawed and a fake allowed him to begin to share information about himself that he had kept hidden. As these secrets were revealed, feelings of shame were also uncovered and shared in the therapeutic relationship. The reenactments, renovations, and new object experiences that occurred in the transference and countertransference were further aspects of the transformative process that allowed James to begin to experience the true self that had been compromised from infancy.

REFERENCES

Ambrosio, G. 2002. "The Analyst at Work: Nina." *International Journal of Psychoanalysis* 83:1233–37.

Bonovitz, C. 2004. "Unconscious Communication and the Transmission of Loss." *Journal of Infant, Child, and Adolescent Psychotherapy* 3:1–27.

Bowlby, J. 1984. "Psychoanalysis as a Natural Science." *Psychoanalytic Psychology* 1:7–21.

Brinich, P. M. 1980. "Some Potential Effects on Self and Object Representation." *Psychoanalytic Study of the Child* 35:107–34.

Caparrotta, L. 2003. "Oedipal Shame, Rejection, and Adolescent Development." *American Journal of Psychoanalysis* 63:345–52.

Edward, J. 1986. "The Renovative Aspect of Psychoanalytic Reconstruction in Psychotherapy." *Clinical Social Work Journal* 14:52–65.

Gleeson, J. P., J. O'Donnell, and F. J. Bonecutter. 1997. "Understanding the Complexity of Practice in Kinship Foster Care." *Child Welfare* 76, no. 6:801–27.

Hodges, J. 1989. "Aspects of the Relationship to Self and Objects in Early Maternal Deprivation and Adoption." *Bulletin of the Anna Freud Centre* 12:5–27.

Hodges, J., and B. Tizard. 1989. "IQ and Behavioral Adjustment of Ex-institutional Adolescents." *Journal of Child Psychology and Psychiatry* 30:76–97.

Lansky, M. R. 2003. "The 'Incompatible Idea' Revisited: The Oft-Invisible Ego-Ideal and Shame Dynamics." *American Journal of Psychoanalysis* 63:365–73.

Lewis, H. B., ed. 1971. *Shame and Guilt in Neurosis*. New York: International Universities Press.

Lynd, H. M. 1958. *On Shame and the Search for Identity*. New York: Harcourt Brace and World.

Minerbo, V. 2002. "A Hypothetical Reconstruction Unveiling a Family Secret." *International Journal of Psychoanalysis* 82:1242–45.

Morrison, A. P. 1986. *Shame, Ideal Self, and Narcissism*. In *Essential Papers on Narcissism*. Ed. A. P. Morrison. New York: New York University Press.

Nickman, S. 2004. "The Holding Environment in Adoption." *Journal of Infant, Child, and Adolescent Psychotherapy* 3, no. 3:329–41.

Russell, P. 1998. "The Role of Paradox in the Repetition Compulsion." In *Trauma, Repetition, and Affect Regulation: The Work of Paul Russell*. Ed. J. G. Teicholz and D. Kriegman. New York: The Other Press.

Schafer, R. 1983. *The Analytic Attitude*. New York: Basic Books.

Schechter, D. 1979. "The Loving and Persecuting Superego." *Contemporary Psychoanalysis* 15:361–79.

Schechter, M. D. 1970. *About Adoptive Parents*. In *Parenthood: Its Psychology and Psychopathology*. Ed. E. J. Anthony and T. Benedek. Boston: Little, Brown.

Siebold, C. 1999. *Vacation Breaks: Opportunities for Partings and Reunions*. In *The Social Work Psychoanalyst's Casebook: Clinical Voices in Honor of Jean Sanville*. Ed. J. Edward and E. Rose. Hillsdale, NJ: Analytic Press.

Smyer, M. A., M. Gatz, N. L. Simi, and N. L. Pederson. 1998. "Childhood Adoption: Long-Term Affects in Adulthood." *Psychiatry* 61:191–206.

Chapter Twelve

Loss, Belonging, Identity, and the Dynamics of an Adoptee's Identification with Her Birth Mother

Jeffrey Seinfeld

In this chapter I will discuss the treatment of a young adopted woman. The major theme will be the relationship between issues of adoption and infantile identification. Fairbairn (1941) introduced the concept of infantile identification as central to object relations theory. Fairbairn states that the original relationship to the object consists of the infant completely identifying with and incorporating the object. Infantile identification gradually gives way to a relationship based on differentiation and selective identification with the object. For Fairbairn, infantile identification is the infant's earliest means of dealing with separation anxiety. I will describe how a client, originally separated from her biological mother a few months after birth, responds to this loss through infantile identification. Though she has minimal contact with her birth mother in the first few years of life, she learns much about her and gradually develops a primitive connection to her that affects her identity formation. As will be described in this chapter, loss, belonging, and identity are key issues among adoptees. This chapter will demonstrate the relationship of those themes with the adoptee's identification with the birth mother.

As Brodzinsky, Schechter, and Marantz Henig (1993) point out, until a generation ago it was believed that there was little difference between adoption and being raised by the family one was born into. Since the 1960s, however, it has been recognized that adoption carries its own difficulties, although the research suggests adoption is better for the child than being brought up in foster care, an institution, or an ambivalent home. According to Brodzinsky, Schechter, and Marantz Henig, adoptees constitute a high percentage of children in outpatient therapy: 5 percent rather than the typical 1–2 percent, and 10–15 percent rather than the typical 1–2 percent in residential treatment and 6–9 percent of adopted children diagnosed by the school system as emotionally or neurologically impaired. The vast majority of adoptees are reportedly well-enough adjusted in adult life. The authors report that 85 percent of adoption placements are viewed as successful by family members and professionals. Nevertheless, adoption appears to be a risk factor in acting out for some children and adolescents.

When adoption does emerge as a problem in an adoptee's life, the most significant issue is a pervasive sense of loss. This theme underlies acting out, and school and interpersonal difficulties. At the same time, Brodzinsky, Schechter, and Marantz Henig (1993) point out that the children whose mothers registered them for adoption at birth but changed their mind and raised the children themselves did worse than adopted children. There are children who feel unwanted and abandoned by their biological parents, while others feel special, chosen, and loved by their adoptive parents. Many children feel a mixture of both.

The following case discussion will focus on a young woman suffering from many of the difficulties associated with adoption, as well as the particular traumas of her own life. The case to be discussed was presented to me by a young supervisee.

FELICIA

Felicia was a twenty-six-year-old client suffering from depression and anxiety. She was attending a martial-arts class and told another student friend about her emotional difficulties, and the friend recommended that Felicia see a therapist. Felicia first responded negatively, but the friend said that she knew a therapist to whom she felt Felicia could relate and who also practiced martial arts. Felicia replied that she would consider going but preferred a female, and the friend said the therapist was female.

Felicia made an appointment for a consultation but did not show up. She was embarrassed and avoided her friend by not attending her martial-arts class, but the friend called and encouraged her to go to see the therapist. Felicia did so a month later.

Felicia was a tall, casually but stylishly dressed, attractive young woman. She had a flair for putting colors together and carried herself with notable pride. Felicia asked the therapist about her martial-arts background. The therapist was impressed with the reading Felicia had done in martial-arts philosophy. Felicia asked the therapist about one of the books on her shelf, and the therapist offered to loan it to her. Toward the end of the session, the therapist asked Felicia why she needed help, and Felicia told her of her anxiety and depression. Over the next few sessions they continued to talk about martial arts, meditation, and philosophy. On one occasion they agreed to meditate for a few minutes, and during the silence, Felicia burst out laughing. The therapist gently asked what had triggered the laughter. Felicia had trouble stopping, then said she didn't know but had had an uncontrollable urge to laugh, "like when you are at a funeral and the last thing to do is to laugh." The therapist thought that Felicia's issues probably had to do with loss. The therapist was willing to engage Felicia in a general discussion about martial-arts philosophy because Felicia already knew of the therapist's martial-arts background from the referral source, and this was a decisive factor in Felicia's seeking treatment.

Over time, Felicia described her background. She was of Puerto Rican descent and was born and grew up in an impoverished area of the Bronx. Her biological parents gave her up when she was a few months old. She grew up in foster care, and her foster parents adopted her during latency. Felicia's birth mother was acquainted with the foster parents, and Felicia would see her occasionally. Felicia later learned that her birth mother was a prostitute and a drug abuser, and that her biological father was a drug addict. Felicia never met her birth father, who left the area shortly after her birth. Her adoptive father was the only father she ever knew. Felicia was close to him but he left the family not long after her adoption, and thereafter, Felicia only occasionally saw him. Felicia's biological mother gave birth to a son when Felicia was eight, and he also went to live with Felicia and her adoptive family. The birth mother disappeared from the area afterward and Felicia never saw her again. Felicia's adoptive family was also Puerto Rican.

Felicia said she felt destined to follow in her mother's footsteps, but could not elaborate. In her early twenties she had lived with a drug addict who violently abused her. She was so badly beaten that her adoptive mother intervened and demanded that she return home. Felicia was grateful that her adoptive mother was protective. Felicia reported a history of occasional drug abuse—marijuana and cocaine—and alcohol abuse.

Her adoptive father, a military veteran, had learned martial arts overseas, and he taught her some very basic moves. They watched kung fu movies together every Saturday morning. Felicia said these films were very popular among the African-American and Latino youths in her community because of the discipline, loyalty, and courage of the kung fu fighters. She especially appreciated the fact that many of the fighters were women. Felicia believed her martial-arts background had saved her from becoming a serious addict. She currently smoked marijuana, but less heavily than before. Martial arts had enabled her to care for her body and to give up drug and alcohol abuse.

When the therapist inquired about her current situation, Felicia vaguely replied that her life had no direction. She lived with a roommate in the Bronx, was unemployed, and formerly had worked in retail. When the therapist asked how she supported herself, Felicia mentioned occasional modeling.

One day Felicia showed up for her appointment visibly shaken. She spoke circuitously and vaguely about the dangers of urban life, the vulnerability of young women, the struggles of people of color. The therapist replied that Felicia appeared quite shaken, and asked if anything had happened. Felicia asked if the therapist had read that week about a prostitute who had been murdered. The therapist vaguely recalled seeing something about it, and Felicia said she knew the girl. She said the murdered young woman was Nigerian, and the murder may have been related to her prostitution activities.

Felicia then said, "I have something to tell you—everything is confidential? You would never repeat anything to our mutual friend? You never judge me. I work in the sex business."

She went on to describe how she believed her anxiety was related to her prostitution activities. She said people typically believe that prostitutes take pleasure in their work and that it is an easy way to make a buck. She said it is actually difficult and dangerous. Many of the men mistreat the women. Felicia worked for a service, and recently she had gone on a call. The man wasn't going to pay her and tried to rape her. She fought him, and he beat her. She managed to escape, but was traumatized. On another occasion, a man was having intercourse with her when he abruptly withdrew, removed his condom, and shot his sperm in her face. Over the years, she had experienced increasing anxiety, but the murder of her acquaintance put her in a panic.

Felicia said that she entered the sex business in a way that was typical of many young women. She started working as a stripper in a club in her late teens. At first she felt extremely uncomfortable, as if the men penetrated her with their stares. The women earned most of their money by being selected for lap dancing. Most of the women selected were white. When Felicia was not selected, she first thought it was because the men preferred white women. Before long, she began to doubt her own attractiveness. Maybe her breasts were not large enough, maybe her nose was too flat, or maybe her legs were not curvaceous. So much of her self-esteem was based on her appearance that she felt quite threatened. In anger, she sometimes stole from the lockers of the other women. One night one of the patrons of the club propositioned her. She thought he was attractive and the type of man she might sleep with. She might as well be paid, she thought.

Before long she had progressed to working in a Manhattan brothel. She considered the madam of the brothel a mentor who taught her valuable lessons. Felicia then began to work for some of the higher-paying escort agencies, sometimes earning one thousand dollars an hour, which she had to split with the agency. She said she was not hired by the elite, highest-paying agencies because they only brought over women of color from exotic places outside the United States and were uninterested in a Puerto Rican girl from the Bronx. She said that she knew she would eventually tell her story, and she had wanted a female therapist because a man might be titillated and excited. She believed a woman would be more accepting and understanding.

The therapist had a complicated and ambivalent reaction that evolved over the next several weeks. This reaction was manifest in the therapist's silent thought process and was not shared with Felicia. The therapist was in her midthirties and, like Felicia, of Puerto Rican descent. The therapist had grown up in a poor neighborhood in Brooklyn and was accustomed to seeing street walkers. But Felicia did not fit the therapist's image of a street walker. In fact, the therapist thought that Felicia could pass for a graduate student dressing "artistically ghetto." Felicia spoke in an articulate, thoughtful fashion, and her language was often poetic and creative.

As a Latina woman who had struggled to receive an education and become a professional, the therapist felt disapproval of Felicia's scandalous lifestyle. She felt Felicia was confirming some of the negative stereotypes about women of color. The therapist's parents had grown up in Puerto Rico and were quite traditional in their values and ideals. Her father worked hard and had wanted to protect his children from the street life: alcohol and drug abuse, stealing, violence, premature sex, and prostitution. The therapist's parents were strictly selective about whom they allowed their children to associate with. Felicia was certainly someone who would have been off limits.

But the therapist realized that, despite her disapproval, she felt positively toward Felicia. She admired Felicia's toughness, street smarts, and survival skills. Though the therapist had grown up in a tough neighborhood, she had been sheltered and protected. She realized that Felicia reminded her of a secret friend the therapist had had in high school. This friend was tough, street savvy, and free with drugs and sex. When neighborhood girls picked on the therapist, the friend had come to her aid. Although identifying as heterosexual in her sexual activity, the therapist recalled feeling sexual attraction toward her admired friend.

This friendship came to an end when the friend was caught shoplifting in the therapist's presence, and all of the parents were called in. The therapist was forbidden to associate with the friend, and given her obedient nature, she complied. She found herself sharing her parents' disapproval of the friend, probably in the service of separating. She let go of the resentment she felt toward her strict parents and grew to appreciate their encouragement of discipline and education. Now she realized that her feelings toward her long-lost friend were reawakened in her countertransference toward Felicia.

The therapist thought of how Felicia had dropped out of high school; Felicia was certainly bright—as smart as the therapist—but she didn't have any of the same encouragement or opportunity. The therapist had a strange, surprising thought: "Felicia ended up selling her ass; I ended up selling my empathy. We each see our clients for an hour. We each create an atmosphere of intimacy. We each say the time is up. Felicia is paid much more by the hour!"

The therapist had grown up with an ambivalent attitude toward her cultural heritage. Her parents were proud of being from Puerto Rico and had an aristocratic bearing. Her father, however, disapproved of New York Puerto Ricans. He believed they glorified street life and neglected their education.

Felicia's biological and adoptive parents were both Puerto Rican. Felicia sometimes questioned whether she belonged to her adoptive parents, but knew she belonged to the greater Puerto Rican family. She studied Puerto Rican history, actively supported Puerto Rican independence, and enthusiastically participated in the parade on Puerto Rican Day. The therapist soon engaged Felicia in discussion about Puerto Rican culture. The therapist grew excited about sharing this interest. The therapist felt that she was adopting Felicia's identification with Puerto Rican culture, and that Felicia was accepting her as a sister Puerto Rican.

Foster (1988) discusses the therapeutic value of client and therapist discussing shared or different cultures. She states that culture is an important aspect of one's psychosocial identity that is often neglected by clinicians. Felicia and her therapist shared a Latina cultural heritage, but were of different social classes. Foster points out that people of shared cultural heritage may nonverbally recognize class differences. The client may believe the therapist makes certain assumptions based on social class and vice versa. Foster argues that such cultural issues may affect the therapeutic relationship, and that by opening up general discussion about cultural issues, the therapist may help reduce anxiety and discomfort.

The therapist came to believe that it was especially important for her to engage Felicia about their shared cultural background. As noted earlier, identification was one of Felicia's central means of object relating. Her identification based on her birth mother was primarily focused on street culture such as prostitution and drugs. Sharing a mutual heritage allowed Felicia to identify with her Latina therapist who valued education and professional success.

During the second year of treatment, Felicia experienced panic attacks about her future. Felicia sometimes spoke as if she was no longer in the sex business, while at other times she sounded as if she was less involved but still active. The therapist believed that the latter was true but did not confront the contradiction because she believed Felicia wished the former to be true. Felicia thought about seeing a psychiatrist, but changed her mind when the therapist offered a referral. As she continued to suffer panic attacks and depression, Felicia reconsidered, but then said she could not afford the fee. The therapist asked whether the issue was only about money, and wondered whether Felicia might be frightened. Felicia said she believed that the therapist genuinely cared and wished to help, but that she automatically felt a wall come up around her. She said that whenever anyone cared for her, she became paranoid. Her biological mother had been described the same way, and she had ended up alone. Felicia felt destined to follow in her biological mother's footsteps. The therapist offered to accompany her to the psychiatrist, and Felicia agreed. When they met to go to the appointment, Felicia said she had nearly called to cancel, but had forced herself to go. After the appointment, Felicia said that the psychiatrist had treated her with respect and concern and that this was the happiest day of the year.

Fairbairn (1944) describes the schizoid defense in which the individual, when threatened with change, withdraws into a closed psychic system in identification with internal objects. Fairbairn describes two internal objects: an enticing, exciting, but non-gratifying object; and a rejecting, abandoning object. Felicia's birth mother had qualities of both objects—her street activities of prostitution and drug abuse were exciting, but Felicia also felt rejected and abandoned by her. Fairbairn states that individuals who suffer abandonment and abuse may tenaciously hold on to such objects because they are better than no objects. Felicia's relationship to her therapist as a potential good object may have threatened her loyalty and her tie and identification with her internal biological mother. As we will see, this identification represented the core of Felicia's sense of identity—even if negative—and her sense of belonging. Thus, as the therapist became significant to Felicia, Felicia resorted to schizoid withdrawal. The therapist persisted in her efforts.

In the third year of treatment, Felicia described her history in greater depth. Themes of abandonment and adoption took center stage. Felicia had begun to act out rebelliously in early adolescence. She would disappear for days as she and her friends drank alcohol and smoked marijuana. Felicia's adoptive mother worried, and they would fight when she returned. The fights sometimes became physical as Felicia would push or strike out at her mother. At the age of fifteen, Felicia engaged in a relationship with a married man. Out of fear and frustration, her adoptive mother would cry out that Felicia was following in the direction of her biological mother—that she would become "a whore and a drug abuser." As a latency-age child, Felicia swore, rebelled in school, and hit other children. Her adoptive mother couldn't understand where Felicia had learned such behavior. She did not swear herself, and she had taught her children never to use foul language and to respect their teachers. Felicia's adoptive mother believed Felicia must have inherited her biological mother's "bad genes." Felicia remembered feeling that if she had been born bad like her mother, she might as well be the baddest girl in the neighborhood. Her badness became her badge of pride.

Jean-Paul Sartre (1963) describes a similar set of dynamics in his biography of Jean Genet. The playwright Genet was born of parents who were poor and criminal. They abandoned him to the welfare system. He was adopted by middle-class people who took pride in being "decent folk." They were determined that, unlike his biological parents, Genet would grow up to become a respectable member of society. In the back of their minds, however, was the sense that it would be an uphill struggle against his base nature. Genet was not permitted to take anything in the home without first asking permission. Once he was seen secretly taking food. So he was designated a thief. Sartre points out that there were other plausible explanations for his behavior. Maybe Genet was testing whether he belonged to the family by seeing whether basic things at home belonged to him. His adoptive parents had an underlying conviction that Genet shared his biological parents' criminality, and he adopted this identity and grew up to be a career criminal as well as a playwright.

Felicia's familial situation was not identical to that of Genet. Her adoptive mother had greater affection and concern for Felicia, and her reaction to Felicia's behavior was more the result of fear and frustration than of punitive moral judgment. Nevertheless, both sets of parents had believed that their adopted children inherited "bad genes" from their biological parents. By the time Felicia was sixteen years old, her mother felt that she could no longer manage her, so Felicia was sent to residential treatment.

Themes of belonging and adoption emerged as Felicia described her relationship with her younger brother, Jose. As I noted above, Felicia was eight years older than her younger brother. Jose had lived with their biological mother for two years, and then came to live with Felicia and her adoptive family. Felicia and Jose had the same biological mother, but different biological fathers. Felicia often assisted her adoptive mother in taking care of Jose. He was the only blood relative that Felicia knew, and they shared the experience of belonging to one another. Felicia told the therapist that neither she nor Jose felt the same sense of belonging with anyone else in the adoptive family.

When Felicia was an adolescent and Jose was a latency-age child, they lived in a tough, dangerous neighborhood. Felicia was very protective of Jose, walking him to and from school, and watching over him. She always felt bad that Jose was growing up without a father. When neighborhood kids picked on him, Felicia would shout at them. She attempted to teach Jose to fight. Sometimes she would get angry at him and shout at or strike him, but never really hurt him. She described him as a good, nerdy-looking kid who never got into trouble. Once, when she shouted at a kid who was picking on him, Jose said, "Felicia, you can't always fight my battles for me." Jose would become frightened when he saw Felicia fight with their mother and push or strike at her.

When Jose reached adolescence, however, the tables were turned. One time when he was fourteen they argued, and Felicia pushed him. To her surprise, he pushed her back and she went flying. She came at him and Jose easily threw her down and pinned her. Felicia laughed hysterically at the thought of her once little, nerdy brother overpowering her. They developed a pattern of play fighting. She would come up on him and playfully jab or tap him then run away. He would catch her and throw her around. Felicia then either surrendered or called her mother for help. She recalled that when Jose had been a child, she would sometimes run after him and he would be the one to call their mother for help.

Felicia described a recent event to her therapist. Her brother and two of his friends had visited her. She began to playfully poke and tease him. He said, "Come on Felicia—I don't want to hurt you." She said, "Try to—come on— you're a pussy." He pushed her and she fell to the floor. He dragged her around by her arms and she laughed so hard that she wet her pants. The therapist remarked that it sounded like sexualized fighting. Felicia did not get defensive but said, "It pays to talk to a professional person. I never thought about it that way."

The therapist continued to think about this sibling relationship and realized that when Felicia described her little brother overpowering her, she glowed with pride. The therapist also recalled that Felicia had assumed a maternal role when Jose was a child, and she had worried about him. Later Felicia had felt bad that Jose did not have a father, and she had tried to teach him to defend himself. The therapist recognized that Felicia was pleased that Jose did not let her push him around, and that she was proud of playing a role in helping him discover his masculinity. She was relieved and proud of him that he could take care of himself.

Brodzinsky, Schechter, and Marantz Henig (1993) describe how adopted children often experience a sense of loss even if adopted at birth. They state,

> Adoptees who are placed in the first days or weeks of life grieve not only for the parents they never knew, but for other aspects of themselves that have been lost through adoption. They feel the loss of origins, of a completed sense of self, of genealogical continuity. Adoptees might feel a loss, too, of their sense of stability in their relationship with their adoptive parents; if one set of parents can relinquish them, they might think, then why can't another? (12)

Brodzinsky, Schechter, and Marantz Henig state that the loss experienced by such early-placed adoptees is not acute or traumatic or consciously experienced until the age of five; there can sometimes develop feelings of grief, alienation, or disconnection. Adopted children either experience a sense of being lost and abandoned, found and loved, or both.

As I mentioned earlier, Felicia went to live with her future adoptive parents after birth. They first became her foster parents and later her adoptive parents. Felicia's living status was initially uncertain. Her future adoptive parents were unclear if Felicia's biological mother would want Felicia back. Brodzinsky, Schechter, and Marantz Henig note that the attitude of the adoptive parents toward the infant can affect the infant's development, as can their anxieties. The parents might be anxious as to whether they can keep the child, or uncertain whether without a blood connection they can care properly for the child. Felicia's future adoptive mother might have initially been restrained in emotionally connecting with Felicia because of the uncertainty of Felicia's future living status. Not much was known of the reasons she originally took Felicia home. Adoptive parents typically have an adoption story that they share with the child, but in this instance the story was vague. Felicia's adoptive mother told Felicia the story when she was able to understand—sometime in early latency. Felicia was told that her biological parents had been in dire straits financially. Felicia's future adoptive mother had found her to be lovable and couldn't help but want to protect her. Felicia's biological mother and adoptive parents lived in the same building at the time, and her adoptive parents agreed to take her in. Felicia's adoptive parents had at the time one grown daughter of their own who no longer lived in the home.

As we have seen, when Felicia was growing up she would sometimes rebel, and her adoptive mother would say that Felicia was following in her mother's footsteps, though she'd never fully spell out what she meant by this. Later in latency, Felicia learned from neighborhood youths that her biological mother had been a prostitute and drug abuser. Felicia questioned her adoptive mother as to the validity of this information, and her adoptive mother confirmed what Felicia had been told.

Brodzinsky, Schechter, and Marantz Henig (1993) describe how the adopted child typically becomes preoccupied with similarities and differences between themselves and the adoptive parents. Felicia and her adoptive parents shared their Puerto Rican origin, which was a source of pride. Felicia was dark skinned, as was her adoptive father, while her adoptive mother was light skinned. Felicia took Oedipal pride in sharing this characteristic with her father and sometimes taunted her mother that she and her adoptive father were more alike. It will be remembered that Felicia also enjoyed watching kung fu movies with her father and attributed her love of martial arts to their relationship.

Felicia was aware of grieving for her adoptive father, who disappeared when she was seven. She acknowledged to her therapist much anger at men. She had lost both her biological and adoptive fathers and had been abused by her first two boyfriends. Felicia said her prostitution activities might have to do with "making men pay." She felt contempt for the "johns" who had to pay for sex. Again, the reader will recall that during her adolescence, Felicia constantly angered her mother by disappearing for several days at a time to smoke marijuana or drink with her friends. Felicia noted to the therapist that she still had this tendency to disappear, and that her family had resigned themselves and no longer sought her out. The therapist commented that significant people had disappeared from her life—her biological parents and adoptive father—and that Felicia sought to turn the tables by becoming the one who disappears instead of the one who is left. Felicia felt there was much truth to this.

Brodzinsky, Schechter, and Marantz Henig (1993) also describe a controversial experiment by Mary Ainsworth (a protégée of John Bowlby) to measure attachment between infant and mother. Ainsworth devised a twenty-minute laboratory experiment designated "the strange situation." A mother and infant are first alone in a room, observed through a one-way mirror. A female stranger enters, and talks with the mother; the mother leaves, and the stranger plays with the child. The mother returns, and the stranger leaves; then the mother leaves, leaving the baby alone. The stranger returns, and the mother returns; then the stranger leaves, and the mother and the child remain together.

The way the infant responds to the mother—especially during the last reunion—measures how well or badly the two are attached. About 75 percent of the infants in this experiment demonstrate *secure attachment*: when the mother returns they make contact, vocalize, and seek comfort. Some children reflect *avoidant attachment*: the infant ignores the mother when in the room, does not turn to her as a secure base, and hardly notices her when she leaves or returns. A small group of infants demonstrate *resistant attachment*: the infant is distressed or anxious when the mother is in the room, does not use her as a secure base, and during reunion, clings to her but can find no comfort in her arms and angrily pushes her away.

During the third year of treatment, Felicia was in an automobile accident in which she was not seriously hurt but was emotionally traumatized and physically bruised. She was taken to the emergency room of a local hospital and her adoptive mother joined her. On the one hand, Felicia was comforted by her adoptive mother's presence, but she also felt anger and a wish to push her away. Felicia reported that throughout her developing years, whenever there was a crisis, she would feel this need for her mother's comfort and this angry inclination to push her away. In this way, she clearly fit Ainsworth's description of resistant attachment.

Felicia continued to feel not only a sense of grief, but also a sense of shame. On the street she often felt people looked at her with hostility, and she covered herself up with large hats and dark glasses. She said it was obvious to connect this shame to her prostitution activities, but she did not feel that this fully explained it. She realized that she was quick to take offense. She noticed that her female friends often acted as if they "walked on eggshells" around her. All of her friends were currently or had been in the sex business. Felicia was not close to them and did not trust them. She did have one close friend, who had recently given birth. Felicia rarely revealed anything of significance. She reflected on how she was often intolerant of other people, harsh, and quick to angrily snap. She said that Jose was sad because his girlfriend had broken up with him. But she also said he lacked ambition in that he did not complete high school and worked at a menial job. Felicia said to Jose, "What do you think? Girls want nice things, jewelry, to be wined and dined, clothes, to be taken to nice places. No girl wants a loser no matter how cute he is. All girls sell their pussy one way or another."

Afterwards she told the therapist that she had been unnecessarily harsh in saying this, and that this was typical. She telephoned Jose to apologize for not being empathic. Felicia recognized that when she was under stress she became panicked and suspicious; every little problem then became a crisis, and she was angry and intolerant of others. On a couple of occasions the therapist spoke in a raised, spirited voice to make a point and Felicia snapped that the therapist was loud. Later Felicia telephoned to apologize for overreacting.

A brief review of Kleinian developmental theory will serve as a framework to demonstrate Felicia's progress in treatment. Melanie Klein (1975) describes human development in terms of the paranoid-schizoid and depressive positions. In this theory, *positions* are not simply stages, but ways in which the individual organizes its experience of itself in the world. The positions occur in sequence in the beginning of life, the paranoid-schizoid preceding the depressive, but both recur as adaptations to situations involving danger and loss.

The *paranoid-schizoid position* is characterized as experiencing oneself as the object instead of the subject of experience. Thoughts, feelings, and life events happen to the individual. It is as if one is always reacting instead of acting. There is the sense that one is not responsible for feelings of love or hate. One loves because the object is irresistible, and one hates because the object is a monster. The ordinary struggles of everyday living are experienced as persecutory. There is a sense of shame at feeling weak and out of control and a feeling of being cursed by life's difficulties. If one fantasizes about the destruction of the hated object, the object returns, raging with the aggression that destroyed it. An example would be a B-rated horror film such as *Halloween* or *Friday the 13th* in which the monster is killed only to return stronger and angrier in a sequel. The paranoid-schizoid position is also characterized by the primitive defenses of splitting, projective identification, idealization, and devaluation. These defenses endeavor to protect the individual from anxiety evoked by the threat of annihilation of the self.

Felicia experienced many of the characteristics of the paranoid-schizoid position throughout her treatment. One of her favorite phrases to describe her life came from the title of a beloved Billie Holiday song: "Everything Happens to Me." When Felicia drank or smoked too much, she would say, "I don't know what happened. Something came over me. I was feeling so good I couldn't stop myself." She also experienced her moods, whether good or bad, as overcoming her. Felicia said she often felt "possessed," either by unwanted thoughts, feelings, moods, or impulses. Klein likens the paranoid-schizoid position to what some religions refer to as "demonic possession." There is also a constant threat of destruction. Felicia often spoke of how she could die from a car crash, an overdose, or at the hands of a "john." She became obsessed with the film *Monster*, in which Charlize Theron plays a prostitute who is attacked by a client and then becomes a serial killer. Felicia often described herself as paranoid; that is, the cards of life were stacked against her. During her three years of treatment, she spoke of her internal states with increasing insight, indicating that she was beginning to experience some aspects of the *depressive position*.

Klein describes the depressive position as characterized by the integration of good and bad part objects. In the paranoid-schizoid position, good (gratifying) and bad (depriving) part objects are experienced as completely separate. Felicia recalled that once on a Mother's Day during her childhood, she gave her adoptive mother a drawing with a heart saying "I Love You Mom." On the other side of the drawing, however, was a picture of a witch Felicia had drawn the week earlier and forgotten. She recalled how her mother had laughed, saying, "Is that me too?"

Klein describes good and bad part objects as now being recognized as parts of the same mother. Thus anger at the bad part threatens to destroy the good part. During the paranoid-schizoid position, there is no guilt over destructive feelings toward the bad object because the object is experienced as all bad. The paranoid-schizoid position can be seen during wartime when opposing countries see each other as all bad and therefore do not have to feel guilt at trying to destroy one another. In the depressive position, there is a developing sense of experiencing oneself as a subject who is responsible for and guilty about destructive feelings. There is a shift from anxiety over the threat of the destruction of the self to anxiety over the destruction of the loved good object. There is also a sense of loss and mourning, as belief in an all-good object recedes and ambivalence is felt toward the whole object with good and bad part objects. As Winnicott (1963) states, the infant has learned that you don't bite the hand that feeds you. Most importantly, there is a sense that one's aggression has sometimes injured the good object—even if only in fantasy—and there is guilt and an effort to make reparation.

In the third year of treatment, Felicia described herself as a very angry adolescent and young adult. She said, "I was so angry I did not know I was angry. It is only recently that I look back and see I was angry. It was my normal state—I was never in another state where I could say, 'Now I am angry.' I still get too angry at times, but now I'm not always angry." Felicia gave evidence of beginning to experience the depressive position as she described feeling guilty about snapping in anger at her younger brother, the therapist, or her friends. The inclination for reparation emerged because Felicia wished to make up for any harm she caused others.

In the paranoid-schizoid position, Felicia split her biological and adoptive mothers into all-good and all-bad part objects. Her biological mother was an all-bad, child-abandoning prostitute and drug abuser, while her adoptive mother was an all-good, self-sacrificing, loving, and morally decent individual. Underneath this split was another split that occurred when Felicia was disappointed in her adoptive mother and current life situation. On such occasions, there was the biological mother who *might* have been, if she had never become a prostitute and drug abuser, and instead had become a good and loving mother to Felicia. This idyllic, all-loving biological mother was placed in opposition to the adoptive mother who sometimes punished and scolded Felicia. However, for the most part, Felicia had been very dissatisfied throughout her life and blamed her all-bad biological mother for abandoning her to a difficult life situation.

Grey (2002) describes how adopted children are inclined to seek out their biological parents to redress traumatic issues of abandonment and establish a sense of identity. Felicia did not experience a wish to reunite with her biological parents. She vaguely remembered her biological mother and knew about her history of prostitution and drug abuse. However, as she started to reflect on her own destructive interpersonal relations, she became interested in learning more about her birth mother. She wondered whether there was more to know, and questioned her adoptive mother and those neighbors who had known her birth mother. Felicia's adoptive mother was not defensive and recollected that Felicia's birth mother enjoyed reading and writing, and that, as a youngster, Felicia had also enjoyed telling and writing stories. Felicia was excited by this information because she had always enjoyed reading Eastern philosophy and the memoirs of women who had been in the sex business. She told the therapist that these women often described the famous men they had encountered and the exotic lives they had led. Felicia sometimes imagined she would write a memoir describing the dark side of this lifestyle—the danger, degradation, drug abuse, and exploitation. In learning that her birth mother enjoyed writing, Felicia felt that this interest might be a part of her nature. Writing was the first positive activity that she shared with her birth mother. Felicia's adoptive mother then put Felicia in contact with her birth mother's cousin—a woman with whom the adoptive mother was close. They met, and the cousin had photographs of Felicia's birth mother. Felicia was fascinated with the similarity of her and her birth mother's olive skin color, attractive facial characteristics, and graceful physical posture. She had previously seen her mother exclusively as a prostitute, but now, looking at the photos, Felicia saw a pretty adolescent, maybe nineteen, her hands proudly on her hips, in a moment in which she was simply herself enjoying her youth— and not in the role of prostitute or drug abuser.

In the paranoid-schizoid position, Felicia grew up maintaining a relationship with her birth mother as an internal object by identifying with her by becoming a prostitute and drug abuser. Felicia felt shame and self-hatred for these activities, which reflected the hatred she felt for her mother for abandoning her for a life of prostitution and drug abuse. As Felicia began to experience the depressive position, she engaged her therapist and adoptive mother in discovering a more complete and balanced understanding of her birth mother and selectively identifying with some of her positive attributes. Felicia now experienced both her birth and adoptive mothers as more integrated and not as exclusively good or bad. At this time Felicia also enrolled in a creative writing program. She was frightened that she would feel as if she did not belong and that she would have to expose her writing to criticism. She explained to the therapist that she was challenging herself in the areas where she was most vulnerable. In her creative writing class, she became friends with persons who were not in the sex business, and she was surprised by their acceptance. In her short stories, Felicia drew on her street-life experience in the Bronx, and the other students and teacher showed interest and appreciation. Felicia was afraid that her stories describing prostitution and drugs might offend some of the students, and instead discovered that they responded favorably. Thus she was able to begin working out some of her issues around shame. Toward the end of the third year of treatment, Felicia moved to a new neighborhood and told her therapist that between her writing course, moving, and therapy, she was beginning a new life.

CONCLUSION

Felicia's adoptive mother had felt threatened and frightened by Felicia's identification with her birth mother. It is paradoxical that Felicia's tie and loyalty to her birth mother had sometimes been strengthened by her adoptive mother's ridiculing Felicia's similarity to her birth mother. Adoptive children may generally suffer from concerns about loss and belonging, and for Felicia this was compounded by the dangerous streets where she grew up and by the loss of her adoptive father. In a sense, Felicia's birth mother belonged to the streets where Felicia grew up, and Felicia's identification with her mother of the streets strengthened her own sense of belonging. In this chapter I have explored some themes of adoption: belonging, loss, and identity in relation to object relations, and the theory of infantile identifications. As Felicia progressed in treatment, her identification grew less infantile and more selective as she identified with newly learned positive aspects of her birth mother as well as aspects of her adoptive mother and therapist.

REFERENCES

Brodzinsky, D. M., M. D. Schechter, and R. Marantz Henig. 1993. *Being Adopted: The Lifelong Search for Self.* New York: Random House.

Fairbairn, W. R. D. 1941. "A Revised Psychopathology of the Psychoses and Psychoneurosis." In *Psychoanalytic Studies of the Personality.* London: Routledge.

———. 1944. "Endopsychic Structure Considered in Terms of Object Relations." In *Psychoanalytic Studies of the Personality.* London: Routledge.

Foster, R. M. Pérez. 1998. *The Power of Language in the Clinical Process.* Northvale, NJ: Jason Aronson.

Grey, D. D. 2002. *Attaching in Adoption.* Indianapolis, IN: Perspectives Press.

Klein, M. 1975. "Notes on Some Schizoid Mechanisms." Orig. pub. 1946. In *Envy and Gratitude and Other Works.* Ed. R. E. Money-Kryle. New York: Free Press.

Sartre, J.-P. 1963. *Saint Genet Actor and Martyr.* New York: G. Braziller.

Winnicott, D. W. 1963. "Dependence in Infant Care, Child Care, and in the Psychoanalytic Setting." In *Maturational Processes and the Facilitating Environment.* New York: International Universities Press, 249-59.

Part II

SPECIAL ISSUES

Chapter Thirteen

Child Custody Disputes in Adoption Cases

Safeguarding the Relationship with the Psychological Parent

Paul Hymowitz

In this chapter I will discuss the various manifestations of adoption in a child custody context. Litigated adoptions are unlike the usual consensual arrangements made through agencies or between individuals by mutual consent. Although litigated adoptions sometimes arise within the context of a family or acquaintance network and then become contested, they may also emerge in the context of a prior disruption of an intact family either through death or divorce. As science, and society along with it, has changed—marked for example by the advent of innovative technologies allowing for procreation outside the realm of traditional marriage (as in gay or single parentage), a burgeoning incidence of international adoptions, and an increase in "blended" families as a byproduct of divorced or never-married parents—the issue of how to evaluate the claims of prospective adoptive parents grows all the more daunting. I will argue for the continued value of the concept of the *psychological parent*, when determining the relative claims of biological parents and everyday caretakers, as a way of best safeguarding the child's bond with a consistent and nurturing adult. Case vignettes, to illustrate the challenging array of adoptive situations faced by the courts, then follow.

MANNY

Let me begin with the experience of Manny, an adopted child, who is now an adult in my psychotherapy practice. He vividly recalls, even from the dim recesses of a two-year-old's experiences, the confusing and frightening sensations of being taken away from his native Portugal and from Maria, the guardian who had been his foster parent for over a year. Manny says that he remembers not speaking and barely eating for weeks that seemed like years

as he slowly adjusted to his adoptive home in Ohio. And although he bonded
and became attached to his loving but rather reserved and strict new parents,
he never felt entirely at home in their world. His adoptive mother's tragic and
untimely death when Manny was about eight years old, following a long
struggle with cancer, and the subsequent lack of emotional availability of his
adoptive father, partly due to his own grief, led to a long-simmering but
heightened resolve to locate his birth mother in Portugal. Nickman (2004) has
discussed the impediment to the "narrative sense" of one's life when the birth
family is not known. Certainly the desperate longing to connect with one's
genetic forebears, so often seen with adopted children, adds a poignant coun-
terpoint to those who would designate the psychological parent as the only
parent. Put in other terms, one always needs to consider the nature as well as
the nurture of parent-child attachments.

Though Manny did ultimately find his biological mother, their reunion was
somewhat disappointing in that he felt little inherent connection with her, and
indeed, his hazy recollections of Maria (who in fact, had been his first attachment figure) did not include or enhance his experience of this stranger
who was his birth mother. In essence, Manny was never able to consolidate a
true sense of belonging to one caretaking figure, the absence of whom had
colored his entire adult life. Manny's situation served to acquaint me with
some of the dynamics of the adopted child, and in this case how the sequen-
tial disruption of Manny's bonding with one consistent psychological parent
had left him with lifelong emotional scars. Our legal system will never erad-
icate human tragedy, and it is in helping to secure the child's bond with the
psychological parent that we can best safeguard that child's future.

Adoption involves a variety of situations in which a nonbiological adult
caretaker assumes legal custody of a child. Adoptive families might thus be
formed in a variety of ways: when a child is given over to an agency by its
parents, and then raised by strangers; in kinship arrangements, whereby rela-
tives of the birth parents raise the child; and in stepparenting families, where
a nonrelated adult marries a biological parent and subsequently adopts the
child. When such adoptive arrangements become the subject of a legal dispute between a birth parent and a nonbiological caretaker, the court's choices
can be particularly agonizing.

A forensic expert is appointed by the court when questions arise as to the
fitness of an adoptive parent or stepparent, when there is a custody dispute between a biological parent and an adoptive parent, or when there is suspected
abuse or neglect on the part of biological parents leading to possible termination of parental rights. While the forensic practitioner is typically mandated
to evaluate the situation from a neutral, "best interests of the child" standard,
child welfare policy has tended to vacillate between a child-protective stance
often involving more rapid removal of a child from a suspected destructive

parent, and a stance that emphasizes family unity, preservation, and rehabilitation of the parents (Roberts 2002). Given such shifting standards and the rather murky and ill-defined parameters of "best interests of the child" considerations, how is the forensic expert to conduct the evaluation?

THE PSYCHOLOGICAL PARENT CONCEPT

The psychological parent concept continues to provide an excellent divining rod for the forensic expert when that expert is faced with the competing demands of biological parent and nonbiological caretaker. The particular utility of this perspective in the context of adoption occurred to me in thinking about the now notorious Baby M case, as described by John Novick and Kerry K. Novick (2005), in which a child was abruptly torn from the only family she had known and returned to her birth father, a stranger to her, under the primacy of a "Blood cries out to blood" doctrine. In contrast, the Elian Gonzalez case (Guggenheim 2005) is an excellent example of an agonized and politically difficult but reasonable decision to restore a child to his birth father (in Cuba), the child's only surviving psychological parent, even though a superior quality of life might have been afforded the child had he not been transferred (and had remained in the United States).

The concept of the psychological parent, formulated in the collaborative efforts of two psychoanalysts working with a law professor (Goldstein, Freud, and Solnit 1996), is an excellent illustration of a psychoanalytic perspective on development because it reminds us to stay close to the individual's experiences and, in particular, to try to "get within the child's skin" (Solnit and Nordhaus 2005) when considering a child's best interests. Goldstein, Freud, and Solnit argue that only a parent who is providing for the day-to-day physical needs of the child, overriding other legal and biological considerations, will become the child's psychological parent. The authors further presume that termination of ongoing contact between primary caretaker and child would be detrimental, thus emphasizing the child's developmental need for continuity of relationship with the psychological parent. The concept, while seemingly self-evident in its simplicity, nevertheless provides a strong foundation for thinking about what Goldstein, Freud, and Solnit term the "least detrimental alternative" for the child. The concept emphasizes that a child's emotional health is enhanced by a parenting figure who makes the child feel valued and wanted, an experience by no means synonymous with biological conception.

In deliberating a custody dispute, Goldstein, Freud, and Solnit recommend a quick resolution of the issue of parentage, considering the abbreviated time-sense of the young child. They also suggest that priority be given to continuity for the child, including an assessment of the person who has been functioning as the psychological parent from the child's point of view. Finally, consideration of circumstances of abuse or neglect of the child must be made. In such cases, the primacy of the psychological parent might have to be overridden, even where the child may cling all the more desperately to that inadequate or destructive parent.

Critiques of Goldstein, Freud, and Solnit have focused on their assumption that there would be only one such adult serving in the role of psychological parent for the child. Indeed, this assumption has been used for decades as an argument against joint custody and in favor of not encumbering the primary parent's freedom in her child-care practices. Given the increasing predominance of the dual-career family, however, two parents usually coordinate the care of their child with the possible assistance of other caretaking adults, such as a nanny. Further, there have been shifts in our theoretical understanding of attachment (Solomon 2005), contributing to the belief that the infant may form primary bonds to more than one adult caretaker. It would thus follow that the role of the psychological parent might similarly involve more than one such adult; indeed, studies have indicated that children benefit from the active involvement of two parents. Such new realities and new theoretical understandings need not detract from the utility of the psychological parent concept in our more complex society, in which many children are now being raised by nonbiological caregivers, because these children still form emotional bonds with those adults who are most consistent in their lives.

The psychological parent may be distinguished from the primary attachment figure, who provides protection and nurturance (Solomon 2005). As Solomon describes it, initially, an infant is likely to form one primary attachment early in its existence, and may have a preference for this primary figure in times of stress, even while forming additional attachments to others. In contrast, the role of psychological parent, while ideally assumed by the same adult to whom the infant has been attached, can be more flexible and is potentially assumed by a number of different adults, based on their active involvement with the child in the context of the child's evolving developmental needs. Both mother and father, and indeed other adults to whom they delegate responsibilities, may be psychological parents to a child relative to their participation in daily caretaking.

A recent American Law Institute (ALI) report (Bartlett 1999) on child custody provides a similar but more mechanical formula than the psychological parent concept for making custody determinations. The ALI formula essentially calculates the proportion of time each parent has spent as primary caretaker of the child prior to separation, and proposes this as the determining factor in subsequent parenting plans, eliminating, in most cases, the need for a forensic expert. The psychological parent concept demands a closer examination of the child's emotional relationship with the adults in question, recognizing that quantity of caretaking time does not provide a direct, one-to-one indication of the bond with the adult, nor does it demonstrate the quality of the caretaking. It is thus likely that there would be some divergence in conclusions reached by either method. For example, in the case of the Rivera family discussed below, the biological father had provided little direct care for his son over a five-year period, failing the ALI standard, but the emotional bond between them was readily observable, hence supportive of the biological father's claim for custody and for his role as psychological parent.

Identifying a child's psychological parent can provide a particularly helpful focus for the forensic evaluator working through the thicket of voluminous and often contradictory data with which the evaluator is confronted when a potential adoption is being considered. Most significantly, it reminds the evaluator to see things from the child's perspective rather than from that of the adults, who are typically consumed by cross-accusations of betrayal and abuse. Beyond this perspective, however, the evaluator has to keep the child's well-being in mind, which sometimes overrides direct implementation of the child's wishes. For the child, the desire to cling to the biological parents, particularly in cases where the child has known them, exerts a powerful emotional pull even where abuse, neglect, or more subtle personal detachment of the parents has predominated. Legal protections for biological parentage continue to hold sway in our society, and attention to the role of the psychological parent provides a valuable balance for the evaluator. The approach being advocated, emphasizing psychological parenthood, while being mindful of the adults' biological claims and similar emotional pulls on the child, will now be described in a variety of child custody disputes involving adoption or stepparenthood.

A QUESTION OF PATERNITY: *JONES V. SMITH*

One clear example of the concept of the psychological parent is provided by the *Jones* case in which the claims of a biological father were pitted against the everyday caretaker of a child, the quasi-adoptive father, a man who had presumed he was the biological father. Mr. Jones was present at the birth of his presumed daughter Janet in 1995 and was raising her with his live-in girlfriend, Ms. Grand, along with their two younger children. In 1999, Ms. Grand left the family home, taking her then newborn girl with her and leaving her two older daughters in the care of Mr. Jones, who then petitioned for their legal custody. Mr. Smith, a former boyfriend of Ms. Grand's, then revealed that in 1998 he had completed a DNA test that identified him as Janet's biological father, and he opposed this petition. He fought to establish his legal paternity of Janet. In this regard, some states have designated a category of *equitable parent* to protect fathers like those in Mr. Jones's situation; that is, a man who has considered himself and has been acting as a father is given legal standing, when the other parent is dead or absent, against the claims of another adult who is subsequently established to be the biological parent. The status of equitable parent may also apply to a stepparent who has been functioning as a parent but who has not legally adopted the child in question (see the L case below).

Ms. Grand presented a contradictory account by claiming to believe that Mr. Jones was Janet's natural father, but nevertheless allowing Mr. Smith to visit Janet in the hospital after her delivery and to have informal contact with Janet during Janet's first three years, after which Ms. Grand withheld visits. The forensic psychologist interviewed the now six-year-old Janet, who "betrayed no memory or knowledge of her biological father. She knew only Mr. Jones as her father." Further, she "presented clinically as well adjusted and resilient."

The examiner decided to restrict his report to recommendations concerning paternity of the child. He thus proposed "disclosure to the child of her pedigree," and offered to conduct "at least one supervised visit" between Mr. Smith and Janet, which he saw as "consistent with the best interest of the child." He found Mr. Jones to be a "socially stable, working father" whose parenting capacity was deemed to be "grossly intact," but who was believed to "lack optimum insight into the advisability of disclosing Janet's pedigree to the child." Given the opportunity to do so with the expert's proffered help, Mr. Jones "volunteered only egocentric explanations as to his failure to disclose to Janet her biological lineage." Although the expert chose not to weigh in on the "ultimate question" of custody, the implications of his recommendations were that it was Mr. Smith who was most sensitive to Janet's needs and that Mr. Jones's refusal to allow access to the biological father raised serious questions about his custodial status.

Had this well-meaning expert kept the concept of psychological parent in the forefront of his considerations, a simpler, less adult-centered recommendation might have followed, and one that was in the child's best interests. Mr. Smith seemed genuinely to have been deceived by Ms. Grand as to his paternity and may well have felt that he was fighting for his parental rights on behalf of his child. Nevertheless, he was a complete stranger to his daughter and had performed none of the day-to-day functions that provide the only real glue that bonds a child to an adult. Despite the above-quoted maxim "Blood cries out to blood," it is the daily caretaking figure to whom the child will turn in times of need. Mr. Jones may well have been conscientious in caretaking only because he thought he was the biological father. However, once the psychological parent-child bond is established, it is one that not even a blood tie can rend asunder.

The expert was also not considering this particular child's developmental needs. A six-year-old is not concerned with "pedigree," nor is that six-year-old struggling with the issues of identity that are more meaningful to an adolescent. The young child is far more focused on the immediacy of day-to-day existence and about being cared for. Given the loss of her mother in the family household, Janet's needs for security and consistency were solely provided by Mr. Jones. She could hardly be expected to take an interest in the paternity claims of a strange male adult. Similarly, it is hard to understand how Mr. Jones's lack of receptivity—described in the report as "egocentric"—to Mr. Smith's claim could be seen as anything more than a normative parental *preoccupation* (to borrow Winnicott's [1957] term) to preserve his unique psychological bond with his daughter.

TWO CASES WHERE THE ADOPTIVE PARENT WAS DEEMED THE PSYCHOLOGICAL PARENT

The Jensen girls present a vivid example in which they were attached to their stepfather, not their biological father. Mr. Jensen was separated from their mother for six years, when the girls were seven and two. He visited them sporadically for several years and then abruptly stopped, claiming the girls were being systematically turned against him by their mother and that he was no longer able to tolerate the "stress" of the visits. Whatever the real reason for this interruption in contact, the girls bonded with their live-in stepfather, Mr. Louis, a man much younger than their mother who had actually been their baby-sitter. During the years when they did not see their father at all, the girls essentially adopted Mr. Louis as their psychological parent in partnership with their mother. When their mother later committed suicide in the midst of a severe depression, they clung to Mr. Louis as the only day-to-day caretaker they knew. Mr. Jensen was notified about the death of the girls' mother by neighbors in the building, and he then came forward as the girls' rightful custodial parent, around which claim a legal battle ensued.

In interviews, both individually and with their biological father, the Jensen girls were adamant that they no longer felt any connection to him, and that he was rather disconnected from and neglectful of them during the years of their visitation; and Gail, the older girl, further alleged that he was never an involved parent when he lived with their mother. In contrast, they described a long-standing relationship with Mr. Louis, who had clearly shared in the parenting with their mother and who indeed may have served as a substitute psychological parent during periods when their mother was emotionally absent. Once their mother died, the girls' attachment to Mr. Louis became deeper, and their resistance to any renewed ties with their rejected father may have intensified this new bond. When it became clear to Mr. Jensen that his daughters were not going to accept his reemergence in their lives, Mr. Jensen proposed that Mr. Louis adopt the girls, thereby relinquishing any further obligation to his daughters, including financial ones, an arrangement that was accepted by the court.

A second case, rather poignant in terms of the travails of its subject, a little girl named Anne, further highlights the utility of the psychological parent concept. In this case, the petitioner requesting custody, Ms. Charles, had provided a guardianship role for Fran, a teenage girl whom she had met while volunteering in an at-risk pregnancy program, by helping Fran take care of her baby and giving her a place to live when she needed it. Over the course of several years, Ms. Charles came to take on much of the day-to-day parenting of Fran's daughter Anne, while also providing a structured home for Fran. Following a long period of simmering conflict, Fran had a falling out with Ms. Charles, who claimed Fran had been stealing from and otherwise abusing her, and Fran left the home. Fran subsequently sent Anne to live with her father, essentially a stranger to Anne. He may then have been physically abusive to Anne, although this was never corroborated. Anne's father then established contact with Ms. Charles, perhaps to get money from her, and ultimately he returned Anne to her.

Ms. Charles then filed for guardianship of Anne, preparatory to an adoption. Fran opposed her petition and requested that Anne be returned to her care. This evaluation was complicated because Anne, now six years old, certainly knew Fran to be her birth mother and still had a bond with her. However, Ms. Charles had been providing a greater part of Anne's daily caretaking and was clearly in a better position to continue to do so. The case was further complicated by racial differences in that Fran and her daughter were African American, and Ms. Charles was Irish American. Fran's lawyer expressed concerns about the possible disadvantage to the child of not being raised by a parent of her own race, arguing about its potential interference with Anne's sense of racial identity.

In such a complex case, how does the forensic expert help the court determine who will best meet the child's need for a psychological parent? Unlike the equal standing of two competing biological parents, the blood tie of one such parent must take primacy over the claims of a nonbiological caretaker if that parent is deemed to be of equivalent fitness and connection with the child. To arrive at such a determination, the evaluator must interview each adult party, using semistructured parenting questionnaires where indicated, and if significant psychopathology is suspected, standard psychological tests. The child is also interviewed, and observations of the child's play as well as projective measures are often used, since the child is typically unwilling or unable to divulge its own wishes directly. Adult-child interactions in the office and, if possible, in the home setting are also observed, preferably with standardized tasks assigned, like having the parent instruct the child in an activity such as building a Lego house or initiate a discussion with the child of an everyday problem, such as resistance to bedtime. The parenting competence of each adult can then be evaluated and added to the observations about the child. Complete histories, document review, and collateral contacts provide supplemental information.

Turning again to Anne's case, observations of her interactions with her two rival caretakers bolstered the clinical impressions of these two adults. Anne was seen to be secure in Ms. Charles's presence, becoming mildly anxious when she left the room, though soon able to focus on the task at hand. Ms. Charles was warm but firm in her interactions with Anne. Some of their discussion indeed centered on Anne's difficulty staying in her own room to play and sleep, and preferring to be with Ms. Charles. The description of Anne's behavior fit the pattern of an anxious attachment whereby the child seems unable to count on the presence of the caretaking figure, an understandable insecurity given Anne's history. In contrast, Fran came across more like Anne's big sister, giggling together with her at some photos Fran had with her. Anne found candy in Fran's bag and began to eat some of it, and though Fran didn't say anything, one had the sense that she hadn't brought the candy for her daughter. Even the appointments with Fran were difficult to set up, as her arrival was always uncertain.

A variety of considerations argued that Ms. Charles was better suited to be Anne's custodial parent, although both adults could claim some aspects of psychological parentage. Fran had a history of coming and going in her child's life, suggesting the lack of her own internalized experience of a bond with Anne. This culminated in her allowing the biological father to take the child with him down South for several months, presumably to allow her some time to "get my act together," with Ms. Charles showing the greater sense of grief and loss at this decision. Further, Fran was still living a kind of adolescent existence, without a stable job or living situation, and had been involved with a series of boyfriends. Finally, in her interview, Fran demonstrated only a limited understanding of her child's developmental needs. In contrast, Ms. Charles had provided the day-to-day caretaking that Anne so desperately required, and a move toward adoption was recommended.

TWO CASES WHERE ADOPTION VERSUS RESTORATION
OF THE BIRTH PARENT'S CUSTODY WAS CONSIDERED

The following two cases involve situations where the biological parent or parents were found to be well-bonded with their child and to have served as psychological parents. Yet each situation raised questions about parental neglect of the child in the context of viable alternative adoptive arrangements. In the end, the forensic expert reached opposite conclusions in these two cases, illustrating the basic maxim that each situation must be decided on its own merits.

The Rivera case illustrates a situation where there is a palpable bond between the biological parent and the child despite many years during which the day-to-day parenting was provided by a foster parent. Juan Rivera was a bright sixteen-year-old who had been living in a stable foster-care setting for five years. He had initially been removed from his drug-addicted mother and placed in the care of his father, Frank. When it was discovered that Frank was continuing to leave Juan with his mother on some nights, even given her precarious condition, Juan, at age ten, was removed from his father and placed in foster care. After several unsuitable placements, Juan ended up in a warm and orderly home where he lived and apparently thrived for the next five years, during which time Frank would visit him. Frank gradually received more extended visitation, including overnights.

The forensic evaluation was aimed at assessing Frank's suitability to regain custody of his son, as opposed to finalizing an adoption by the foster mother, Ms. Wilson. Interviews with Juan revealed his ongoing strong bond with his father, and the feeling of Frank's having been a true psychological parent for Juan, who clearly stated his desire to return to his father. Frank emerged in the evaluation as a still somewhat unreliable man, living a rather unfocused existence, supporting himself with the odd construction job while playing in a band on weekends. Though Frank was charming and personable in his manner, and clearly persistent in maintaining contact with his son, it seemed unlikely he would be able to provide Juan with the structure and consistency of care that Juan had been receiving. Nevertheless, the father-son bond was undeniable, and the boy was at an age and level of maturity where his preference to return to his father carried considerable weight. In this case, the developmental considerations for a child well into his adolescence suggested yielding to Juan's stated preferences despite the evaluator's misgivings. It was thus suggested that custody should revert to Mr. Rivera, and the adoption was averted.

A second and contrasting case involved a ten-year-old boy with special needs, Joey, who had been raised for varying lengths of time by both of his parents, by his parents alternating once they had separated, and by his maternal aunt for other periods of time. Specifically, the aunt had taken Joey for almost a year at age two when her sister, Ms. Evans, had accused her husband of molesting Joey. Given the poorly justified basis of the allegations, Ms. Evans's own mental state was then put in question. With an upsurge in marital cross-accusations during the boy's tenth year, he was again placed with his aunt. A forensic evaluation was then ordered, with consideration of the custodial suitability of the two warring parents, as well as the possibility of a full adoption by the aunt.

Each parent emerged from the evaluation with significant flaws, amply highlighted by an adversarial spouse. Mr. Evans emphasized his wife's emotional instability, further depicting her as an absent parent who had abandoned her son. Ms. Evans, in turn, alleged that she had been driven out of the home by her husband's abuse and that he was a chronic and habitual pot smoker. The fact that she had left Joey in Mr. Evans's care for an entire fall without taking appropriate action, however, was undeniable. As for Mr. Evans's parenting, the school reported that Joey came late to school, had homework unprepared, and then often fell asleep in class. It was assumed that Joey was "up until all hours" at home. Temporary placement of Joey with his aunt immediately yielded an improvement in his school functioning, academically and behaviorally.

The evaluation's conclusions in this case hinged on the major drawbacks in each parent's parental competence, despite Joey's manifest attachment to both of them and despite the fact that either adult could justifiably lay claim to being his psychological parent, particularly Mr. Evans, who was home far more than his wife. Further, Joey spoke in favor of returning to live with his father, and such desires are taken into account, though they are certainly not determinative at such an age. Unique factors in this family situation, however, argued against either adult becoming the designated custodial parent. First, Joey's special needs had to be taken into account. He had been diagnosed with attention deficit hyperactivity disorder (ADHD) and a specific reading disability, in addition to showing aggressive and oppositional/defiant behavior toward school authorities, and he had been placed in a special education class. He thus appeared to be in desperate need of a structured and consistent home environment.

Joey was observed to be openly defiant and contemptuous of his mother who, with her inappropriately casual and whimsical demeanor, presented in a way consistent with her husband's allegations against her. Mr. Evans, while unquestionably seen as the adult closest to Joey, was nevertheless demonstrably incapable of providing the necessary parental guidance, supervision, and role-modeling required, and allegations of his drug abuse had also been substantiated. It was thus advised that Joey be placed with his aunt on a permanent basis, despite the ability of the biological parents to pass the psychological parent standard. In this situation, there was reasonable certainty of ongoing parental neglect by either parent, which would have been particularly damaging given the cognitive and emotional vulnerability of their child.

CONCLUSION

Considerations of adoption in a few child custody cases provide some instructive examples of the broader issues involved. Adoption is best done early in a child's life when there is a greater flexibility in bonding with a caretaking adult. However, this is not always possible, and the older child still has a need for the psychological parenting that may not have been experienced with the birth parents. As illustrated in the Evans case, a relative known to the child, when available for a kinship adoption, may best safeguard the child's need for consistency and for the familiarity of the caretaking figure. Such considerations of nurture and optimum daily care must be juxtaposed with what is often the adopted individual's lifelong quest for discovery of or connection with their biological parents, a yearning that must be considered where removal of a child from the child's birth parent is being contemplated.

Keeping the role of psychological parent in mind when one or more parties in a custody dispute is a prospective or current adoptive, nonbiological parent helps to maintain the focus where it ought to be: on the child's needs as opposed to the adults' legal rights. Open adoptions, where the birth parents are known by and accessible to the child, and which have gained greater acceptance today, are a welcome way to facilitate a child's access to their biological parents, particularly as the child struggles with the identity issues of late adolescence. As with Manny, the patient I described in the introduction to this chapter who never felt bonded with his adoptive parents, some youngsters harbor an inextinguishable longing for their real or imagined roots. In addition, a girl like Anne will likely always feel some sensitivity about the racial divide between her and her adoptive mother or father, as may many of the increasing number of international adoptees. Even more wrenching are those situations in which children remain emotionally attached to an incompetent or abusive parent.

The custody evaluator in an adoption case is advised to keep the focus on the more immediate question of which party has been and will be most responsible for the child's daily needs, for in doing so, the evaluator will have identified the psychological parent and will have best protected the growing child's needs. As many experts have noted, the rotating child-care arrangements of today's dual-income families make it likely that the child will have more then one adult serving in the role of psychological parent, but having more than one adult serving such a function should not invalidate the importance of that role. An assessment determining which parent has provided the daily work of caretaking tends to put the child's experience and well-being squarely in the center of the evaluation. Ultimately, it is the unique context of each adoptive situation that requires the professional's careful scrutiny.

REFERENCES

Bartlett, Katherine. 1999. "Child Custody in the Twenty-first Century: How the American Law Institute Proposes to Achieve Predictability and Still Protect the Individual Child's Best Interests." *Willamette Law Review* 35:467–83.

Goldstein, Joseph, Anna Freud, and Albert Solnit. 1996. *In the Best Interests of the Child*. New York: Free Press.

Guggenheim, Martin. 2005. "When Should Courts Be Empowered to Make Child-Rearing Decisions?" In *A Handbook of Divorce and Custody: Forensic, Developmental, and Clinical Perspectives*. Ed. Linda Gunsberg and Paul Hymowitz. Hillsdale, NJ.: Analytic Press, 129–38.

Nickman, Stan. 2001. "Affect Tolerance: A Crucial Requirement for Substitute Parenting." In *Stepparenting*. Ed. Stanley Cath and Moisey Shopper. Hillsdale, NJ: Analytic Press, 51-67.

———. 2004. "The Holding Environment in Adoption." *Journal of Infant, Child, and Adolescent Psychotherapy* 3, no. 3:329–41.

Novick, John, and Kerry K. Novick. 2005. "Soul Blindness: A Child Must Be Seen to Be Heard." In *A Handbook of Divorce and Custody: Forensic, Developmental, and Clinical Perspectives*. Ed. Linda Gunsberg and Paul Hymowitz. Hillsdale, NJ: Analytic Press, 81–90.

Roberts, Dorothy. 2002. *Shattered Bonds: The Color of Child Welfare*. New York: Civitas.

Solnit, Albert, and Barbara Nordhaus. 2005. "Divorce and Custody in a Changing Society." In *A Handbook of Divorce and Custody: Forensic, Developmental, and Clinical Perspectives*. Ed. Linda Gunsberg and Paul Hymowitz. Hillsdale, NJ: Analytic Press, 139–42.

Solomon, Judith. 2005. "An Attachment Theory Framework for Planning Infant and Toddler Visitation Arrangements in Never-Married, Separated, and Divorced Families." In *A Handbook of Divorce and Custody: Forensic, Developmental, and Clinical Perspectives*. Ed. Linda Gunsberg and Paul Hymowitz. Hillsdale, NJ: Analytic Press, 259–80.

Winnicott, Donald. W. 1957. "Two Adopted Children." In *The Child and the Outside World*. London: Tavistock, 45–51.

Chapter Fourteen

Consultation during the Adoption Process

Working with Families Adopting Older Russian Children

Laurie Sloane

In this chapter, I will discuss my experience working as a consultant to a Russian hosting program sponsored by an international adoption agency. Russian hosting programs are unique within the adoption community. The agencies attempt to match up families interested in and willing to consider adopting older children from Russia while the specific orphanage determines the selection of children sent to this country, ostensibly for a two-week vacation. It is viewed as a humanitarian effort providing hope for a new life for both the children and the families. It gives the families the opportunity to meet and get to know a Russian child while beginning to integrate him or her into their lives. It can be a very stressful time, particularly for the children who come with little or no preparation, speak a different language, and need to adjust to a completely different lifestyle. As a consultant, I was asked to use my clinical background to help the agency provide more effective training for their staff to support the emotional needs of the adoptive families. I will describe what I learned about life in Russian orphanages and about Russian adoptions in general. I will also detail my experience with the hosting program, including problems that were identified with the homestudy workers and with the families.

ADOPTING A CHILD FROM RUSSIA

During the past four years, over twenty thousand visas[1] were issued to Russian children traveling to the United States, most of whom came to begin new

---

1. U.S. State Department, http://travel.state.gov/family/adoption/stats/stats_451.html.

lives with an American family. According to a recent *New York Times* article, seven hundred thousand Russian orphans are waiting to be adopted.[2]

In Russia, orphanages are called "children's homes" and provide care for children up to the age of sixteen. The children share rooms and beds, and refer to each other as "brothers and sisters." This is their family, sometimes the only family they have ever known or can recall. Children are brought to the home by parents or other family members for a variety of reasons including death, illness, poor economic conditions, and drug addiction. Sometimes parents or aunts and uncles come to visit or keep in touch by mail, but for many children, these visits and letters become less frequent over the years and gradually cease. For others, there is the hope of a family reunion when economic conditions improve. In Russia, parents can place their children voluntarily for up to one year while the parents get back on their feet. During this period, it is not uncommon for biological parents to visit their children in the homes and in this way maintain their connections.

Developmental theory stresses the importance of attachment between a baby and a primary caregiver. Reports from visitors to Russian "baby homes" suggest care is provided in a group with individual attention given in varying degrees depending on the ratio of caregivers to babies. Babies may form attachments to each other and to some of their caregivers, and this may be enough to move them forward developmentally. Others, who arrive in the orphanage with certain vulnerabilities, require more individualized attention and may get lost in the shuffle. These children will suffer from developmental deficits and delays that will have an ongoing effect as they grow older. They may not be recommended for adoption, but if they are adopted, problems may emerge in their interpersonal relationships and academic performance.

Once a family in the United States decides to pursue adoption, the agency conducts a homestudy, which can take several months to complete. These homestudies, which are part of the procedure in all international adoptions, become the basis of a psychosocial profile of the family. Sometimes additional psychological testing is recommended to assure the stability and appropriateness of the prospective parents. The challenge is to help the family see this assessment as useful to them rather than as an invasion of their privacy and a scrutiny of their mental health. The family is often unprepared for what is being asked of them as they begin the process of adoption, and many emotional hurdles remain once the family is approved. Generally, it takes another two to three months before the family

---

2. Peter Fin, "Russian Adoptions Orphaned by State," *Washington Post*, June 19, 2005, A01.

makes their first visit to Russia, which happens only after volumes of documentation have been submitted to the Russian government. Once a family is given the approval to travel, they will spend an estimated two weeks in a Russian hotel, visiting a specific children's home in hopes of bonding with a particular child. If the family and the Russian agency personnel agree, then paperwork is submitted to begin the actual adoption process. The family then goes back to the United States and waits for a call to return to Russia for an adoption hearing. This process can take several months before the final trip is made.

Russian bureaucracy is similar to ours, but the different language and culture create a vastly different experience for waiting families. American families are scrutinized by government agencies while at the same time the families are investigating the status of the children they hope to adopt. Health and mental health professionals examine the children to determine if they have physical impairments, developmental delays, or learning disabilities. The wait ends when the family is brought before a Russian court for a final examination to determine their fitness and suitability to be parents of a Russian child.

The question of suitability has created many dilemmas for the adoption community. It is a theme that has repeated itself over the last few years and caused a great deal of distress among prospective adoptive parents and the Russian children they are hoping to adopt. It has raised the level of anxiety within this group and caused concern among the professionals in agencies on both sides of the Atlantic. For example, recently a single parent who had already successfully adopted one Russian child returned to Russia to adopt a second child. She was denied the adoption, reportedly because her mortgage was too big, her debt too high, and her car inadequate. She returned a third time to Russia, and successfully adopted another child. It is unclear why she was denied the second attempt at adoption. But the politics of some of the regions in Russia affect the proceedings, and in addition, there is a growing trend among foreign governments to request fuller clinical assessment and psychological testing of all prospective foreign parents. Preparing families for this type of exploration and evaluation is a challenge for adoption professionals.

THE HOSTING PROGRAM

When a family hosts a child, the Russian agencies view that as comparable to the first visit to the Russian children's homes. If the hosting period is successful, the family pursues the adoption and travels to Russia for a final trip to bring the child home with them. This is a unique program that affords prospective parents considering older child adoption an opportunity to meet and spend time with the child prior to adoption. Often, the prospective parents are a bit older than most first-time parents. Some have postponed having children until later in life and others have tried fertility treatments and been unsuccessful. A number of the prospective parents may have pursued other avenues of adoption that failed. The personnel in the Russian children's homes select children who are eligible for adoption, and who they believe will be able to function in a family with different habits, culture, and language. As the date of formal adoption grows closer, pictures and information about the children are sent to the agency and then shared with the families. By contrast, the children are not told anything until a few days before they leave Russia, and then only that they are going on a trip. The rationale for this practice is to avoid upsetting or disappointing the children. But if other children from the home have previously participated in the hosting program, a child might have a clue about a possible adoption growing out of their trip. Therefore, some children arrive well aware of this possibility, while others have no idea of the purpose of this visit when they meet their host families.

In my role as consultant, I attended a parent orientation meeting at the agency and had the opportunity to hear about this experience from both the parents and the social workers. The agency staff reviewed the visit schedule with the families, beginning with the children's arrival. The children, they said, travel with a Russian representative and meet an interpreter when they arrive at the agency in the United States. The families pick up the children a few hours later. Each child is matched with a family based on the family's requests, including gender and age. For example, if the family already has a child, consideration is given to the age of the second child, and whether he or she will fit in with the needs of the first child.

The interpreter from the agency is available to the families on an as-needed basis. The Russian representative goes from home to home and stays with the host families, often helping to facilitate bonding between family and child. Generally this is a female staff member from the specific children's home, who helps the family learn a bit about Russian culture, and herself hopes to learn about American culture through the visit. Sometimes she shares information about the child's life in the home, which helps create a living history for the family and helps to promote more empathy for the child's experience both in Russia and while visiting this country. The availability of this history can help anchor the experience for some families; for others, the absence of any information makes the bonding more difficult. The Russian children are sometimes lonely for their "brothers and sisters" during the visit. Some parents understand the need for mutual support and exchange phone numbers with other hosting families, arranging play dates if possible. The agency offers a family picnic where all the visiting children reconnect and the parents can spend time with one another.

At the orientation meeting, many parents asked questions about concrete issues such as food and toys for the children and expressed anxieties about meeting their young visitors. Imagine a child who doesn't speak your language or know your customs and who will be sleeping in a room with your son or daughter. What will that experience be like for you or the children in your family? The adoption agency worker reminded the families that these children don't need a lot of things, that less is more, and that they should keep their plans simple. I talked about the possible psychological states of the visiting children. We discussed attachment and how it develops and the possibility of attachment disorders occurring in this population. Specifically, I emphasized the importance of making good eye contact and of making an effort to recognize what the child is thinking and feeling. For example, I told them that if a seven-year-old boy is sitting on the floor, it is a good idea to sit on the floor with him and follow what he is playing. Play is a good way to communicate since the language of play is universal. A lot of the prospective mothers seemed to relax, and they nodded as if to say, "Oh, I can do that." Someone asked about sending a child to day camp along with another adopted child already in the family. This parent asked, "Do you think it's a good idea? It would allow this little girl to be with other children and have fun all day." I asked this mother how she was feeling as the date got closer. She told me she was scared and anxious. She was worried about providing this child with a good experience, thereby ensuring that the visit would result in her wish to be adopted. This mother was concerned about being rejected by her host child.

The social workers who conducted the homestudies attended the parent orientation as well. One of the workers, a Russian social worker, spoke about the importance of understanding Russian culture. She emphasized that keeping to a routine and providing structure would be most comforting to the children. She suggested plain foods, a few toys, a few changes of new clothing, and limiting television and video game exposure. She hoped that this information would be useful to the host families and to the children during the two-week visit.

As I looked around the room at the twelve families attending the meeting, I became aware of the diversity of the group and began to get a sense of what they might be experiencing. They had already covered a lot of emotional ground in a journey that began with their wanting a biological child, continued through the enduring of fertility treatments, and ended in their pursuing adoption. Many of them had initially wanted to adopt infants, but then had compromised, agreeing to explore older child adoptions. The agency staff and the families were visibly forming relationships during the orientation. The tone, the laughter, the hugs at the end of the meeting all confirmed this.

At a staff meeting a month after the orientation, I spoke with a group of seven master's-level social workers who conducted homestudy visits. Many of them had other full-time agency positions as substance-abuse counselors or school social workers and supplemented their incomes by doing homestudies in the evenings or on weekends. Their understanding of psychodynamics was limited, and as they spoke about the families they had been assigned, many of the workers emphasized the more practical aspects of the study including sleeping arrangements, size of the apartment or house, and so on. I wondered about this with the group. One of the workers summed up the group's feelings by saying, "We have a limited amount of time to collect a lot of information. The parents are often anxious about our presence and want to ask a lot of questions about how everything works."

When asked to discuss their feelings, the workers noticeably shifted to their observations of the families. One worker raised doubts about the family she had interviewed. She felt that they were going to "squeeze" the child into an already crowded room and that they expected the child to immediately fit in, following the family's routine, because as the mother had said, "That is what we need." The worker had become frustrated with this family, and her tone was hostile and judgmental. I felt as if she and the mother were becoming equally rigid and that a power struggle had already begun. I asked the group to talk about their reactions to this mother, hoping to open a space for understanding her experience. After one of the workers characterized this mother's lengthy quest, her disappointments and fear of future ones, and her wish to finally meet a little girl who could become a part of her family, the atmosphere in the room palpably shifted. The caseworker finally backed off from her judgmental stance and began to reflect on the mother's need for control. This dialogue felt very productive and important because these families are so in need of support and understanding.

For the most part, the parents hope that the children will bond with them and be a good fit for their families. During one of the family group sessions, I had the opportunity to meet Mr. and Mrs. White, a charming older couple who were seeking to complete their single child family. They had decided to participate in the hosting program, hoping to get to know a young girl who might fit in with their family. As it turned out, the child they hosted, Marina, was an adorable, petite ten-year-old with an engaging smile and a personality to match. She immediately charmed the family. Their eleven-year-old son Roger wanted to adopt her the day he met her and was very upset when she returned to Russia at the end of the two-week visit. Roger White struggled with a chronic illness that limited his outdoor activities and required lots of bed rest. Mrs. White told the agency, "This was the happiest I've seen Roger in a very long time. All that smiling and laughing helps boost his immune system. I am sure of it."

Marina had heard from another child in the children's home that this might be an opportunity for her to get a new family. Even before she met the Whites, she told the interpreter how excited she was at the possibility. During her stay she willingly visited the White family's pediatrician who, after a routine exam, referred her to the international adoption unit at a nearby hospital for a developmental assessment. With the trend toward foreign-based adoptions, many hospitals in regions nationwide have decided to add special units to address the ongoing needs of this group.

Marina's weight was of particular concern, alerting the medical team to the possibility of an untreated thyroid problem. The White family was all too familiar with chronic health problems and the care required. What started as a wish for a second child now turned into a concern and resembled the experience with intensive care they had already encountered with their son. Could they handle this situation, and did they want to take a chance, not really knowing if Marina's health and developmental needs would respond to medical treatment? These were the questions the Whites struggled with during their two-week hosting period.

It is my impression that adoption of an older child from a foreign country requires a leap of faith, a vision about the future, a sense of optimism, and hope. The Whites embraced their faith and hope, and decided to adopt Marina, knowing that answers to their questions about her health history might not be found in the children's home in Russia. Marina went home knowing that the family wanted her, but she was feeling very conflicted. She said,

> I love them all and have prayed for a family to belong to, but what about the family I have in Russia? I had a family that might want me back, might be waiting for me, and I have many brothers and sisters at the home where I live. I am not sure about giving that up.

Marina's words echo the sentiments of many of the children thinking about adoption. They hope for the opportunity, but struggle with their fears of abandonment, trauma, and rejection. Can another bond be forged?

When Marina returned to Russia, the Whites went to work completing the adoption papers with the agency. They made arrangements for their son to stay with a relative while they were gone, but they worried about his medical care as his health faltered, and wondered how Roger would manage in their absence. For the Whites as for many families in this process, child-care arrangements for a child left at home became a source of anxiety. Several months later, the agency called telling the Whites to get ready to travel. The Whites traveled many hours to Moscow, and then boarded a prop plane for several more hours before reaching their final destination. They traveled to attend a final hearing, which would lead to the approval of Marina's adoption. They spent three weeks in a hotel in a small Russian village waiting for a court date and visiting with Marina daily.

Each morning they went to the home where Marina lived. They met her friends, her "brothers and sisters," and her caretakers. They saw her room, a large room with ten beds, each separated by a sheet for privacy. The home was clean and pleasant, but sparsely furnished, with some toys, and only a few televisions. The children spent a lot of time outdoors, but according to the Whites, had minimal sports and playground equipment. Teachers traveled to the home to teach the children and told the Whites what a "nice girl" Marina was, and that "she is very well liked and behaves very well." They didn't tell the Whites that Marina couldn't read or write, or that she was dyslexic. Nor did they tell them that they relied on Marina to help control her classmates by being "good." The Whites found this out much later after Marina was enrolled in a public school in their metropolitan area.

During the court appearance, the judge asked Marina how she felt about being adopted. She shocked the Whites by replying, "I don't want to be adopted. I will miss my brothers and sisters too much." This is a good example of the ambivalence experienced by these children when asked to make such a big decision, one that involves severing their attachments to their "brothers and sisters," caretakers, country, and culture. In addition, they have to relinquish their wish to be reunited with their biological parents. It is a great deal to ask of a ten-year-old girl. In this case, however, Marina had already formed a bond to the White family, and as it turned out, after a brief court recess, she appeared before the judge and said, "Yes, I want to belong to the White family." Shortly after that, she came home to the United States to begin her new life.

Another family was not as successful in their hosting experience, and ultimately did not adopt the child they hosted. Their experience highlights the need to explore the expectations these families have of the children they host, as well as the emotional experience of the individual child at the time of their visit to the United States. In this particular case, the Martin family welcomed a twelve-year-old girl named Nadia into their home. She was very sullen and withdrawn from the moment she met them. A representative from the children's home in Russia stayed overnight with her, but Nadia did not reveal the reason for her grief. It was later learned that right before her trip, she had received news of the death of an older sibling, living in another facility in Russia. The staff in Nadia's Russian home had decided a trip would do Nadia good, and had sent her along for her two-week "vacation." This lack of communication and information is not uncharacteristic. Occasionally, information is held back or forgotten, or the person traveling with the children is someone who works for the Ministry of Education in a particular region, but not in the children's home, and who therefore is unfamiliar with the children's backgrounds. This was the case with Nadia and the Russian representative sent here for the hosting program.

A social worker from the adoption agency was brought in to meet with the family and Nadia. Through an interpreter, the details of Nadia's loss were communicated to the family. The Martin family felt empathically toward Nadia, and she was able to perceive that in their responses to her they opened the way for a better experience during their remaining time together. Nadia continued to be sad, but was appreciative of the Martins' hospitality. At the end of the two weeks, no one was sure about how to proceed, but they all agreed that more time was needed. Meanwhile, Nadia was already twelve years old and by her next birthday would no longer be eligible for the hosting program. Each year older is a year further away from the possibility of an older child adoption. As it turned out, the Martins had hoped for a younger girl, a girl who would be more "upbeat" and more appreciative of "what an opportunity she was being offered." It was not a good fit for anyone, and so Nadia went home and the Martins decided that the visit had been worthwhile, but for now, they were going to hold off on adoption.

These examples illustrate some of the struggles families find themselves engaged in and the hopes, expectations, disappointments, and losses they are confronted with along the way. The more the agency staff understands these dynamics and becomes attuned to them as they evolve, the more successful the hosting experience becomes. Hosting programs are problematic for everyone involved: the matches are not always right, and the stress of a child from another culture who arrives homesick and disoriented is sometimes too much to bear. The wish for a "normal child," versus the reality of meeting a child who has difficulty speaking, reading, writing, making eye contact, or simply playing can be very difficult for the hosting family. On the other hand, it is an amazing opportunity for parents and children alike to meet, become involved with each other, and live together twenty-four hours a day, as they do. Many families feel enriched, and believe they are making a significant contribution by participating in the hosting program. If you ask the agency staff, they will agree with the families and are proud of their participation in the process as well. It seems to make the space between the two cultures smaller and more

understandable. It also gives children of all ages a chance to have a better life
and the opportunity for a brighter future.

Let's consider the notion of opportunity from the child's point of view. Can
a child of seven or twelve really know what they would be agreeing to? They
would probably know a lot more about what they might be giving up. Imagine having to let go of the wish to be reunited with your mother and father.
Imagine having to say good-bye to your "brothers and sisters" and caretakers
at possibly the only home you've known and breaking your ties to your culture and country. Can you imagine the pulls and pressures on these young
children and the challenges the families are faced with once their newly
adopted children arrive here? Marina was certainly aware of the pull she felt
from the past and the familiarity of the children's home contrasted with the
excitement of a future in a new home with a new brother, father, and mother
in a new land. Fortunately, Marina had many strengths, and with her positive
attitude and good interpersonal skills, she made a good adjustment.

Her new family understood and talked with her about her losses. This was
very helpful in Marina's transition to her new family life. Some families find
it hard to talk with the children about their past life. They can't relate and are
reluctant to ask questions, thinking they are sparing the children sad memories. In fact, bearing witness as the children recount their stories helps everyone become a family together. In Marina's case, her new parents understood
that she needed time and love to adjust to life here. When she started school,
her motor delays interfered greatly. The Whites provided Marina with speech,
language, and occupational therapies weekly for several years. Marina's special education classification allowed her school to address her learning needs.

The White family grappled with Marina's frustrations as well as their own disappointment that she wasn't a perfect child, that she wasn't a child who could
rise above her own limitations just by working hard. Her past was real; the lack
of early intervention in Russia shaped her academic struggles. Because she was
likable, children invited Marina into their world; they asked her to play with
them on the playground and to sit with them at lunchtime. This helped her
through a difficult first year. Marina's parents encouraged these friendships,
knowing how important they were to her. As Marina's confidence grew, she became more willing to ask for help. Slowly she built trust in these relationships
and came to believe that she could count on her new friends and family.

DISCUSSION

Families like the Whites struggle with disappointments, with the loss of what
was hoped for and the need to accept what is true in their new lives. The Rus-

sian children come with their own unique histories and limitations, so it is not an easy road for them either. Three years after arriving here, Marina continued to struggle academically. More difficulties emerged, and a different school placement was considered. Marina herself asked to stay with her new American friends; she didn't want any more change, and who could blame her? The Whites considered Marina's needs along with her school's recommendations. They concluded that Marina's need for continuity should take priority, and decided not to make any other changes.

For older couples and single people wanting to raise families, this hosting program might be the last opportunity to achieve this dream. Multiple losses, unmet hopes and wishes, and the drive to have a child to love ultimately fuel these efforts. No one is prepared for the unpredictability of the adoption process in Russia, the bureaucracy and paperwork involved, or the waiting to hear when a trip to a children's home will take place. Hosting seems to offer families a bit more control. It is very important to them to meet the children, to try on the possibility of raising an older child, a possibility they might have never considered before. After the children go back to Russia, the hosting families are comforted by the firsthand knowledge they possess. They now have a specific child in mind, and that makes the process of waiting easier.

Children want to belong to families, but for this group of older Russian children, belonging seems to come at a price. In order to belong to an American family, they have to choose to give up their hopes and wishes of being reunited with their Russian families of origin and to leave behind their "brothers and sisters" in the orphanages they call home. Will they retain their culture and ties to their country? Most adoptive families try to preserve this connection, but Russia is far away, and not all of the children will make a trip back after settling in America.

CONCLUSION

The mandate of this agency is to facilitate adoptions and, in this case, place Russian children with American families. The willingness of this and other international adoption agencies to expand their services to include more clinical training for their social workers would contribute to the success of the program. Homestudy workers should be more prepared to effectively evaluate and support the emotional needs of the families and children. Domestic and foreign-based adoptions have risen significantly in the last five years. The need for better-trained and better-educated professionals has led to the development of postgraduate training for adoption workers. Presently, this training is available at two universities in the United States. The New York State Office of Child and Family Services is exploring these models and working with professionals in the adoption community to develop a curriculum for postgraduate training to be implemented in New York State in the near future.

The provision of pre-adoption groups would give families an opportunity to discuss their questions and concerns as well as address the underlying anxieties that can often interfere with the adoption process. The use of such a group model was very helpful to the families participating in the hosting program. The need for post-adoption counseling and group support within the community is also essential to help new parents of older children form relationships. Learning about each other, understanding each other's culture and history, and addressing the special needs of the group may all be aspects of the post-adoption experience. The hosting program itself requires a particular sensitivity to the special needs of the American families and the Russian children who participate in the program. Most families and agency staff agree that although it is complicated, it is worthwhile.

Chapter Fifteen

Birth Parents and Adoptive Parents

Who Are the "Real" Parents?

Alice van der Pas

Fairy tales and mythology reflect basic patterns in our thinking about parents who are not *parents* in the biological sense of the word. Remember the jealous stepmothers of Snow White and Cinderella. The older, and more gruesome, story of Oedipus tells about parents who abandon their child. Little Oedipus is rescued by a shepherd (social worker) who rescues the child, and entrusts him to a royal but childless couple. They adopt him, rename him, and take good care of him. Oedipus thinks of them as his real parents. The story is not about them, however, but about how fate punishes Oedipus's birth parents. It does so through the hands of Oedipus himself—even though he is not aware of what he does. The messages seem clear: giving up one's biological child cannot go unpunished; even optimal adoption does not make one a real parent; and the only real parents are the birth parents who raise their own child. Stepparents are not worth any mention in this respect.

WHAT, OR WHO, IS A "REAL" PARENT?

Adoptive parents themselves often wonder: Am I a real parent, or a surrogate? Is my parenting the real thing? When authors in our field write about parenting and child rearing, they usually have the prototypical, biological parent in mind. Long-term foster parents or adoptive parents may be included through phrases like "parents and their replacements" or "parents and other parental caretakers"—the implicit suggestion being that these are not parents in the true sense of the word. Many an adopted child voices the same message at some point: "You are not my real parents. My real parents live in Bogotá." And whenever there is a problem with their child, adoptive parents are reminded of their tenuous status. When a biological child stirs up a crisis in the parent-child relationship, the relationship itself is not an issue. It is a given. With an adoptive child, an argument is not only about rules or demands, but also about the relationship. The parental position is at stake.

The birth parents, though biologically tied to the child who has been adopted, often wonder whether they have the right to call themselves parents. And if they don't have such doubts themselves, others do, and will express these. After all, parents who do not bring up their own child do not fit the most basic definition of parenting: "Parenting is the behavior and roles of mothers and fathers" (Harkness and Super 1995). They do not behave as parents, and have given up most, or all, of their parental roles.

But is parenting, indeed, a matter of behaviors and roles and an unwavering relationship? Of biological ties? Of concrete responsibilities? These seem legitimate questions for the clinician who deals with the uncertainties of birth and adoptive parents. As such, these questions pertain to more than the particular problems of particular adoptive parents. They go beyond the subject of adoption itself to the question of what it is that makes a person a "real" parent—any person, regardless of biological or legal ties, and regardless of parental or unparental behavior. The essence of being a parent is the central theme of this chapter, and not specific circumstances such as adoption. Ample attention is paid, however, to the ramifications of my argument for professional work in the area of adoption.

A DEFINITION OF "PARENT"

I define a "parent" as a person who has an awareness of being responsible for a child. This awareness, and its all-or-nothing quality, distinguishes a "parent" from those persons with children who are *not* parents. Being a "parent" means that a man or woman can no longer be indifferent to a particular child, even if the parent should want to become indifferent. Such a state is no longer possible. Once one is a "parent," one can only acknowledge an unconditional and timeless *me voici* toward the child.

But how can you or I be responsible for a future that is not ours and that, nevertheless, is put into our arms? How can anyone be responsible for someone who is utterly separate—simply because he or she is someone *else*? I think that exactly this paradox is the basis and foundation of what we call "bringing up a child," or "being a father," or "being a mother" (van Rhijn 1999). Usually, parents have this *non*-indifference without their conscious knowledge. It is, indeed, not a matter of making a choice or decision. That which is experienced consciously, is the awareness of already *being* responsible.

The Unconditionality and Timelessness
of the Parental Awareness of Being Responsible

Thus, the person who has an awareness of being responsible for a particular child can never again be indifferent to that child, regardless of who the child is and what it does, regardless of who the parent is and that parent's capacities and circumstances. The unconditionality of *me voici* thus encompasses being both responsible *and* not in control, being both at a loss *and* accountable, encompasses both helplessness *and* authority. Parents have little actual control over a child's life. They can feed the child, but cannot make it swallow. They have to ensure that the child adjusts to certain norms, but to reach this goal they have to say at some point, "Figure this out for yourself." And then they wonder, "Was this the right decision? Was this the right moment?" And when a child is different from the child one hoped for, when it is ill, disturbed, or handicapped, being a parent implies an even more intense awareness of being responsible.

Once parents accept being responsible for a child, the awareness of their commitment is not only unconditional; it remains with them throughout the child's life—and even after the child's death, until the parent dies. "*Once* responsible, *forever* aware of being responsible," as parents will testify. This awareness is not to be viewed as a continuous state or as an attitude; it is, rather, a repeatedly renewed consciousness of one's non-indifference toward this child.

When and how does it start? By definition, it precedes conscious awareness. Also, parents have different timetables for acquiring the awareness of being responsible. It does not come automatically when a woman discovers that she is pregnant, nor does it necessarily come immediately after the child's birth. It can, on the other hand, be acutely present before the child is born. Parents who mourn a stillborn child sometimes feel accountable for the child's untimely death, and they certainly consider the child to be *their* child. In the following example, a first-time father describes his first conscious awareness of being responsible.

Halfway through the bottle, all of a sudden she laid, on the left and on the right, a minuscule little hand on my large hand that held the bottle. Those little hands were less than one-tenth of my hand; it was a wonderful experience. Immediately I made up my mind: no less than unconditional love. Whoever has this kind of experience, should no longer carry on about hair in the drain or who is going to do the shopping on Saturday. He should not carry on either about divorce and who has the children which weekend. He knows his task: take very good care of these riches. (Kager 1993)

The father suddenly senses that this child's well-being is up to him, and him alone. He translates this awareness into the words "unconditional love," and the importance of this assignment outweighs the importance of almost anything else. Things he got worked up about until then—hair in the drain, his freedom on Saturdays, and marital bliss—pale beside being responsible toward this child.

But the baby was already several days old! Did this father lag behind out of lack of interest? Was he not aware of being responsible prior to this bottle-feeding experience—or was he not yet *consciously* aware of it? Several authors on the transition to parenthood (Michaels and Goldberg 1990; C. Cowan and P. Cowan 1992; Belsky and Kelly 1994; Feeney et al. 2001) refer not only to different timetables for mothers' and fathers' commitment to parenthood, but also to the different paths men and women seem to take as soon as parenthood looms on the horizon. C. Cowan and P. Cowan (1992) found that men tend to express awareness of being responsible by attempting to secure more income for the future family; women, by "nest-building." If ever gender roles push themselves to the fore, it is with respect to tasks related to parenting! But the fact that, for centuries, both schedule and program have differed for male and female parents does not detract from the timeless quality and unconditionality of both fathers' *and* mothers' awareness of being responsible.

What Does Having an "Awareness of Being Responsible" Imply?

Being a parent seems like hubris and humility rolled into one. It is *hubris* because the parent signs, so to speak, a blank contract with an unknown person: "Whoever you are, however you turn out, I'll vouch for you. Always. No strings attached." Is this not sheer recklessness? What makes a person think that he or she, of all the people in the world, is going to be a parent to this child? Probably for that same reason, custom prescribes in most primitive cultures that grandparents, women of the village or neighborhood, or an entire tribe actively assist in turning the parental awareness of being responsible into responsible child rearing. So-called allo-parents (Hrdy 2000) fill in the birth parents' blanks. Adoption is not an issue.

Being a parent is *humility* because the elevated aim, its limitlessness and vague contours, is almost synonymous with failure. Parents sense this, although for sanity's sake they forget that every day is a day of reckoning, and that humiliation is waiting on their doorstep.

But what *is* "being responsible?" My definition refers to a present and future where, in both an abstract and a personal way, the indefinable best inter-

est of the child *equals* the best interest of the parent, and where the best interest of the parent serves that of the child. On this level the interests of both
converge, while in the reality of daily child rearing the short-term interests of
parent and child clash every few minutes (Dix 1991). At those moments, the
awareness of being responsible functions merely as a compass needle quiver-
ing in the direction of that distant and never-to-be-realized entity: the best interest of the child.

"Nature offers no clues about the concrete rights, duties or responsibilities
of parents," states philosopher van Rhijn (1999): these are not a given of *nature*; they come with *culture*, and cultural conditions vary greatly. Of all
norms and values, those regarding parenting are particularly changeable. It is
specific for the human species that our behavior is prepared, but *not* prede-
termined, by biology. Nor is a biological or genetic tie a prerequisite for an
awareness of being responsible, as I define it. Biological ties and the awareness of being responsible belong to different categories of relationships: biological and ethical. Being an aspect of culture, the parental awareness of being responsible does not belong to the categories of rights, duties, and
generally assumed responsibilities and abilities that require parents to be in
control, and hold them *formally* accountable.

Thus, a stepparent may be a parent according to the definition, as may a
permanent foster parent, an adoptive mother, and the mother who gave up the
child for adoption—and also those parents who have been divested of
parental authority because of blatantly incompetent functioning. A real parent
may also be the man or woman, single perhaps, or homosexual, whose path
was crossed by a "cast-away" child and who said, "Come in, I'll take care of
you." I have known several—like an older sister who, together with her husband, legally adopted her two much younger sisters who had been neglected
by their parents. All these persons are postulated to be parents because they
hold themselves unconditionally and timelessly accountable vis-à-vis the
child and the child's best interest.

In view of my focus on the ethical quality of a parent's stance vis-à-vis a
child, I briefly consider the philosophical approach to responsibility of the
Lithuanian-French philosopher Emmanuel Levinas. Although his ideas were
not specifically concerned with parents, his thinking enlightens my definition
of the word *parent*; it also offers a philosophical foundation for the structural
unrest and unease of parents.

In his lifelong search for a philosophical interpretation of responsibility,
Levinas endeavored to find terms that would break through the restrictions of
Western philosophical *discours*, with its focus on man as a rational being.
Levinas argues that "in being responsible I am confronted with an other who
resists being fitted into my world view and who remains absolutely different"

(Kalshoven 1998). For Levinas, being responsible always means "*I am* responsible," or the French *me voicí*, "Here I am," without and before any explicit appeal from the other. Not any Other is responsible; but only I. My definition of the word *parent* points to the same realm: a relationship to an Other whose face and interest we can no longer not acknowledge. Levinas summarizes this relationship as a "hostageship": it makes us insecure—not in the psychological sense of this word, but structurally, because we are responsible *beyond our reach*.

The reader may feel taken aback by the ethical tenor of the definition, and to avoid misunderstanding of the word *ethical*, I shall outline briefly what it does and does not imply in the context of speaking about parents. It does imply that a person has an unremitting uneasiness regarding the "goodness" of that person's functioning as a parent. However, this uneasiness does not give any clue or direction regarding sound parenting. Ethical is not *about* anything, like concrete qualities and responsibilities, that we tend to associate with parenting. Being a parent only implies that the child's fate has become the parent's fate, irrevocably, and that the center of gravity of the parent's existence has shifted.

Levinas assumes two "deliveries": first a child is born, and then there is the ethical, equally birth-like event of finding oneself a parent. And Levinas does not use this kind of terminology in a naïvely optimistic way; he does not expect the parent who gives birth to be automatically ethically "intrigued" by the infant; nor does he expect the ethically "intrigued" parent to be automatically a good parent. On the contrary: for Levinas, being responsible fundamentally means "being late" (Kalshoven 1998), and any awareness of being responsible is at least one step behind some (ir)responsible fact.

Parents have no reason to expect that their being responsible will ever be fully realized, not even the adoptive parents who so consciously choose to parent. But not actualizing one's responsibilities does not preclude an awareness of being responsible. In other words, parents may act irresponsibly toward a child, without having lost the awareness of being responsible. For Levinas, being responsible does not exist on one side of a chasm, with behavior on the other. Rather, being responsible *is* "being late." Every parent is familiar with the experience of a divide, sometimes a deep one, between being responsible and actualizing one's responsibilities. Thus, where Levinas sees "being late" as the deepest meaning of "being responsible," the deepest meaning of being a parent may be the humiliating experience of never quite living up to one's awareness of being responsible—while divining what one ought to do, and striving to accomplish this, in a "surplus de conscience" (quoted in De Boer 1988, 55). *Parents* in this sense of the word, and in my definition, know themselves to be responsible, certainly before others talk about responsibilities in the traditional sense, and they know themselves to be accused before making any mistake.

PHENOMENA OF PARENTING IN
RELATION TO THE PROPOSED DEFINITION

Concomitant with this definition, one may assume that some biological parents do *not* have an awareness of being responsible—but who are they? I briefly discuss some of the various ways in which biological parents seem to justify this assumption.

Absent Biological Parents

Some men who have donated sperm, many men who have directly sired a child, and some women who have had an abortion or who have given a child up for adoption do not seem to consider themselves parents. They appear to have no awareness of being responsible for their child. The number of biological parents-who-do-not-parent is unknown; therapists and other practitioners do not usually meet them professionally, nor have these parents, as such, been the object of research. For the purpose of this chapter, I want to stress that it would be unwarranted to judge their stance as lacking in responsibility. We simply know too little about them.

Many birth parents, though, do count the absent child among their children, and consider themselves parents, albeit undeserving ones. TV programs dedicated to finding lost parents illustrate time and again that these parents' main concern was, and is, that the child lives and is happy.

The first words an American mother spoke when she learned that her child, who had been adopted, was trying to find her, were "Is she alright?"—after which she expressed immense relief about the good news, and her wish not to see the child.

The first words a Peruvian mother spoke after reunion with her son, adopted by Dutch parents, were "May I call you my son?" In other words: "May I still call myself "parent"? (Spoorloos)

The Peruvian mother's plight may be that of a great number of birth mothers (indeed, *mothers*) who give up a child for adoption: they expect to be judged nonparents.

Parents Who Put Parental Care on Hold

We know more about the phenomenon of parents who put parental care "on hold," or who do not immediately feel affection but do seem aware of being responsible. In the rural Brazilian poverty cultures that Scheper-Hughes (1985, 1992) describes, mothers keep a "protective distance" from any newborn with signs of weakness until it is evident that the child will live. When the child dies, the mother is supposed to refrain from crying. Her "single responsibility is to thrust a candle into the dying infant's hands to help light the path on the journey to afterlife" (1992, 383). These mothers weigh the best interest of the weak child against that of the other children and of the family as a whole, and are supported in this by their family and community. Adoption is not an option. Hrdy (2000), in a sociobiological study of motherhood, states that under certain conditions this is "an adaptive rather than a pathological behavior," and "millions of infant deaths can be attributed directly or indirectly to 'maternal tactics' to mitigate the high cost of rearing them"(49)—and not, I might add, to lack of awareness of being responsible.

Parents Who Put *Me Voici* on Hold

Robson and Kumar (1980) report that an initial indifference toward the baby is not uncommon among mothers. It is not intentional, and of short duration. In a group of 119 British primiparas, these authors found that about 40 percent of the mothers "recalled that their predominant emotional reaction when holding their babies for the very first time had been one of indifference. . . . [It took most mothers one week] to develop affection for their babies" (347). "All were married or had stable relationships, most had wanted and planned their pregnancies and had been through careful preparation in ante-natal classes" (352). And yet,

> a number of women likened their early feelings of indifference to "baby sitting" and some said their babies hadn't really belonged until they got home; in a very few instances the "strangeness" did not dissipate until 2–3 months later. Guilt about the early feelings of detachment was rarely admitted although mothers often recalled feeling puzzled and distressed at the time. (351)

These mothers performed their motherly duties and took good care of the child, but with "indifference." In Levinas's terms, biological birth had taken place, but not yet the ethical event of a *me voici* toward the child. The mothers had not yet become *parents* in the sense of my definition.

Similar reactions are reported by the Dutch author Duijves (1999), who interviewed fifteen mothers of different ages, social classes, and cultures about becoming a mother:

> I did not think at all "What a sweetie." I even felt a slight disappointment at first. I swear to it. I did not permit myself to feel it, but I still remember thinking: she is not at all attractive.

> I was scared to pick her up. They said: pick her up and I thought: do I have to? Can't you people do it? You take care of her. . . . For a long time, I had this feeling that I could not accept that I had a child. For about a year. (136)

The findings of Robson and Kumar, and Duijves, may point to the "being late" that, as Levinas suggests, is implicit in the awareness of being responsible. Or to present-day social expectations of motherhood: that any woman feels comfortable with it and intuitively knows what to do. These mothers *did* "baby sit," though, or *did* admonish others to take care of the child.

Awareness of being responsible prompts very poor parents such as the Brazilian mothers noted above to refrain from child rearing until it is clear that the child is worth the investment; and it prompts mothers in more affluent societies to feel distressed when they do not feel affection immediately. They "baby sit," or ask others to take over. It suggests that giving birth to a child, taking care of the child (perhaps in the sense of "baby sitting"), feeling affection, and having the awareness of being responsible are very different phenomena. These activities refer, respectively, to a biological process, child-rearing behavior, and emotions, and to a stance that belongs in an ethical realm. They do not represent a temporal or causal sequence in which, for example, the arrival of the child triggers affection, prompting parents to have an awareness of being responsible, which then sets off child rearing. Rather, the awareness of being responsible does not seem at all related to biological ties between parent and child, or to affection, or to actual child rearing or the signing of adoption papers. It is not biological in nature, behavioral, psychological, legal, or emotional—but ethical.

Parents Who (Try to) Flee from Acting Responsibly

Our proposed definition of *parent* implies no more than it states: an awareness. It is not prescriptive. It does not assume acting responsibly or any of the qualities we tend to expect in parents: insight, competence, altruism, self-control, and so forth. On the contrary, fol-lowing Levinas's view, being aware of *ir*responsibility implies having already acted *ir*responsibly. With parents this can take a mild and innocent form.

> My husband and I had absolutely no experience with babies. I felt overwhelmed. All I could do without feeling extremely anxious was to breast-feed the baby. "I am the only one who can do this," I told myself. "Nobody else can do this in my stead." Those were the only moments that I felt a tiny bit competent as a mother. (HM, personal communication, 1996)

It can also be more dramatic, as in the next example. This child has Down's syndrome. His parents are experienced, but their family and the hospital staff suggest that it would be unwise for them to bring their son up themselves. They do this instead of helping the parents cope with the shock of having given birth to a child for whom being responsible will be an immense task, and instead of helping the mother nurse a child who does not suck well.

> She had tried to nurse her baby in the hospital, but he had poor sucking reflexes. As she increasingly left his care to hospital staff, some of them hinted that she might refuse to take him home. Family members advised her to leave the baby. The new child would ruin his sister's future. (Bardin 1992, 75)

The parents stopped even the most minimal baby sitting in the hospital. Parental care and affection were put on hold. After several mistaken efforts at counseling, a new therapist focused on the ramifications of *not* taking the baby home: the couple would then in fact be giving him up for adoption. The pain that came with the sudden realization that they had deserted their son during those weeks was grueling.

> They finally began to deal with their child's existence, their feelings of attachment and responsibility, and their dislike of themselves for not living up to their own values. They felt that they were now unable not to care for their son. Their tears turned to sobs and then to a wailing of despair that neither had known before. (Bardin 1992, 76)

Adoption was the last thing they wanted. It would have made them feel like bad parents.

While parents learn to know themselves better through daily parenting, a fifth or sixth child is equally as unknown as the first. In 1809 this was subtly expressed by an English mother, some days before her sixth child was due: "Martha has sent me a beautiful robe for the young stranger whom I expect" (de Jong-IJsselstein 1999).

Expectation and apprehension go hand-in-hand, even the sixth time around, and the awareness of being responsible may exacerbate feelings of incompetence, as in the inexperienced mother of the first example, or when the surrounding network is not helpful, as in the second one. When apprehension turns into overwhelming insecurity, child rearing may deteriorate to a bare minimum (Webster-Stratton and Herbert 1994), or worse, neglect (Weille 1994). We assume that in many adoptions, child rearing is permanently delegated because a parent is not, or does not feel, adequately equipped to bring up the child—perhaps due to deleterious circumstances.

In the following vignette of a deeply insecure young mother, delegation (to a grandmother) takes place despite optimal circumstances. The father of the child goes along, and the parents' flight from actual parenting is masked by the resources that can be employed by the very rich.

> It never occurred to my nineteen-year-old mother or to my forty-four-year-old father that it was in any way singular, immediately after my February birth in New York, for them to take off to Europe, leaving my maternal grandmother and my Irish nurse to take the newborn to Newport, mother and father not returning until August in time to supervise the annual fancy-dress ball, given at my father's 240-acre estate. . . .
>
> . . . When we did get to know each other a little towards the end of her life, [mother] told me how frightened she had been of me as a baby, afraid to pick me up, to hold me. (Vanderbilt 1997, 9, 44)

Although Vanderbilt's mother was too frightened even to hold the baby, she did see to it that Gloria was well taken care of.

But what is one to think of the mother who leaves her family: does she have an awareness of being responsible? Jackson concludes from interviews with some sixty mothers who left their families that

> the circumstances that compel the separation are always complex and far-reaching, and usually more by default than by choice or design. Contrary to popular assumptions, I found that *no mother leaves a child lightly, easily, entirely willingly, or in cold blood.* Many mothers are separated from children involuntarily, or through selfless decisions about what seems to be in the children's best interest (Jackson 1994).

A smaller group of Dutch mothers who had left their family was interviewed by van Hennik (1996). Each of these mothers emphasized that she had known that the father would take good care of the children. Could the same be true for the fathers who desert their family without leaving a trace? We tend to doubt it, but in fact, we lack knowledge on this subject.

Parents with Handicaps or Psychiatric Disturbances

Can a person with a mental handicap or psychiatric disturbance be a responsible parent? Often these parents are handicapped in relation to the execution of parenting in the home, and may require compensatory measures in terms of daily help. Such conditions need not, however, affect these parents' awareness of being responsible. Their fear that they are not providing good enough care, and that the future may bring a worsening of the situation, may be a heavy burden, and may worsen their own condition.

In sum, the awareness of being responsible for a child does not tell a parent *when* to do *what*, or *how*. Nor does it prevent parents from being misled by social pressures, anxiety, or discouragement. Arranging one's life in accordance with an ethical stance requires qualities that do not automatically flow from the stance itself. Instead, this stance makes parents vulnerable. The more a parent misses the mark, the more painful that parent's awareness of not actualizing their responsibility. Falling short may lead parents to rant and rave defensively about the child, to welcome the offer of grandma to take over—or to wait for professionals to force a takeover.

For adoptive parents, it may be reassuring to realize that their awareness of being responsible for the child is in line with, and of the same kind as, the birth parents' awareness of being responsible. The adoptive parent is not a surrogate parent, nor is the birth parent of their adopted child a second-rate parent. Both are real parents.

THE ISSUE OF PROFESSIONAL ETHICS

The idea that an abusive or neglectful mother can be approached as having an awareness of being responsible stirs up skepticism if not alarm among practitioners. In this section I shall explain why the safety of child, parent, and practitioner may best be guaranteed when those who work with parents adhere to my definition of "parent."

At regular intervals a pendulum swing takes place in the helping professions regarding family violence. The pendulum moves from an understanding and psychological, or "soft," approach regarding family violence to a moralizing and law-and-order approach, and back. Among the "soft" approaches toward parents I would place "partnership with parents" (Sheppard 2001). Kaganas (1995) expresses a similar concern:

> There are very serious obstacles to meaningful partnerships with parents. On the one hand, if workers cling too faithfully to its tenets in practice, partnership might place children at risk. And on the other hand, the discourse of partnership might be developed as rhetoric to mask the very real coercive power that responsible authorities have over families judged to be irresponsible.

The risk of being lenient toward parents is as real as the temptation to hide professional authority and power behind a smokescreen of partnership. Worse, the notion of a partnership with parents suggests a sharing of responsibilities, which runs counter to *both* the parents' awareness of being responsible *and* the practitioner's professional responsibility. The concept of a partnership with parents treats the two responsibilities, parental and professional, as if they were comparable and equal. But these responsibilities do not belong under the same heading. The parental awareness of being responsible is not comparable to a professional's responsibility, and remains inviolable regardless of the parents' behavior. Whether parents are young or old, at home or at work, driving a truck or presiding over a meeting, they hear the call of duty of their being responsible at every moment, and the practitioner should never cease to be aware of this.

Yet, a parent's functioning may be such that a child-protective intervention is unavoidable, to protect both child and parent against further mishaps. I subscribe to R. Kempe and C. Kempe's statement: "We firmly believe that a child's rights must be independently recognized" (1982), and I believe equally firmly that it may be up to a professional to make decisions that go against a parent's immediate wishes. However, when professional power is used, for example, to enforce a permanent foster placement, the worker should keep in mind that (1) malfunctioning parents, too, have an awareness of being responsible, and (2) professionals are accountable to parents in much the same way as the parents are accountable to their child.

Entirely in line with my definition of "parent" is the concept of the "working alliance" (Sanders and Childress 1992). This is a stance in which *both* the parental awareness of being responsible *and* the responsibilities of the professional are acknowledged. Within a working alliance, a child-protection worker may, if necessary, remove a child from the home against the parents' wishes, but the worker will never call into question the parents' awareness of being responsible. The working alliance remains intact because the concept itself opens up space for cooperation—a bond even—between professional and parents, despite these differences in responsibility and power.

How to maintain this stance? A professional's empathy, however determined one is to "stick with the parents," soon runs thin when confronted with parental dysfunction, or with the professional's own inability to effect change. To be fully able to appreciate the parents' experience and at the same time to fully appreciate the seriousness of a problematic situation—while not falling prey to negative countertransference, moral indignation, disapproval, or the wish to escape it all in the emotional denial that goes disguised as "understanding" or "empathy"—those who work with parents, I propose, should treat my definition of *parent* as an axiom. The Greek root of the word *axiom* suggests that "deeming worthy" has precedence over "judgment," and

> this applies to both the parent-child relationship and the practitioner-parent relationship. It is not relevant that I *know* of the parent being responsible, but that I *respect* it without saying "you are accountable" and regardless of whether the parent himself *knows* it. (Kalshoven 1998)

Thus, the postulate of the parental awareness of being responsible—when used as an axiom—forces practitioners to think at least twice before judgmentally labeling parental behavior that does not seem to serve the interest of the child. It reminds them of the fact that even the gravely dysfunctional parent once had the best of intentions—and still has them.

Clinging to the proposed definition as an axiom prevents being moralistic. "An *ethical* climate is a different thing from a *moralistic* one. Indeed, one of the marks of an ethical climate may be hostility to moralizing" (Blackburn 2001). The axiom need not change a professional decision, but will change one's tone of voice during its execution, and one's choice of words in reporting about it. Parents respond accordingly, and thus a child-protective measure need not be detrimental to the relationship between parents and helper. Child-protective interventions will always be necessary, and practitioners will need at times to question a parent's behavior, judgment, or feelings, but they are never entitled to question a parent's awareness of being responsible. Child protection and parent protection need not clash.

The following example of an informal, never officially acknowledged "adoption" may illustrate how the parental awareness of being responsible may remain intact even when parents dysfunction—and why a helper's professional ethics or the legal prescriptions of child protection should never call this into question.

Rosie

Rosie's teenage parents married because of the pregnancy, and divorced when Rosie was six months old. One year later the mother deposited Rosie at her father's doorstep. The father and his girlfriend did not know what to do with Rosie, took her along to bars or locked her up in her bedroom with a bowl of food. They considered placing her in a children's home, but then friends— who could no longer bear the sight of Rosie's neglect—offered to be her foster parents. The friends took Rosie in when she was five years old. She was a difficult child, and the foster parents applied for help at our agency. Rosie received psychotherapy, and I worked for five years with the foster parents. The father was not interested in further contact with Rosie.

When Rosie was about fourteen years old, she told her foster mother that for several days an unknown woman had been waiting near her school, watching her intently. The foster parents had feared something like this for a long time. Rosie's mother worked as a prostitute, and because Rosie was stunningly beautiful, her mother might want to employ her. The unknown woman—indeed the mother—hired a lawyer to demand visiting rights. The lawyer called our agency for advice. With the consent of the foster parents, I offered to discuss our viewpoint directly with Rosie's mother. Rosie's mother agreed, and so it happened that I had a long talk with her about what had gone amiss in Rosie's early years, and how Rosie had developed since then. I explained that from Rosie's vantage point, it was too early for a reunion with her mother. The precarious gains of her stay with the foster parents, and of her therapy, might be put in jeopardy by that experience. Contact might be possible after Rosie's adolescence, but preferably not yet. I wrote these considerations down for the mother, without blaming anyone and without obscuring any of the unpleasant facts. The mother withdrew her request.

Six years later, Rosie called to get information about her troubled childhood. She was grateful to hear that her "irresponsible" mother had, after all, acted in Rosie's best interest.

While painful experiences which a child has had with its biological parents should be acknowledged and never slighted, no child should ever get the message, spoken or written, explicitly or between the lines of a report, that the child's parents do not deserve respect. A child's affection is never wasted, even if given to parents who raise badly, or chose not to raise at all.

It is the task of those who work with parents, any parents, to postulate that the parents *have* an awareness of being responsible, without their having to offer proof.

PARENTAL RESILIENCE AND VULNERABILITY

Awareness of being responsible renders many parents capable of more patience, endurance, fighting spirit, and courage than they knew they could muster—making them stronger and more resilient. It can also lead to resistance in the face of a helper's good intentions—or to stubbornness. Parents may not agree with a diagnosis, refuse a treatment plan, or demand (or refuse) placement of the child in an institution. Whether parents are valiantly holding on to their own good judgment, or are misled by some belief or anxiety, the underlying force, probably, is the awareness of being responsible.

Parental resilience need not be expanded on here, but another aspect of parents' awareness of being responsible does deserve attention: the vulnerability that comes with the daunting if not reckless nature of the *me voici*. Commitment can lead to high achievement, but it also contains the possibility of failure; the chance of breakdown, and of the concurring feelings of shame and guilt, tends to be proportionate to the height of the aim. While aiming at the lofty goal of raising an infant to full adulthood, one learns to know one's own best and worst features. Each foible in one's personality becomes magnified. If a parent does not notice them, the child will point them out, or the other parent. Family, neighborhood, and wider society, however supportive, look over parents' shoulders: are they doing what they are supposed to? Also, in public and in scholarly debates, we tend to forget some sober facts.

Something is amiss with one out of every four children, intellectually, physically, or emotionally (Meadow-Orlans 1995, 58; Verhulst 1985). Parents never fail to wonder, "Is it *my* fault?" and they expect an embarrassing assessment from real or imagined representatives of larger society. But when things go well, they thank the child for it.

Healthy and unhealthy, strong and weak, perfect and imperfect children are rather randomly distributed among healthy and unhealthy, strong and weak, perfect and imperfect parents. Being a parent may come to appear absurd, or futile, when one's best efforts meet with the "indifference" of the autistic child (Reid 1999), or with the unswayable differentness of any child—not to mention the final "message" of a confused child who commits suicide and seems to say that it was all for naught. And in any child's life, a trauma, large or small, can occur. Traumatic events, such as an act of violence, sexual abuse inside or outside the family, a traffic accident, or the sudden loss of a parent occur regardless of the child's ability to take them in stride, and of the parents' capacity to cope with the aftereffects.

Today's parents are yesterday's children. The awareness of being responsible does not necessarily change them into more mature individuals, or cure any psychopathology. They belong to the same vulnerable species as their child. And, just as the child they once were ten or fifteen years earlier, they deserve understanding and trust, sensitivity and patience. As professionals, we are hindered in this by the fact that

> the conflict between self-interest and the love of the child which is felt by the parent, which is no simple reawakening of infantile narcissism but a conflict accompanied by the capacity to destroy the child—for the parent possesses the power the infant dreams of—is a conflict unrepresented in developmental models of the transition to parenthood. (Datan 1982)

Each and every parent, however, knows the defeat of having acted monstrously, or of not having acted when action was called for.

THE SHARED, UNFAMILIAR CHILD

When encountering problems of adoption, the professional deals with the best and the worst among parents: those who dedicate their life to bringing someone else's child up, and those who cannot manage to raise their own child. These two groups of parents appear to be worlds apart; in fact, they have important things in common:

The child—Each set of birth parents and adoptive parents shares at least one child.

The un-(family)-arity of the child—For the adoptive parent, there is the mystery of the child's unknown background: genes from a different family, and untraceable characteristics. For the birth parent who is still in touch with the child, the child's clothes and speech have become unfamiliar. This parent does not know the names of the child's classmates or teachers. When the child is adopted abroad, the parent may not even have a clue as to where the child lives, and the child looks forever to them like the baby or toddler of years ago.

The experience of failing the child—The adoptive parent cannot undo what has happened to the child; the birth parent cannot repair having failed the child.

The awareness of being responsible—In the ethical sense of my definition both birth parent and adoptive parent are real parents. It is the professional's responsibility to be, and to remain, aware of this, and hopefully my definition will help in this endeavor. My definition does help to explain both the fallibility and the resilience of everyday parenting. It makes us sensitive to the tension behind one parent's violent efforts to straighten out a child, and to the tension behind passive neglect by parents like the Vanderbilts and like Rosie's parents. These parents' deeply hidden tension was a product, my definition assumes, of their shameful experience of having missed the mark.

The definition does not in and of itself explain the dynamics that enable one parent to succeed and cause the other to falter and fail. It does create space, however, for a value-free theory of parenting (van der Pas 1996, 2003, 2006), and for professional work with parents without a moralizing agenda.

CONCLUSION

I have attempted to capture the core experience of being a parent by proposing a definition of *parent* that will reflect the experience of prototypical and atypical parents themselves, and that can enlighten professional work with adoptive or birth parents—that is, any parents. The definition focuses on the ethical kernel of the typical parental stance vis-à-vis the child, and is distinguished from both procreation and actual child rearing. Thus, the word can be broadened to encompass both nonbiological parents, and parents who do not themselves bring up their child. Certain practical implications of this definition, and some methodological misgivings, have also

been addressed in this chapter; more particularly, how the proposed definition may be of use to the professional who deals with adoption.

REFERENCES

Bardin, A. 1992. "Less than Perfect: A Couple's Struggle to Accept Their Down's Syndrome Baby." *The Family Therapy Networker* 16, no. 6: 75–81.

Belsky, J., and J. Kelly. 1994. *The Transition to Parenthood: How a First Child Changes a Marriage*. New York: Delacorte.

Blackburn, S. 2001. *Being Good: A Short Introduction to Ethics*. Oxford: Oxford University Press.

Cowan, C. P., and P. A. Cowan. 1992. *When Partners Become Parents*. New York: Basic Books.

Datan, N. 1982. "After Oedipus: Laius, Medea, and Other Parental Myths." *Journal of Mind and Behavior* 3, no. 1:17–26.

de Boer, T. 1988. *Tussen filosofie en profetie. De wijsbegeerte van Emanuel Levinas*. Baarn: Ambo.

de Jong-IJsselstein, M., ed. 1999. *The Diary of Elizabeth Richards (1798–1825)*. Hilversum: Verloren.

Dix, T. 1991. "The Affective Organization of Parenting: Adaptive and Maladaptive Processes." *Psychological Bulletin* 110:3–25.

Duijves, D. 1999. *Het Moedergevoel (The Motherfeeling)*. Utrecht/Antwerpen: Kosmos-Z&K.

Feeney, J. A., L. Hohaus, P. Noller, and R. P. Alexander. 2001. *Becoming Parents*. Cambridge: Cambridge University Press.

Harkness, S., and C. Super. 1995. "Culture and Parenting." In *Handbook of Parenting*. Vol. 3. Ed. M. H. Bornstein. Mahwah, NJ: Lawrence Erlbaum.

Hrdy, S. B. 2000. *Mother Nature: Maternal Instincts and the Shaping of the Species*. London: Vintage.

Jackson, R. 1994. *Mothers Who Leave*. London: Pandora.

Kagan, J. 1998. *Three Seductive Ideas*. Cambridge, MA: Harvard University Press.

Kaganas, F. 1995. "Working with Children." In *Legislating for Harmony: Partnership under the Children's Act 1989*. Ed. F. Kaganas, M. King, and C. Piper. London: Jessica Kingsley.

Kager, K. 1993. Untitled contribution for a special issue on parents and children. *Vrij Nederland*, July 31, 49.

Kalshoven, A. 1998. "Tragisch ouderschap? Marginalia inzake verantwoordelijkheid [Tragic parenthood? Marginalia concerning responsibility]." *Systeemtherapie* 10, no. 4:274–80.

Keller, H., R. D. Yovsi, and S. Voelker. 2002. "The Role of Motor Stimulation in Parental Ethnotheories." *Journal of Cross-Cultural Psychology* 33, no. 4:398–414.

Kempe, R. S., and C. H. Kempe. 1982. *Child Abuse*. Orig. pub. 1978. Cambridge, MA: Harvard University Press.

Meadow-Orlans, K. P. 1995. "Parenting with a Sensory or Physical Disability." In *Handbook of Parenting*. Vol. 4. Ed. M. H. Bornstein. Mahwah, NJ: Lawrence Erlbaum.

Michaels, G. Y., and W. A. Goldberg, eds. 1990. *The Transition to Parenthood: Current Theory and Research*. Cambridge: Cambridge University Press.

Reid, S. 1999. "The Assessment of the Child with Autism: A Family Perspective." *Clinical Child Psychology and Psychiatry* 4, no. 1:63–78.

Robson, K. M., and R. Kumar. 1980. "Delayed Onset of Maternal Affection after Childbirth." *British Journal of Psychiatry* 136:347–53.

Sanders, J. S., and B. L. Childress. 1992. *Severely Disturbed Youngsters and the Parental Alliance*. New York: Haworth.

Scheper-Hughes, N. 1985. "Culture, Scarcity, and Maternal Thinking." *Ethos* 13, no. 4:291–317.

———. 1992. *Death without Weeping*. Berkeley: University of California Press.

Sheppard, M. 2001. "The Design and Development of an Instrument for Assessing the Quality of Partnership between Mother and Social Worker in Child and Family Care." *Child and Family Social Work* 6:31–46.

"Spoorloos" (Without a Trace). Nederland 3, KRO network. Original broadcast date unknown.

van der Pas, A. 1996. *Naar een psychologie van ouderschap* [*Toward a psychology of parenting*]. Amsterdam: SWP.

———. 2003. *A Serious Case of Neglect: The Parental Experience of Child Rearing; Outline for a Psychological Theory of Parenting*. Chicago: University of Chicago Press.

———. 2006. *Eert uw vaders en uw moeders* [*Honor thy fathers and thy mothers*]. Amsterdam: SWP.

van Hennik, L. 1996. *Ik ga—moeders die hun gezin verlaten* [*I'm leaving—mothers who leave their family*]. Utrecht: Scheffers.

van Rhijn, A. 1999. "Ouderschap als list van de natuur [Parenthood as a ruse of nature]." *Ouderschap and Ouderbegeleiding* 2, no. 2:173–80.

Vanderbilt, G. 1997. *A Mother's Story*. New York: Plume.

Verhulst, F. C. 1985. *Mental Health in Dutch Children*. Doctoral thesis. Rotterdam: Erasmus Universiteit.

Webster-Stratton, C., and M. Herbert. 1994. *Troubled Families / Problem Children*. Chichester, UK: John Wiley and Sons.

Weille, K. L. 1994. "Getraumatiseerde ouders: Hun gevoelens van schaamte en de onze [Traumatized parents: Their feelings of shame and ours]." In *Getraumatiseerde ouders* [*Traumatized parents*]. Ed. K. L. Weille et al. Rotterdam: Sectie Ouderbegeleiding NVRG.

Epilogue

Diana Siskind

Adoption is a transformational process bringing parenthood to those who long for but cannot bear children and giving stranded children home, family, and their place in the world. But every adoption is preceded and followed by its story, and when these stories are told in the offices of psychotherapists, we begin to understand the impact of adoption in all its complexity. We learn from parents how their quest to have and raise a child has played out in real life, and what shadows might have fallen between the dream and the reality. And we learn from the children the many ways that being adopted shaped their development, their sense of identity; what went wrong along the way, and how we may help in the ways that help is needed. Our clinical work with parents and children as well as with adults who were adopted is the focus of this book. Because adoption has become widely practiced, accepted, and accessible, and because it has greatly changed the composition of families, it is a timely subject for study. We hope that our readers will join us in continuing to undertake the exploration of this important terrain of loss and connection, and of the fragility and resilience of human bonds.

But there is another way to view the adoption story, one that has been most eloquently described not in clinical writing, but in literature. It has, I suspect, been prompted by the novelist's fascination with our most primitive fear, a fear going back to earliest life, the fear of abandonment; in the hands of master writers, this archaic fear has turned the plight of the foundling, the orphan, the homeless child, into fiction. In Charles Dickens's great works, his homeless and stranded children suffer severe abuse and neglect, and their fight for and success at survival holds the reader's rapt attention. In contrast, Hector Malot's gentler *Sans Famille* (*Without Family*), a book for children written in French in 1878, gives us a generous view of love and attachment. It begins with the story of a foundling, living happily though in extreme poverty in the

French countryside, whose descriptions of his caretakers capture the essence of motherliness and of fatherliness, and also convey a quality of responsiveness in this young child that we do not have a name for, a quality that combines empathy with deep awareness of the other person. Perhaps we could call it a precocious capacity to love. The book begins in this way:

> I am a foundling.
> But until the age of eight I thought that like other children, I had a mother, because when I cried a woman held me gently in her arms and rocked me until my tears stopped flowing.
> Never did I go to bed without this woman coming to kiss me, and when the winds of December whitened my window panes with snow, she took my feet between her two hands and stayed with me rubbing them while singing me a song the tune of which and some of the words I can still find in my memory.
> When I was tending our cow along the grassy road or the fields and was surprised by a sudden downpour she would run to get me and would insist on shielding me under her wool skirt with which she covered my head and shoulders.
> And when I had a quarrel with one of my friends, she insisted on hearing about my upset, and she almost always found kind words to comfort me and to take my side.
> Because of all this, and for many other reasons as well, because of the way she spoke to me, because of the way she looked at me, because of her caresses, and because of the gentleness of her scolding, I felt certain that she was my mother.[1]

When several terrible tragedies befell the home of this very poor woman and there was literally no food to eat, she was forced to give this boy to a traveling musician who promised to take very good care of him. The man and boy went off together, and the following is the child's description of fatherly care:

> A father could not have taken better care of his own child. He taught me to read, to sing, to write, and to count. During our long hikes he always used the time to give me lessons, sometimes on one subject, sometimes another depending on chance or the circumstances at hand. During days of bitter cold he divided his coverings with me and during times of great heat he always helped me carry our luggage and the items that were normally under my charge. When we ate our meals he never gave me the lesser piece, keeping the best for himself, on the contrary, he shared with fairness the good and the bad equally with me. At times, it is true, he would pull my ear or give me a reprimand but this was normal for a father to do and never caused me to forget his care, his kind words, and all the

---

1. Translated by Diana Siskind.

signs of tenderness from the beginning of our time together. He loved me and I loved him.

Although the above is fiction, Hector Malot's paragraphs serve as a good reminder of what is simple and yet not simple, a reminder we sorely need in our complicated twenty-first century. Adoption can be difficult and emotionally risky for parent and child, but ultimately is it not the ability to connect and to form a reciprocal relationship that matters most? As we end this book, we might do well to hold this clear and balanced thought, a guiding principle to anchor our work with adopted children and their parents.

REFERENCE

Malot, Hector. 1933. *Sans Famille*. Paris: Nelson Editeurs.

Index

abandonment, 187

abuse, 187

adaptation, 93, 165

adolescence: adoption fantasies in two girls, 138–47; identity development during, 137–38; separation and, 138, 147

adopted children: constricted affect, 54–55; developing emotional regulation in, 58–59; difficulties in expressing anger, 155–56; early development and life in orphanages/institutions, 48; feelings of ambivalence and, 41; full impact of adoption felt during latency, 18–19; increasing contact with the birth mother, 4; of infertile couples, 14; informing of their adoption, 115–34; integration of loss and trauma, 77; intermingling of loss with adoptive parents, 19–20; internalization of shame or defect, 166–67; loss as an experience of, 182, 189–90; mental representations of biological parents and, 11; percent in outpatient therapy, 181–82; problems arise in the third year of life, 48; psychological problems and, 115; search for biological parents

and, 159–60; self-soothing, 59; "shadow parents" and, 74; "splitting" of parental images, 156; unconscious communication and transmission of loss, 20–28; underrepresentation of older children in psychodynamic research, 5; vulnerability to adoption fantasies, 137, 138

adopted foster children: assessment process, 94–95; birth stories and, 111; complicated feelings within, 94; condition of internal fragility in, 93–94; continued feelings of insecurity and loss, 112; developmental vulnerability in an infant, 99–102; effects of trauma, neglect, and caregiving disruptions on a toddler, 102–5; identity formation and, 111; need for prolonged period of adaptation, 93; prolonged adoption case in latency, 105–8; separation from family of origin, 95

adoption decision: made when parents experience personal loss, 80–83; same-sex families and, 66–67

adoption fantasies: clinical cases in adolescent girls, 138–47; vulnerability of children to, 137, 138

About the Editors and Contributors

Kathleen Hushion, **MSW**, is a child and adult psychotherapist and psychoanalyst practicing in New York City and Huntington, New York. She is a member of the Institute for Psychoanalytic Training and Research (IPTAR) and the International Psychoanalytic Association (IPA). She is also on the faculty of and a supervisor for IPTAR's Child and Adolescent Psychotherapy Training Program. She specializes in working with internationally adopted children and their families, does adoption homestudies, and lectures to adoptive parents.

Susan B. Sherman, **DSW**, is on the faculty of the Advanced Training Program of the Jewish Board of Family and Children's Services, and the Psychoanalytic Psychotherapy Study Center. She has published articles on psychoanalytic theory and practice. She has a private practice for adults, adolescents, and children in New York City.

Diana Siskind, **MSW**, is on the faculty of the New York School for Psychoanalytic Psychotherapy and Psychoanalysis, and she is in private practice in New York City. She is the author of three books: *The Child Patient and the Therapeutic Process* (1992), *Working with Parents: Establishing the Essential Alliance in Child Psychotherapy and Consultation* (1997), and *A Primer for Child Psychotherapists* (1999).

Christopher Bonovitz, **PsyD**, is on the Adjunct Clinical Faculty of the Derner Institute of Advanced Psychological Studies, Adelphi University, City University of New York; and the faculty of the Child and Adolescent Program, National Institute for the Psychotherapies.

Jerrold R. Brandell, PhD, is professor and chairperson of the Graduate Concentration in Interpersonal Practice at Wayne State University School of Social Work, Detroit, where he teaches psychodynamic theory and practice. The founding editor of the journal *Psychoanalytic Social Work*, he has published seven books, including *Psychodynamic Social Work* (2004) and *Of Mice and Metaphors: Therapeutic Storytelling with Children* (2000), and also maintains a part-time practice in psychoanalysis and psychotherapy.

Jane Hanenberg, EdD, is a psychologist who works with children and adolescents. She practices outside Boston.

Paul Hymowitz, PhD, is a child psychologist and psychoanalyst with a private practice in Manhattan, where he also conducts child custody evaluations for the courts. He is coeditor of the 2005 volume *Divorce and Custody: A Clinician's Handbook*.

Carole Lapidus, MS, CSW, is a clinical social worker in New York City where she is in private practice. She is on the faculty of the Institute for Infants, Children, and Families.

Jeffrey Seinfeld, PhD, is a professor at the New York University School of Social Work. He is the author of *The Bad Object*; *The Empty Core*; *Holding and Interpretation*; and *Rage, Terror, and Despair*.

Janet R. Shapiro, MSW, MA, PhD, is an associate professor of social work and social research, and director of the Center for Child and Family Well-Being at Bryn Mawr College. She holds dual degrees in social work and developmental psychology, and is coauthor of *Neurobiology for Clinical Social Work: Theory and Practice*, and *Complex Adoption and Assisted Reproductive Technology: A Developmental Approach to Clinical Practice*.

Vivian B. Shapiro, MSW, PhD, is an associate professor emerita at the University of Michigan School of Social Work. Her clinical research is in the field of infant mental health. She is coauthor of the article "Ghosts in the Nursery," and the book *Complex Adoption and Assisted Reproductive Technology: A Developmental Approach to Clinical Practice*.

Sandra Silverman, LCSW, is a supervisor and faculty member at the Psychoanalytic Psychotherapy Study Center and the Institute for Contemporary Psychotherapy. She is in private practice in New York City.

Cathy Siebold, DSW, is on the faculty and is a supervisor and training analyst for the Psychoanalytic Psychotherapy Study Center, and the New Jersey Training Institute for Psychoanalysis. She is also an author, having published articles on psychoanalytic theory and practice, and Education Chair of the National Membership Committee on Psychoanalysis.

Laurie Sloane, LCSW, BCD, is executive director of the Psychoanalytic Psychotherapy Study Center, a psychoanalytic training program in New York City. In addition to her psychotherapy practice in Manhattan and Long Island, NY, she provides consultation to adoptive families and adoption agencies.

Alice van der Pas, PhD, MSW, is the author of a ten-volume handbook on parenting and professional work with parents. Earlier she was on the editorial boards of the *Dutch Handbook of Family Therapy* and of the journal *Systeemtherapie*, and in 1998 she founded the *Dutch Journal on Parenting and Parent Guidance*.

Susan C. Warshaw, EdD, ABPP, is a diplomate in psychoanalysis, American Board of Professional Psychology; an associate professor, Ferkauf Graduate School of Psychology, Yeshiva University; a supervising analyst on the faculty of the New York University Postdoctoral Program in Psychotherapy and Psychoanalysis; and on the faculty and a supervisor of the William Alanson White Institute, Child, Adolescent Training Program and the Institute for Child, Adolescent and Family Studies.